Revised Edition

Pocket Cruisers & Tabloid Yachts

Volume 1

Building Plans for Six Small Cruising Craft
From the Boards of the Benford Design Group

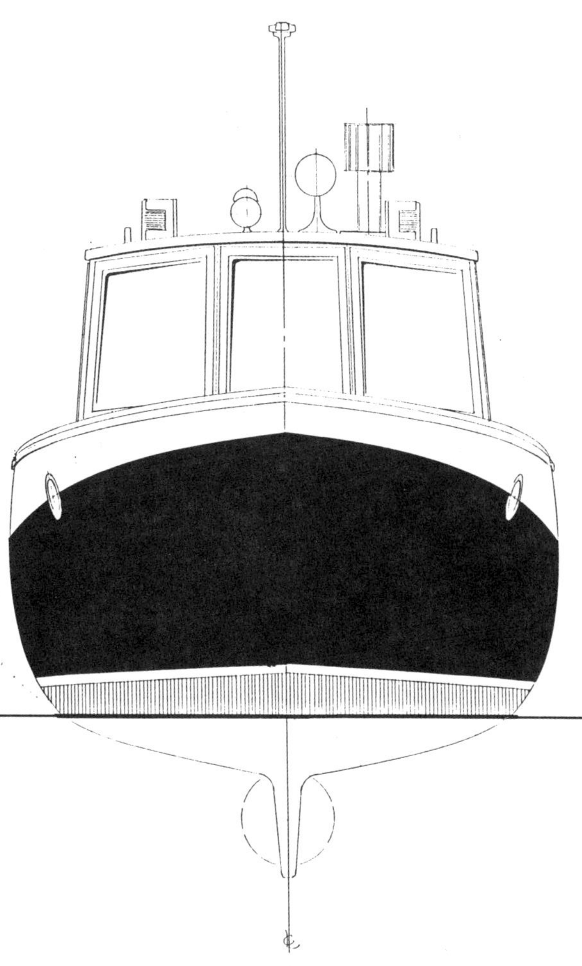

Benford Design Group
P. O. Box 447
605 Talbot St.
St. Michaels, MD 21663

Voice: 410-745-3235
Fax: 410-745-9743

Published by:

Tiller
Publishing
P. O. Box 447
St. Michaels, MD 21663

Phone: 410-745-3750
Fax: 410-745-9743

Photo credits:

Front cover: Clockwise from upper left, JRB, Gene Coan, JRB, Carl B. Ziesmer, M.D.

Back cover: Clockwise from upper left, JRB, JRB, JRB, Carl B. Ziesmer, M.D., JRB, JRB, JRB, Clarence Butz, Joe Failing, and center photo by JRB.

DEDICATION:

To **John Atkin**, whose design work provided inspiration for a young designer, and who, three decades ago, kindly provided that young designer the apprenticeship needed to follow his dream.

Many heart-felt thanks, John!

BY THE SAME AUTHOR:

BOATBUILDING & DESIGN FORUM, 1973. A monthly newsletter with more information on ferro-cement boatbuilding & other boatbuilding information. OP*

THE BENFORD 30, 3 editions in 1975, 1976 & 1977. An exposition on the virtues of this design and general philosophy on choosing a cruising boat. OP*

CRUISING BOATS, SAIL & POWER, 4 editions in 1968, 1969, 1970 & 1971. Design catalog and article reprints. OP*

CRUISING DESIGNS, 4 editions in 1975, 1976, 1993 & 1996. A catalog of plans and services and information about boats and equipment.

CRUISING YACHTS, 1983. A hard cover book with a selection of Benford designs covered in detail, including several complete sets of plans, a lot of information about the boats and how they came to be. Eight pages of color photos. OP*

DESIGNS & SERVICES, 7 editions, 1971, 1972, 1987, 1988, 1990, 1993 & 1996. Catalog of plans & services of our firm.

DESIGN DEVELOPMENT OF A 40 METER SAILING YACHT, 1981. A technical paper presented to the Society of Naval Architects & Marine Engineers, at the fifth Chesapeake Sailing Yacht Symposium, and in the bound transactions of that meeting.

THE FLORIDA BAY COASTERS, A FAMILY OF SMALL SHIPS, 1988. A book of study plans of these Benford designed freighter yachts. OP*

PRACTICAL FERRO-CEMENT BOATBUILDING, with Herman Husen, 3 editions in 1970, 1971 & 1972. Best-selling construction handbook, a how-to on ferro-cement. OP*

SMALL CRAFT PLANS, 2 printings in 1990 and 1991. A book with fifteen sets of full plans for 7'-3" to 18'-0" dinghies and tenders.

SMALL SHIPS, 3 editions, 1990, 1992 & 1995. A book of study plans for Benford designs for tugs, freighters (like the Florida Bay Coasters), ferries, excursion boats, trawler yachts, houseboats & fishing vessels. Ten pages of color photos.

* OP = Out of print

Table of Contents

Introduction

In the beginning....

My cruising began on a tabloid yacht, a 21½' gaff sloop that my parents bought the summer before I arrived. My parents took me sailing before I could walk, and I remind them that my subsequent life with boats and living aboard always seemed perfectly normal to me....

I spent my first twenty years cruising Lake Ontario on this boat, developing a great fondness for the lifestyle to be found on such a boat.

I was fortunate to be able to continue my education and learn more to pursue a career in yacht design by apprenticing with John Atkin about thirty years ago. John's father, Billy Atkin, had started designing in 1906 and John was ably carrying on the tradition by designing a variety sizes and types of interesting cruising boats. I particularly liked the small ones, for they were the ones I could personally aspire to, and relate to, in those times.

Small cruising yachts have always been the most popular boats. They're big enough to be comfortable staying overnight aboard, and small enough to be affordable and easily handled.

Over the last three decades in the yacht design business, I've designed quite a number of small cruising yachts, both sail and power. This book is the first of a multi-volume set that we have planned. We hope you will enjoy both this book and the pleasure of using one of these boats.

The plans printed here are for the use of people wanting to build just one boat for themselves. Professional builders wanting to offer any of them as stock boats should write us regarding royalties for production boats and for details on how we can be of assistance in marketing them. As always, prices noted in this book are subject to change without notice, particularly years hence....

What are Pocket Cruisers & Tabloid Yachts?

The simplest definition is that they are small power and sail cruising yachts, respectively. Thus, a pocket cruiser is a small cruising powerboat and a tabloid yacht is a small cruising sailboat.

While these definitions are not in as common usage as they were a couple generations ago, they are such nice ones that I want to do what I can to perpetuate their usage.

Patterns & Kits:

Full sized patterns are available for both the 14' Tug and 17' Fantail. These are for the full loft floor, whereas most of our larger boat design patterns are only for the body plan or frame shapes. The 20' Catboat or Tug Yacht is available as a molded fiberglass hull kit, from a bare shell to a completed boat. For current pricing on these, write or call us.

Building Questions:

While we're usually generous with our time in answering quick questions, this is part of our consulting work that was included in the stock plan price. If your questions are long and/or involved, or you are interested in a design variation on one of these or another of our boats, you should be prepared to pay a consulting fee for our assistance in helping you get the boat done in a manner that will please both of us.

Acknowledgments:

Others, besides myself (JRB on the drawings), whose drawing talents have contributed to these drawings are Peter Dunsford (PAD or Dunsford), Tom Fake (TWF), Jeff Patterson (JRP), Bob Perry (Perry), Jon Stivers (JSS), and Bruce Williams (BEMW). Many thanks to them for their help.

Jay R. Benford, June 1992

Benford Design Group
P. O. Box 447
St. Michaels, MD 21663
Voice: (410) 745-3235
Fax Machine: (410) 745-9743

Chapter One

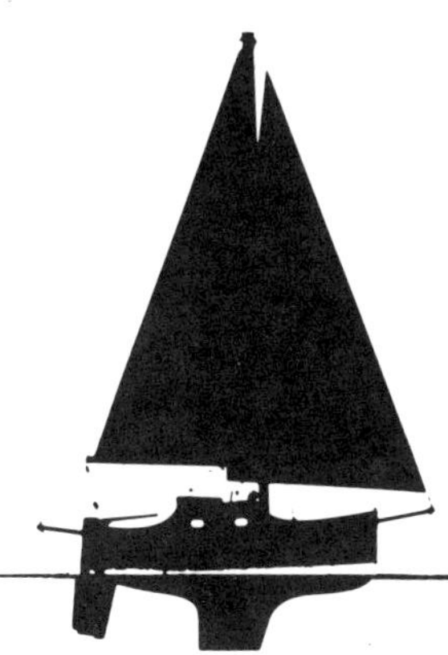

14' Long Distance Cruiser *Happy*

Design Number 168

1978

John Guzzwell made yachting history when he sailed back into Victoria, B.C., in 1959 aboard ***Trekka***. He had set a record for the smallest boat on a solo circumnavigation that stood for many years. In recent years several sailors have set out to break his record and at least one has succeeded.

When Howard Wayne Smith came to us in December of 1977, he was a crewman on a tugboat on the Canadian West Coast. He'd been reading and planning his new boat project for some time. His dream was to create a distinctly smaller boat to break the record set by his hero, John Guzzwell.

To a smaller group in the boating world, John Guzzwell is equally famous for his skill in fine yacht construction. Earlier in 1977, he had set up shop on Orcas Island, the next ferry stop over from where we then had our office, on San Juan Island. Over there he had the first of the 37' pilothouse cutters of our design, ***Corcovado***, under construction, and we were able to talk with him about some of the questions we had about his voyaging and about ***Trekka***.

Howard Wayne Smith's specification to us was to try to get the maximum amount of boat we could in under 14 feet of length. After considering many alternatives, we came up with the plumb ended cruiser shown in the accompanying drawings. Howard wanted everything kept as simple as possible, for each pound of weight would be important.

The designed auxiliary power was a small outboard engine. The locker in the stern was designed to be watertight, sealed off from the rest of the boat. This locker holds the engine as well as the fuel tanks.

The companionway hatch is hinged, making it easier to seal against water coming inside. The boat can be well ventilated in warmer climates through the 6 opening ports, 2 dorade vents, the foredeck hatch, and the companionway hatch.

The raised deck amidships provides an area in which there is sitting headroom below. The pipe berths shown on the drawings extend aft under the cockpit seats, keeping the crew in the area of least motion when at sea. The forward part of the boat is devoted to storage and has space for the very simple galley that is used for cooking aboard.

The mast is stepped through to the keel creating a very strong mounting. The jib and genoa can be poled out opposite each other for downwind runs. A wind vane, mounted on the boomkin, is hooked to the trim tab on the rudder. Mooring and rigging cleats, not shown on the deck plan, were through bolted to the deck. The pair of small winches are more than adequate for sheeting the genoa.

The small area of hollow in the keel amidships gives a place for bilge water to collect and makes it easier to pump it out. This is one of the ideas that were incorporated in the design as a result of comments from John Guzzwell.

"Hull speed" is just about 5 knots. Howard wanted to be able to average 3 knots for most of his passage making. The motion on a short and fat boat like this is much better off the wind than bucking to weather. With the NACA foil sectioned keel, she has the lateral plane and lift to sail to weather, but Howard prefers to do most of his sailing off the wind.

The basic hull construction was done by Finn Nielsen at Maple Bay on Vancouver Island. Howard did a lot of the outfitting himself. Most of the construction materials in her are native to the Pacific Northwest, including a lot of fir and cedar. The construction is cold-molded cedar planking over fir longitudinal stringers.

Howard's story of working his way from the idea for a solo circumnavigation in such a small craft through the design, construction, transportation and sailing phases is highly entertaining. He writes in a personable style, and a number of magazine and newspaper articles by and about him have been published around the world. His plans include a book or two and we'd recommend the reader keep an ear out for news of these if stories of adventure, determination and skill are of appeal. Excerpts from some of his early writings follow:

"Once Jay and his young associate, Peter Dunsford, heard more of the story and saw my preliminary plans, their eyes lit up and they were tossing ideas back and forth a mile a minute. They were enjoying themselves. I sat there fascinated. Realizing that this might have been the last time I could go custom with a boat, I wanted to go all the way: all wood, with lots of varnish and bronze, tan bark sails, etc. I had been thinking in terms of single carvel or strip planking for the hull, but Jay immediately informed me that for my size vessel, these were too heavy a medium, and we'd have to go with a cold molding method...Well, we talked for a few hours that day, and I was very pleased when Jay agreed to start work on the design even though he said it would take about three months by trying to squeeze it in with other work."

"By March, 1978, the design was completed, and as you can see, ***Happy*** turned out really nice. Jay did a fine job. I think he really enjoyed himself on this one, as she's a little out of the ordinary, and that's his bag really."...

"With the 8 hp diesel engine I installed and plenty of plywood (there are bins and drawers in every available space), ***Happy*** really gained some weight, and is now about 2500 to 2600 pounds."...

"I found that, for her size, ***Happy*** is pretty stable, and I could walk around on her deck without heeling too much."...

After a slow trip across the Gulf Stream for a shakedown cruise to the Bahamas, and a holiday there, Howard sent us another report: "The trip back across the Stream was a very quick one, just under 12 hours. We were surfing about half of the way back, and averaged a little over five knots!"...

After sailing 10,000 miles from Miami, Florida, through the Panama and across the Pacific, touching at the Galapagos, Marquesas, Fiji, Tahiti and on towards Australia, he touched a little too hard on a reef off Noumea, New Caledonia. There, towards the end of November, 1982, the beautiful ***Happy*** was lost, an hour before Howard was due on watch in the early hours before dawn. Howard was able to scramble into his dinghy and surfed his way over a number of treacherous reefs (spending the night on the overturned hulk of a steel wreck), landing in Noumea the next day. Friends he'd met in the Marquesas took him back to **Happy** to salvage all possible gear, but she was otherwise a complete loss.

However, Howard Wayne Smith was a determined adventurer. With the aid of an aluminum builder in Noumea, he put together yet another miniature offshore yacht. Economics and record-breaking tables ever in mind, the **Happy II** came from our drawing boards at 9 1/2 feet. Howard felt that his most-used space on the 13' 10" **Happy** was really the equivalent of the space he had available in the smaller vessel. He had to mainly forego stores-carrying ability and speed.

This vessel was built, with the stern fore-shortened to make her under nine feet long and he sailed her to Australia. There he had a series of misadventures with the Australian Customs and lost her to them. At that point, thoroughly frustrated, Howard returned to Toronto, setting aside his plans to complete the voyaging.

Particulars		English	Metric
Length overall		13'-10"	4.22 m
Length designed waterline		13'-8"	4.17 m
Beam		6'-3"	1.91 m
Draft		3'-7"	1.09 m
Freeboard:	Forward	3'-1"	0.94 m
	Raised deck	3'-3 5/8"	1.01 m
	Aft	2'-4½"	0.72 m
Displacement, cruising trim		2,240 lbs.	1,016 kg.
Displacement-length ratio		392	
Ballast		750 lbs.	340 kg.
Ballast ratio		33%	
Sail area, sq. ft.		180	16.72 sq. m
Sail area-displacement ratio		16.82	
Wetted Surface		84.4 sq. ft.	7.84 sq. m
Sail area/wetted surface ratio		2.13	
Prismatic coefficient		.55	
Pounds per inch immersion		285	50.9 kg./cm
Entrance half-angle		28°	
Headroom		4'-10½"	1.49 m

***CAUTION:** The displacement quoted here is for the boat in cruising trim. That is, with the fuel and water tanks filled, the crew on board, as well as the crews' gear and stores in the lockers. This should not be confused with the "shipping weight" often quoted as "displacement" by some manufacturers. This should be taken into account when comparing figures and ratios between this and other designs.

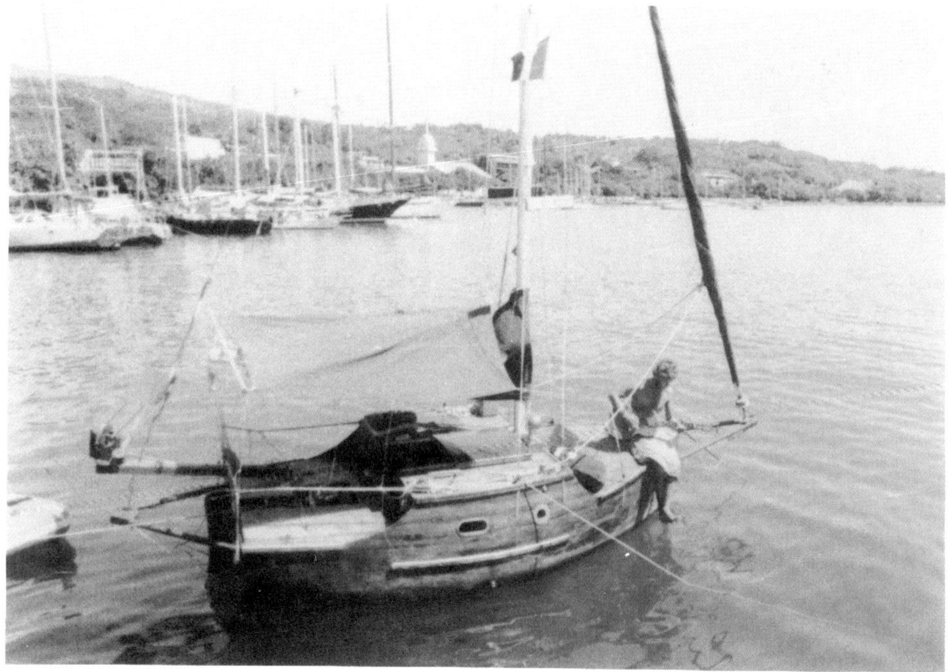

__Happy__ at anchor off Tahiti. She'd made a good passage and Howard Wayne Smith was resting and preparing for the next part of his voyaging. Photo courtesy of the owner.

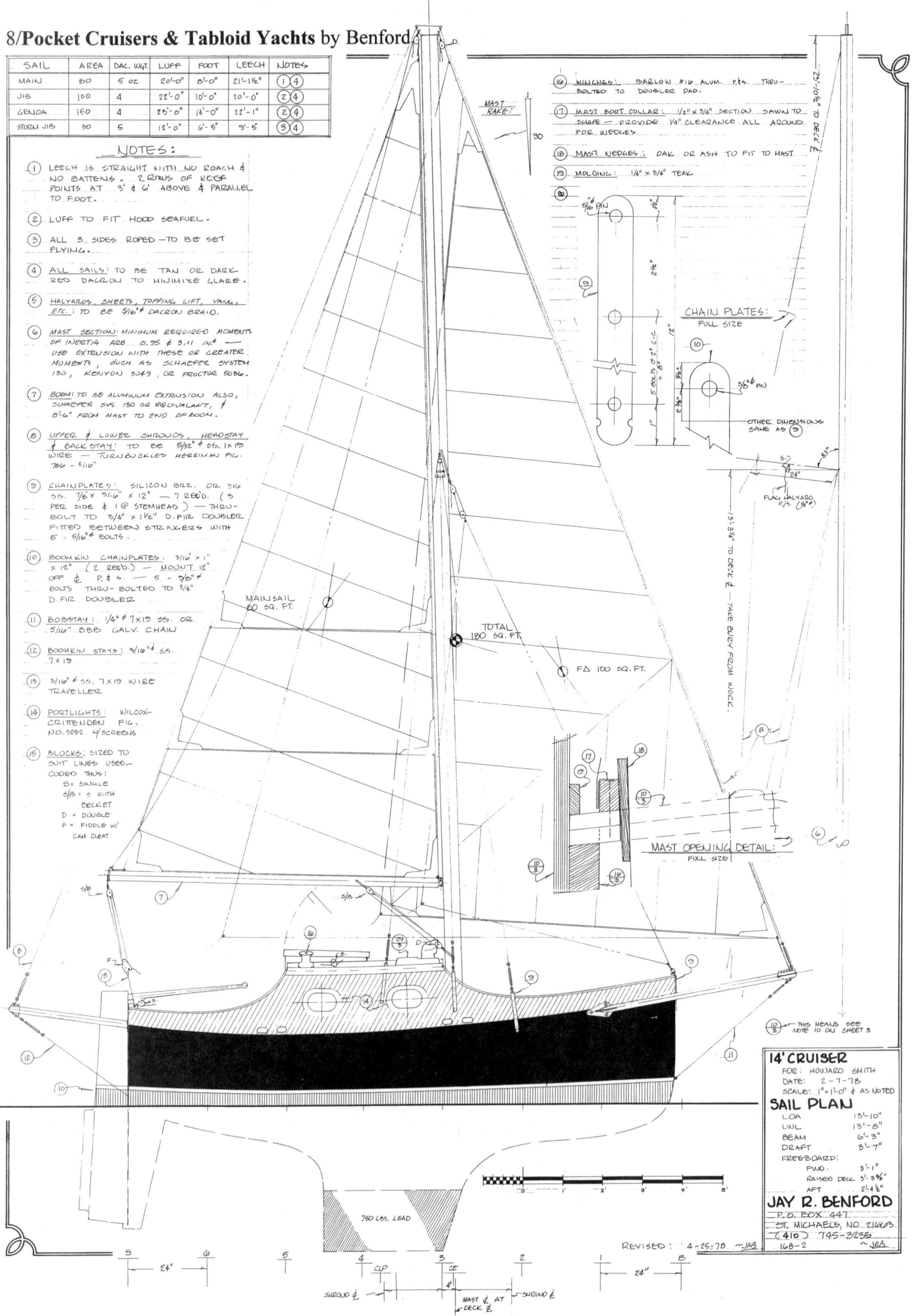

SAIL | AREA | DAC. WGT. | LUFF | FOOT | LEECH | NOTES
MAIN | 80 | 5 OZ | 20'-0" | 8'-0" | 21'-1½" | 1 4
JIB | 100 | 4 | 22'-0" | 10'-0" | 20'-0" | 2 4
GENOA | 150 | 4 | 23'-0" | 13'-0" | 22'-1" | 2 4
STORM JIB | 30 | 5 | 12'-0" | 6'-5" | 9'-5" | 3 4
NOTES:
1 LEECH IS STRAIGHT WITH NO ROACH & NO BATTENS. 2 ROWS OF REEF POINTS AT 3' & 6' ABOVE & PARALLEL TO FOOT.
2 LUFF TO FIT HOOD SEAFURL.
3 ALL 3 SIDES ROPED — TO BE SET FLYING.
4 ALL SAILS: TO BE TAN OR DARK RED DACRON TO MINIMIZE GLARE.
5 HALYARDS, SHEETS, TOPPING LIFT, VANG, ETC.: TO BE 5/16"ϕ DACRON BRAID.
6 MAST SECTION: MINIMUM REQUIRED MOMENTS OF INERTIA ARE 0.95 & 3.11 IN.⁴ — USE EXTRUSION WITH THESE OR GREATER MOMENTS, SUCH AS SCHAEFER SYSTEM 130, KENYON 3049, OR PROCTOR 5086.
7 BOOM: TO BE ALUMINUM EXTRUSION ALSO, SCHAEFER SYS. 130 OR EQUIVALENT, & 8'-6" FROM MAST TO END OF BOOM.
8 UPPER & LOWER SHROUDS, HEADSTAY & BACKSTAY: TO BE 5/32"ϕ SS. 1X19 WIRE — TURNBUCKLES MERRIMAN FIG. 786 - 5/16"
9 CHAINPLATES: SILICON BRZ. OR 316 SS. 7/8" X 3/16" X 12" — 7 REQ'D. (3 PER SIDE & 1 @ STEMHEAD) — THRU-BOLT TO 3/4" X 1½" D.FIR DOUBLER FITTED BETWEEN STRINGERS WITH 5 - 5/16"ϕ BOLTS.
10 BOOMKIN CHAINPLATES: 3/16" X 1" X 12" (2 REQ'D.) — MOUNT 12" OFF ℄ P. & S. — 5 - 3/8"ϕ BOLTS THRU-BOLTED TO 3/4" D.FIR DOUBLER
11 BOBSTAY: 1/4"ϕ 7X19 SS. OR 5/16" BBB GALV. CHAIN
12 BOOMKIN STAYS: 3/16"ϕ SS. 7X19
13 3/16"ϕ SS. 7X19 WIRE TRAVELLER
14 PORTLIGHTS: WILCOX-CRITTENDEN FIG. NO. 5252 W/SCREENS
15 BLOCKS: SIZED TO SUIT LINES USED — CODED THUS:
S = SINGLE
S/B = S WITH BECKET
D = DOUBLE
F = FIDDLE W/ CAM CLEAT
16 WINCHES: BARLOW #16 ALUM. P.&S. THRU-BOLTED TO DOUBLER PAD.
17 MAST BOOT COLLAR: 1/2" X 3/4" SECTION SAWN TO SHAPE — PROVIDE 1/4" CLEARANCE ALL AROUND FOR WEDGES
18 MAST WEDGES: OAK OR ASH TO FIT TO MAST
19 MOLDING: 1/4" X 3/4" TEAK
20
MAST RAKE:
30
5/16"ϕ PIN
CHAIN PLATES: FULL SIZE
3/8"ϕ PIN
OTHER DIMENSIONS SAME AS 9
FLAG HALYARD P./S. (1/8"ϕ)
24"
MAINSAIL 80 SQ. FT.
TOTAL 180 SQ. FT.
FΔ 100 SQ. FT.
13'-3¼" TO DECK ℄ — TAKE BURY FROM WICK.
MAST OPENING DETAIL: FULL SIZE
THIS MEANS SEE NOTE 10 ON SHEET 3
750 LBS. LEAD
14' CRUISER
FOR: HOWARD SMITH
DATE: 2-7-78
SCALE: 1"=1'-0" & AS NOTED
SAIL PLAN
LOA 13'-10"
LWL 13'-8"
BEAM 6'-3"
DRAFT 3'-7"
FREEBOARD:
FWD. 3'-1"
RAISED DECK 3'-3⅜"
AFT 2'-4½"
JAY R. BENFORD
P.O. BOX 447
ST. MICHAELS, MD 21663
(410) 745-3235
168-2
REVISED: 4-25-78 ~JRB
CLP
CE
SHROUD ℄
MAST ℄ AT DECK ℄
SHROUD ℄
24"
24"

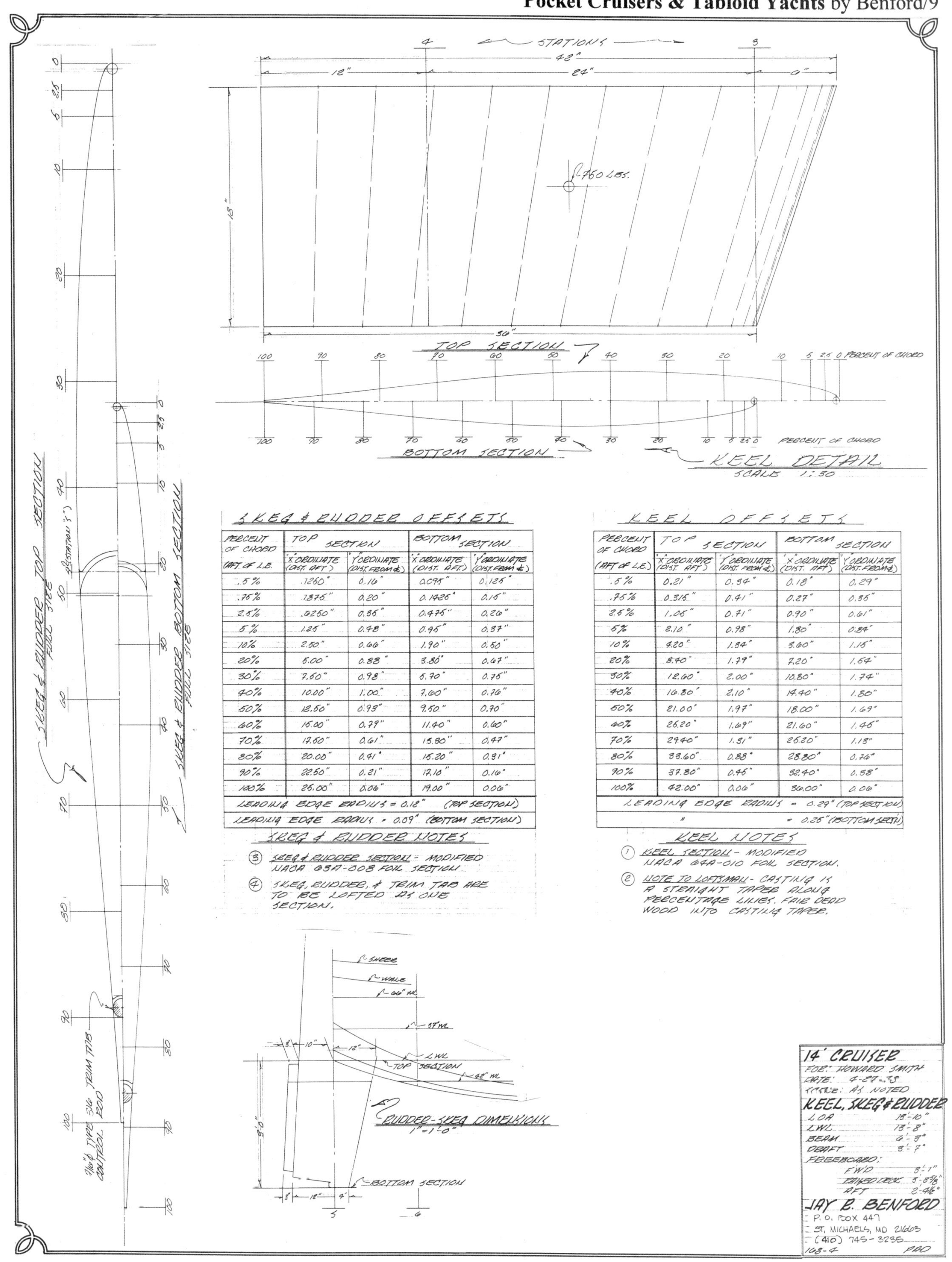

SKEG & RUDDER OFFSETS

PERCENT OF CHORD (AFT OF L.E.)	TOP SECTION "X" ORDINATE (DIST. AFT)	TOP SECTION "Y" ORDINATE (DIST. FROM ℄)	BOTTOM SECTION "X" ORDINATE (DIST. AFT.)	BOTTOM SECTION "Y" ORDINATE (DIST. FROM ℄)
.5%	.1250"	0.16"	0.095"	0.125"
.75%	.1875"	0.20"	0.1425"	0.15"
2.5%	.6250"	0.35"	0.475"	0.26"
5%	1.25"	0.48"	0.95"	0.37"
10%	2.50"	0.66"	1.90"	0.50"
20%	5.00"	0.88"	3.80"	0.67"
30%	7.50"	0.98"	5.70"	0.75"
40%	10.00"	1.00"	7.60"	0.76"
50%	12.50"	0.93"	9.50"	0.70"
60%	15.00"	0.79"	11.40"	0.60"
70%	17.50"	0.61"	13.30"	0.47"
80%	20.00"	0.41"	15.20"	0.31"
90%	22.50"	0.21"	17.10"	0.16"
100%	25.00"	0.06"	19.00"	0.06"
LEADING EDGE RADIUS = 0.12" (TOP SECTION)				
LEADING EDGE RADIUS = 0.09" (BOTTOM SECTION)				

SKEG & RUDDER NOTES

③ SKEG & RUDDER SECTION - MODIFIED NACA 63A-008 FOIL SECTION.

④ SKEG, RUDDER, & TRIM TAB ARE TO BE LOFTED AS ONE SECTION.

KEEL OFFSETS

PERCENT OF CHORD (AFT OF L.E.)	TOP SECTION "X" ORDINATE (DIST. AFT)	TOP SECTION "Y" ORDINATE (DIST. FROM ℄)	BOTTOM SECTION "X" ORDINATE (DIST. AFT)	BOTTOM SECTION "Y" ORDINATE (DIST. FROM ℄)
.5%	0.21"	0.34"	0.18"	0.29"
.75%	0.315"	0.41"	0.27"	0.35"
2.5%	1.05"	0.71"	0.90"	0.61"
5%	2.10"	0.98"	1.80"	0.84"
10%	4.20"	1.34"	3.60"	1.15"
20%	8.40"	1.79"	7.20"	1.54"
30%	12.60"	2.00"	10.80"	1.74"
40%	16.80"	2.10"	14.40"	1.80"
50%	21.00"	1.97"	18.00"	1.69"
60%	25.20"	1.69"	21.60"	1.45"
70%	29.40"	1.31"	25.20"	1.13"
80%	33.60"	0.88"	28.80"	0.76"
90%	37.80"	0.45"	32.40"	0.38"
100%	42.00"	0.06"	36.00"	0.06"
LEADING EDGE RADIUS = 0.29" (TOP SECTION)				
" = 0.25" (BOTTOM SECTION)				

KEEL NOTES

① KEEL SECTION - MODIFIED NACA 64A-010 FOIL SECTION.

② NOTE TO LOFTSMAN - CASTING IS A STRAIGHT TAPER ALONG PERCENTAGE LINES. FAIR DEAD WOOD INTO CASTING TAPER.

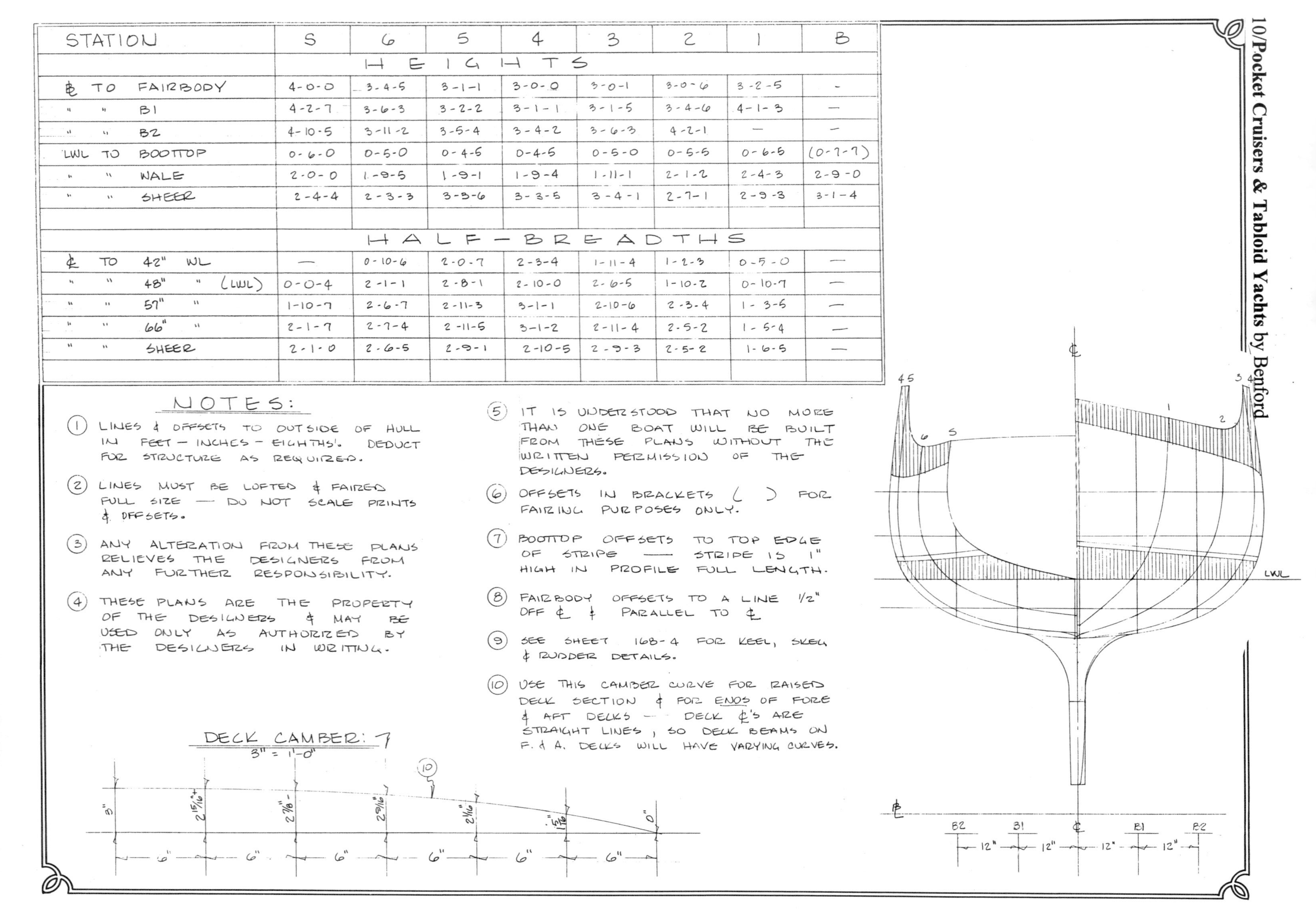

STATION	S	6	5	4	3	2	1	B
	HEIGHTS							
℄ TO FAIRBODY	4-0-0	3-4-5	3-1-1	3-0-0	3-0-1	3-0-6	3-2-5	-
" " B1	4-2-7	3-6-3	3-2-2	3-1-1	3-1-5	3-4-6	4-1-3	—
" " B2	4-10-5	3-11-2	3-5-4	3-4-2	3-6-3	4-2-1	—	—
LWL TO BOOTTOP	0-6-0	0-5-0	0-4-5	0-4-5	0-5-0	0-5-5	0-6-5	(0-7-7)
" " WALE	2-0-0	1-9-5	1-9-1	1-9-4	1-11-1	2-1-2	2-4-3	2-9-0
" " SHEER	2-4-4	2-3-3	3-3-6	3-3-5	3-4-1	2-7-1	2-9-3	3-1-4
	HALF-BREADTHS							
℄ TO 42" WL	—	0-10-6	2-0-7	2-3-4	1-11-4	1-2-3	0-5-0	—
" " 48" " (LWL)	0-0-4	2-1-1	2-8-1	2-10-0	2-6-5	1-10-2	0-10-7	—
" " 57" "	1-10-7	2-6-7	2-11-3	3-1-1	2-10-6	2-3-4	1-3-5	—
" " 66" "	2-1-7	2-7-4	2-11-5	3-1-2	2-11-4	2-5-2	1-5-4	—
" " SHEER	2-1-0	2-6-5	2-9-1	2-10-5	2-9-3	2-5-2	1-6-5	—

NOTES:

1. LINES & OFFSETS TO OUTSIDE OF HULL IN FEET – INCHES – EIGHTHS!. DEDUCT FOR STRUCTURE AS REQUIRED.
2. LINES MUST BE LOFTED & FAIRED FULL SIZE — DO NOT SCALE PRINTS & OFFSETS.
3. ANY ALTERATION FROM THESE PLANS RELIEVES THE DESIGNERS FROM ANY FURTHER RESPONSIBILITY.
4. THESE PLANS ARE THE PROPERTY OF THE DESIGNERS & MAY BE USED ONLY AS AUTHORIZED BY THE DESIGNERS IN WRITING.
5. IT IS UNDERSTOOD THAT NO MORE THAN ONE BOAT WILL BE BUILT FROM THESE PLANS WITHOUT THE WRITTEN PERMISSION OF THE DESIGNERS.
6. OFFSETS IN BRACKETS ( ) FOR FAIRING PURPOSES ONLY.
7. BOOTTOP OFFSETS TO TOP EDGE OF STRIPE — STRIPE IS 1" HIGH IN PROFILE FULL LENGTH.
8. FAIRBODY OFFSETS TO A LINE 1/2" OFF ℄ & PARALLEL TO ℄
9. SEE SHEET 168-4 FOR KEEL, SKEG & RUDDER DETAILS.
10. USE THIS CAMBER CURVE FOR RAISED DECK SECTION & FOR ENDS OF FORE & AFT DECKS — DECK ℄'S ARE STRAIGHT LINES, SO DECK BEAMS ON F. & A. DECKS WILL HAVE VARYING CURVES.

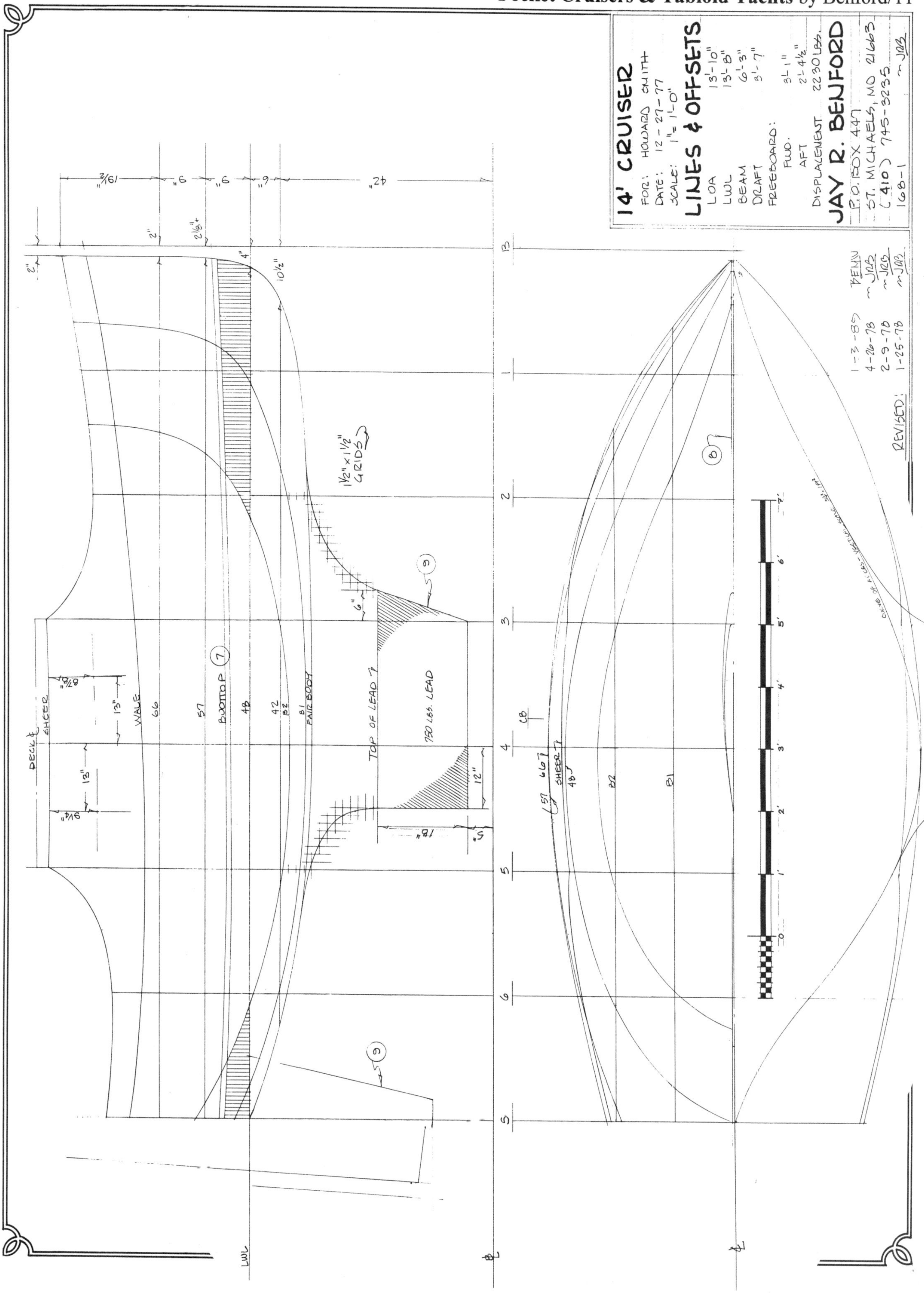

14' CRUISER

FOR: HOWARD SMITH
DATE: 12-27-77
SCALE: 1" = 1'-0"

LINES & OFFSETS

LOA	13'-10"
LWL	13'-8"
BEAM	6'-3"
DRAFT	3'-7"
FREEBOARD: FWD.	3'-1"
AFT	2'-4½"
DISPLACEMENT	2230 LBS.

JAY R. BENFORD
P.O. BOX 447
ST. MICHAELS, MD 21663
(410) 745-3235

168-1

REVISED: 1-25-78, 2-9-78, 4-26-78, 1-3-85

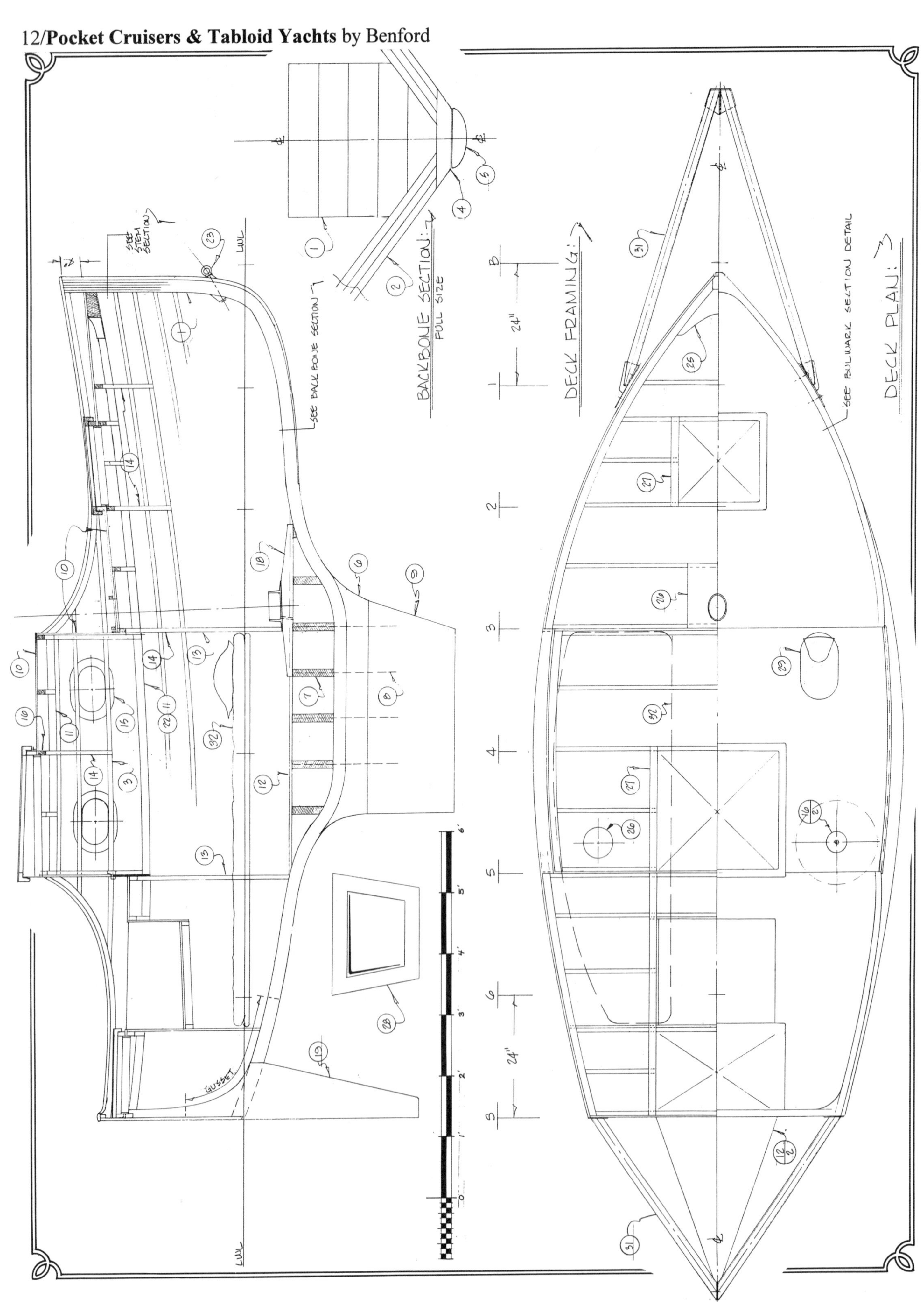
BACKBONE SECTION:
FULL SIZE
DECK FRAMING:
DECK PLAN:
SEE BULWARK SECTION DETAIL
SEE BACK BONE SECTION
SEE STEM SECTION
GUSSET
LWL
24"

NOTES:

★ ALL FRAMING TO BE V. G. D. FIR UNLESS OTHERWISE SPECIFIED.

(1) STEM & BACKBONE: LAMINATED TO SHAPE — 2½" × 2½", EXCEPT WIDER IN WAY OF KEEL.

(2) PLANKING: 3 DIAGONALLY OPPOSING LAYERS OF 1/8" RED CEDAR GLUED TOGETHER.

(3) LONG'L. STRINGERS: 3/4" × 3/4" ON 4" TO 5" CTRS. — FIR OR SPRUCE

(4) STEM CAP: 3/4" TAPERING TO 1/4" AT STA. 1 & ENDING NEAR STA. 2.

(5) STEM GUARD: 1" BRZ. HALF-OVAL — RUN FROM STEM HEAD TO NEAR STA. 2

(6) TIMBER FILLERS: SIDED SAME AS KEEL

(7) FLOORS: SIDED 1½" — LOCATE AS SHOWN.

(8) KEEL BOLTS: 1/2"⌀ EVERDUR BRZ. — ALTERNATE ANGLE OFF ℄ P. & STBD. — DRILL & TAP INTO BALLAST.

(9) BALLAST: 750 LBS. — LEAD WITH 5% ANTIMONY

(10) DECK: 10 MM BRUYNZEEL OR 1/2" FIR MARINE PLYWOOD

(11) CLAMP: 1½" × 1½"

(12) SOLE: 10 MM BRUYNZEEL OR 1/2" FIR MARINE PLY

(13) FRAMES: 2 PCS. 3/4" × 3/4" LAMINATED TOGETHER OVER STRINGERS — NOTCH ONE PIECE OVER CLAMP AS SHOWN.

(14) KNEES: 3/4" STOCK, SHAPED AS SHOWN.

(15) FILLER BLOCKS: 3/4" — SHAPED TO FOLLOW OUTLINE OF PORTS AS SHOWN

(16) DECK BEAMS: 3/4" × 1½" SPACED AS SHOWN.

(17) TOERAIL: FROM 3/4" × 2⅛" TEAK — RABBET OUT AS SHOWN (LOWER PART 1/2" × 1⅛")

(18) MAST STEP: FROM 2½" × 5" — TAPER TO 1" × 5" FORE & AFT AS SHOWN.

(19) SKEG: FROM 2" STOCK — SHAPE LOWER PORTION PER 168-4 — FIT 1/4" CHEEKS ABOVE BACKBONE (SLOT BACKBONE IN WAY OF SKEG) & ADD 10MM BRUYNZEEL OR 1/2" FIR PLY GUSSETS AS SHOWN.

(20) BULWARK FRAME: 3/4" × 1⅛"

(21) RAILCAP: FROM 5/8" × 1¼" TEAK — SHAPE AS SHOWN

(22) TOP OF CLAMP AT WALE HEIGHT IN OFFSETS

(23) BOBSTAY FITTING: W-C. FIG 2220 1/2" × 6" BRZ. SHOULDER EYEBOLT — MOUNT AT 30° TO LWL & ON WEDGE PADS AS SHOWN.

(24) SHEATHING: 6 OZ. FIBERGLASS CLOTH SET IN EPOXY RESIN OVER ENTIRE EXTERIOR OF VESSEL FOR IMPACT RESISTANCE — DOUBLE IN THICKNESS OVER KEEL

(25) BREASTHOOK: FROM 2½" — TO SHAPE SHOWN

(26) DECK DOUBLERS: SAME AS DECK (10) — LOCATED AS SHOWN FOR MAST & HARDWARE.

(27) CARLINS: 1/2" × 1½" — LOCATED AS SHOWN

(28) COMPANIONWAY DROP BOARD: 3/4" × 3" FRAME WITH 1/4" LEXAN — ALSO MAKE ONE WITH 3/4" × 1½" FRAME & INSECT SCREEN IN PLACE OF LEXAN.

(29) DORADE VENTILATION BOX — 4"⌀ VENT — PLASTIMO FIG 45.16.18.4 — P. & S.

(30) HATCHES: (A) SILLS 3/4" — FRAMES (C) FROM 1½" × 1½" — (D) TOPS 1/4" LEXAN — PROVIDE GOOD GASKETS (B)

(31) BOWSPRIT & BOOMKIN: 2" O.D. × 1/8" WALL ALUM. TUBES — 3/16" ℞ MOUNTING PADS, 1/4" LUG ℞S FOR STAYS.

(32) PIPE BERTH: P. & S. AS SHOWN — USE AIREX TYPE 530.50B FOAM & COVER TO SUIT.

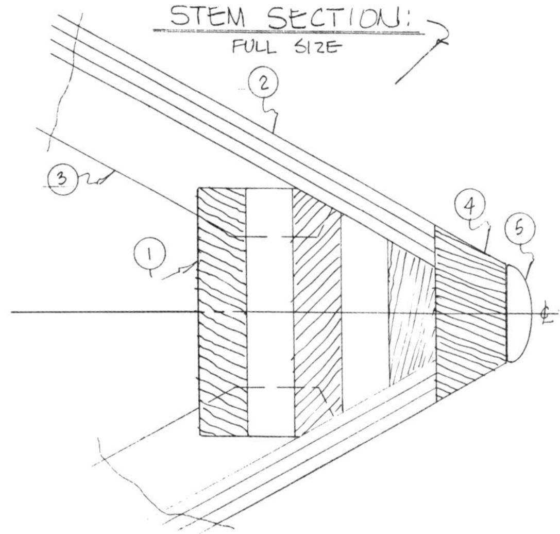

14' CRUISER

FOR: HOWARD SMITH
DATE: 4-25-78
SCALE: 1" = 1'-0" & AS NOTED

CONSTRUCTION

LOA	13'-10"
LWL	13'-8"
BEAM	6'-3"
DRAFT	3'-7"
FREEBOARD:	
FWD.	3'-1"
RAISED DECK	3'-3⅝"
AFT	2'-4½"

JAY R. BENFORD
P.O. BOX 447
ST. MICHAELS, MD 21663
(410) 745-3235

168-3 ~JRB

REVISED: 11-5-79 ~JRB

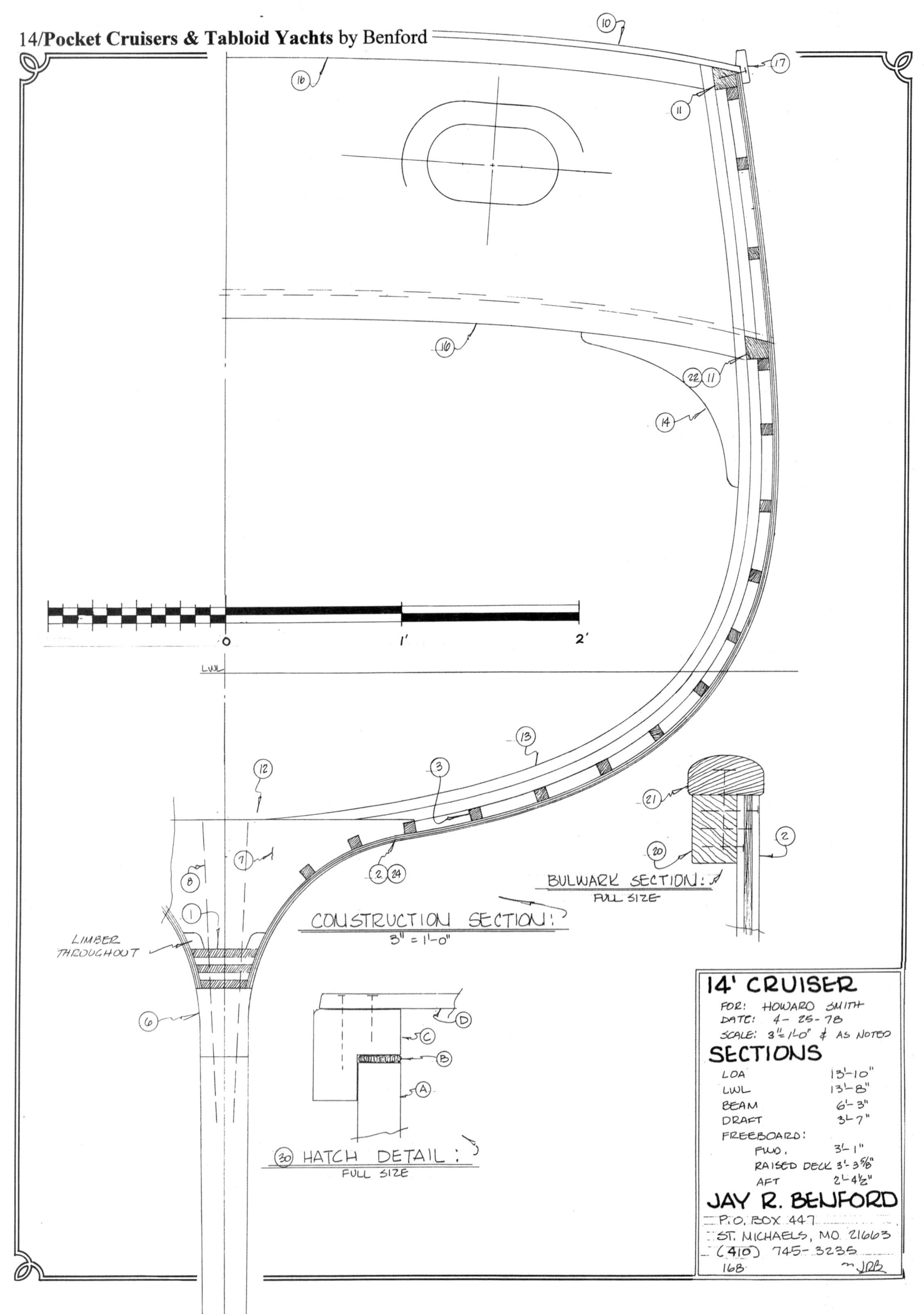

CONSTRUCTION SECTION:
3" = 1'-0"
BULWARK SECTION:
FULL SIZE
30 HATCH DETAIL:
FULL SIZE
LIMBER THROUGHOUT
LWL
0
1'
2'
14' CRUISER
FOR: HOWARD SMITH
DATE: 4-25-78
SCALE: 3" = 1'-0" & AS NOTED
SECTIONS
LOA 13'-10"
LWL 13'-8"
BEAM 6'-3"
DRAFT 3'-7"
FREEBOARD:
FWD. 3'-1"
RAISED DECK 3'-3 5/8"
AFT 2'-4 1/2"
JAY R. BENFORD
P.O. BOX 447
ST. MICHAELS, MD. 21663
(410) 745-3235
168
JRB

Chapter Two

14' Tug Yacht, Tug-Cruiser ***Grivit***, & Trawler Yacht ***Bullhead***

Design Number 98

1972

14' Tug Yacht

What one of us has not indulged in daydreams of being captain of a powerful tugboat, bustling about the business of towing and ship handling? Herein is presented a means to fulfill those dreams for those still young at heart and of spirit.

This husky little workboat will make a handsome tug for use in moving boats, docks and floats at marinas and yacht clubs. As a race committee boat, yacht club tender or for towing logs, she offers promise in satisfying a number of requirements. She'll also be a fun boat to go camp-cruising and day-fishing in for the yachtsman who enjoys just "messing around with boats".

For the man wanting to try out some differing construction techniques, but not wanting to get in over his head, this 14-footer will provide just the right amount of work for a "taste" of what boatbuilding is all about.

The 14' Tug Yacht will also make a sturdy transportation boat around marinas and yacht harbors, for if the Coast Guard allowed it, she'd take up to ten average-sized people aboard before her decks began to feel water coming in through the scuppers! The bulwarks being eighteen to thirty-three inches high, they give those aboard a feeling of being securely inside the vessel, rather than perched atop her, as is usually so common with small craft. The pilot house again defies the imagination, allowing a headroom of 6' 5"!

Depending upon the engine used, the 14' Tug Yacht will prove quite adept at moving and towing and most practical for maneuvering objects into tight corners, where larger vessels couldn't fit.

Having a displacement similar to much larger planing boats, she will provide close to the same proportion of work in building the hull as they would, while the work in out-fitting will be much simplified.

Her cost in materials will prove proportionately less, also fitting in with the first builder's "try-out" budget. The inboard engine, if purchased new, will be the largest single expense. The conscientious buyer can find used and rebuilt engines at more attractive costs.

***Grivit** shown below in Gene Coan photo.*

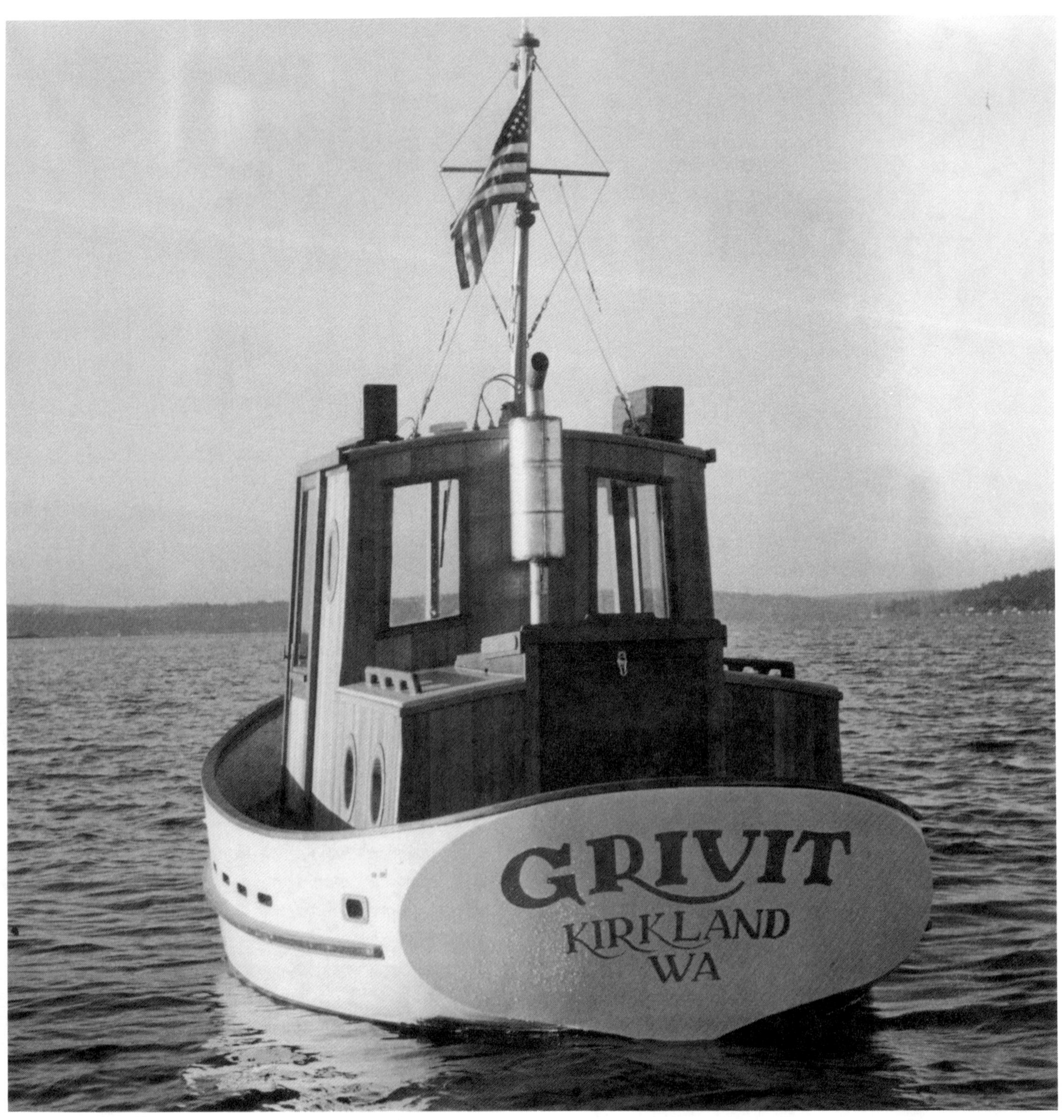

Bullhead - 14' Trawler Yacht

In response to the tyranny of high moorage rates, as well as high costs of fuel and maintenance for large cruisers these days, we have come up with a serious little packet who snubs her nose at such nonsense. Dubbed the **Bullhead**, she offers many at-home creature comforts. Such as 6'-5" standing headroom in her pilothouse (with comfortable sitting headroom fore and aft.) Such as a head (with skylight over.) Such as a pilotseat for two, a stove, an icebox, a sink, and an extension double berth. And all in fourteen feet.

You've heard of compact cars? Well, we thought it high time that someone came up with the economical compact boat. Measuring fourteen feet overall (thirteen feet on her waterline), with her beam half her overall length, this pocket cruiser has a draft of three feet. She displaces 3,675 pounds, and sports a displacement - length ratio of 747. (!) With a flank speed of 5 knots, she requires about 5 to 7 horsepower, and burns about one quart of diesel fuel per hour. Just try that with any typical gin palace!

As our design shows, she has sliding doors port and starboard, with a surprising amount of stowage space in the way of outboard shelves along the starboard midships area, and also aft to port. The head is in the foc'sle, and can be made private by hanging a drop curtain aft of it, between the steering console and the starboard shelf. Ventilation in the head is a natural with the overhead skylight - hatch...which also makes standing up in the area a simpler affair. When the head is not in use, the hatch is handy for poking one's head out to tend dock lines, or to drop anchor without going above decks in nasty weather.

The pilotseat is over the engine midships, and the large windows and ports afford great visibility at the helm, as do the convenient sliding doors (which are also large windows) on each side of the pilothouse. The icebox and stove are situated to port and starboard respectively, with a wood bin aft, convenient to the stove. A sink is planned to be installed just aft of the icebox. The crew can sit comfortably on the great cabin's four and a half foot wide settee, and feel cheerfully lit by the surrounding ports and overhead skylight. Extending the settee to a full-size, double bed (6'-8" long) at night, the crew can then gaze through the skylight at the stars overhead. And just think ... they won't even have to get up out of bed to have that morning cup of hot coffee, for the stove is right at hand!

Maneuvering this little rascal is sweet indeed. We recently had the good fortune to take a short spin aboard one of **Bullhead's** sisters, a 14' Tug, which one of our clients built and cruises on Cayuga Lake, in upstate New York. She literally turns like a top, and charges right along with little effort and negligible wake, looking very businesslike.

How did we create her, you may ask? Well, we were sitting around the drawing board one week-end last spring, shortly after toying with some sketches for a marvelous Lake Union Dreamboat style pocket cruiser (See Chapter Four). As we were the proud owners of one of our 14' Tugboat hulls, the question was asked, "Why couldn't we do something similar to the Lake Union Dreamboat to our 14-footer?" With little more conversation, pencil was set to paper, and the drawings in this chapter are the result....

Particulars		**English**	**Metric**
Length overall		14'-0"	4.27 m
Length designed waterline		13'-0"	3.96 m
Beam		7'-0"	2.13 m
Draft		3'-0"	0.91 m
Freeboard:	Forward	3'-6"	1.07 m
	Least	2'-0"	0.61 m
	Aft	2'-4¼"	0.72 m
Displacement, cruising trim		3,675 lbs.	1,667 kg.
Displacement-length ratio		747	
Ballast		850 lbs.	386 kg.
Ballast ratio		23%	
Prismatic coefficient		.56	
Pounds per inch immersion		310	55 kg./cm
Fuel tankage		17 Gals.	64 litres
Headroom		6'-5"	1.96 m

Grivit -- 14' Tug-Cruiser

People who've owned both large and small boats will probably agree that they had more fun and got more use out of the little ones. The little ones are easier to get underway quickly and can be operated without having to depend on having several crew members along to help handle the heavier gear on the larger boats.

Grivit, the 14' Tug-Cruiser, fits this little boat description. She's fun to look at, fun to be aboard, and fun to own. She's the third version designed on this hull.

The first was a working yard tug, with the deck aft of the pilothouse clear except for a towing bitt. The second was a pocket trawler yacht, with the afterdeck covered with a cabin with cozy accommodations for two. A friendly two, that is.

Grivit, the third version, was designed for Gene and Fran Coan. They use her on Lake Washington, visiting friends and various waterfront restaurants in the Seattle area. Kept on a mooring in front of their place most of the year, they have the pleasure of looking at her daily, even if they aren't using her.

Grivit was outfitted to the Coans' wishes by Howard Cain at his shop in Seattle. They make extensive use of cedar, teak, and bronze. There's good headroom (6' 4") in the pilothouse, and comfortable sitting headroom in the after house.

A word of caution here: Anyone aspiring to own a spiffy pocket yacht such as ***Grivit*** had better enjoy talking to people — you'll be besieged with questioners everywhere you go. Or, of course, you could anchor out for peace and privacy....

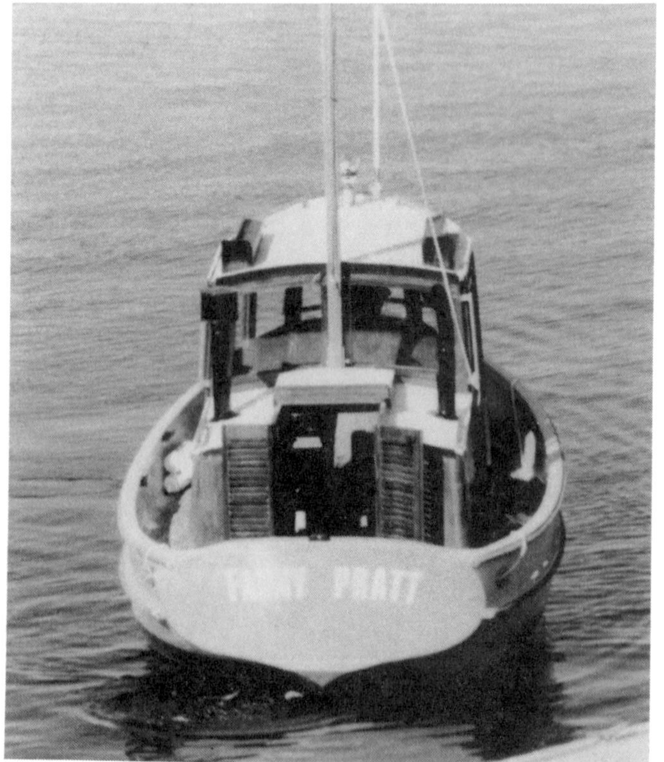

*Gene Coan's **Grivit** (above) and Jim Lesovsky's **Fanny Pratt** are sisterships, built to the Tug-Cruiser version of the 14' Tug plans. Underway and at anchor they are the personification of a small ship.* Photos courtesy of the owners.

Two of the tug versions are shown above. Clarence Butz's **Bullhead** is above left and Joe Failing's 14-footer is rafted alongside the bigger working tug.

Below is Gene Coan's **Grivit** on her mooring on Lake Washington looking the personification of a small ship. Photos courtesy of the owners.

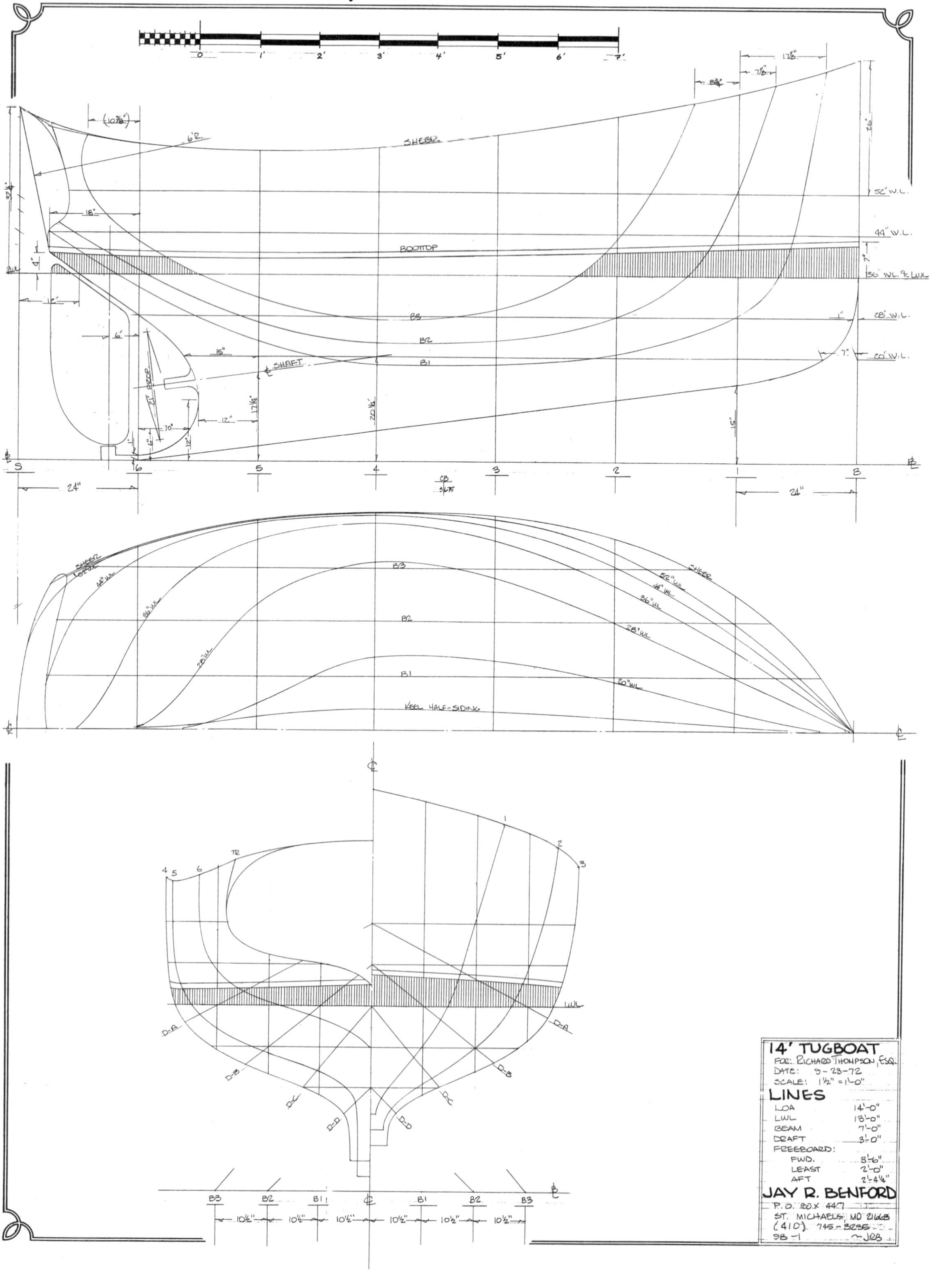

14' TUGBOAT

FOR: RICHARD THOMPSON, ESQ.
DATE: 9-23-72
SCALE: 1½" = 1'-0"

LINES

LOA	14'-0"
LWL	13'-0"
BEAM	7'-0"
DRAFT	3'-0"
FREEBOARD:	
FWD.	3'-6"
LEAST	2'-0"
AFT	2'-4¼"

JAY R. BENFORD
P.O. BOX 447
ST. MICHAELS, MD 21663
(410) 745-3235
98-1 ~JRB

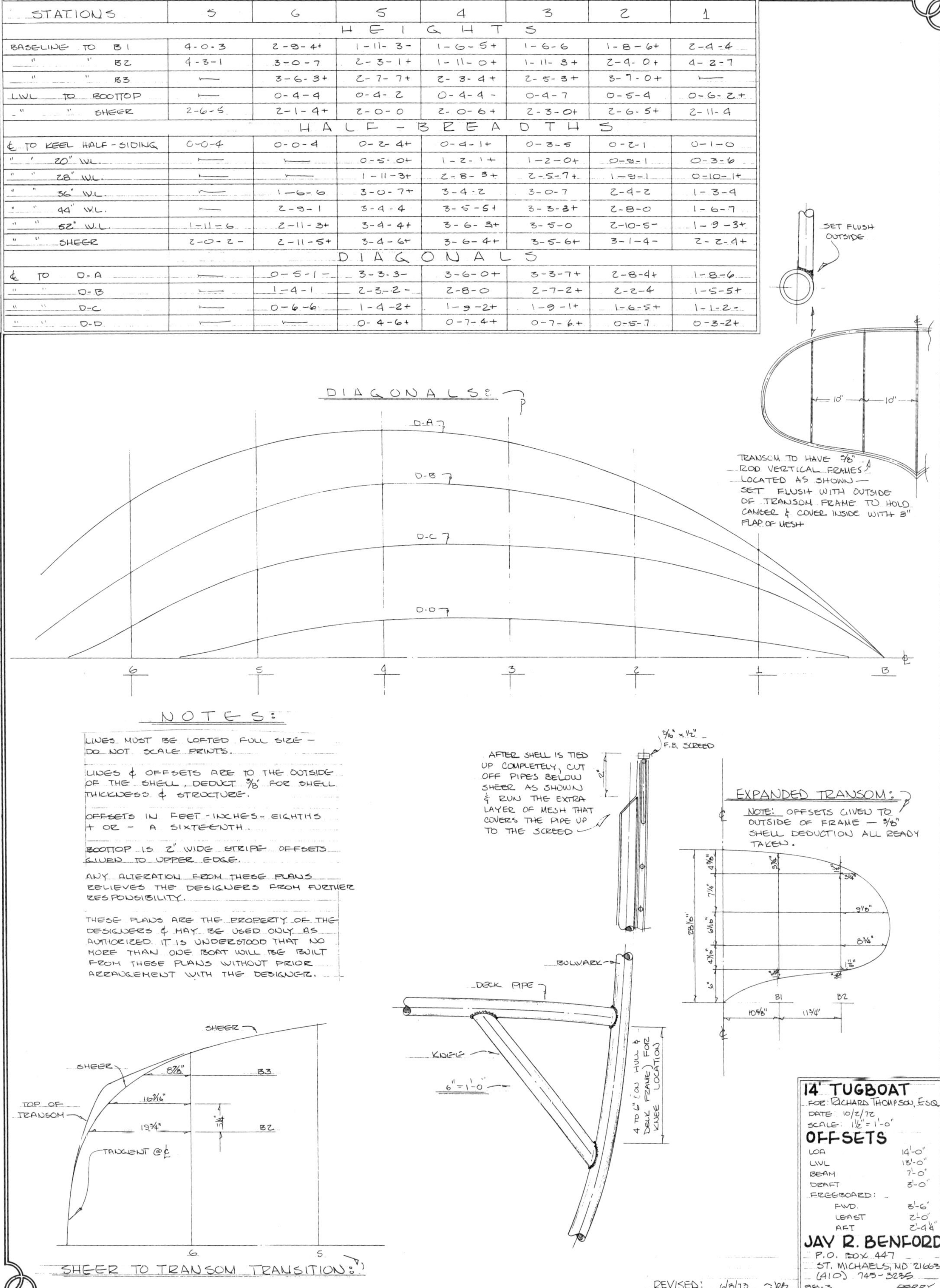

STATIONS	5	6	5	4	3	2	1
HEIGHTS							
BASELINE TO B1	4-0-3	2-9-4+	1-11-3-	1-6-5+	1-6-6	1-8-6+	2-4-4
" " B2	4-3-1	3-0-7	2-3-1+	1-11-0+	1-11-3+	2-4-0+	4-2-7
" " B3	—	3-6-3+	2-7-7+	2-3-4+	2-5-3+	3-7-0+	—
LWL TO BOOTTOP	—	0-4-4	0-4-2	0-4-4-	0-4-7	0-5-4	0-6-2+
" " SHEER	2-6-5	2-1-4+	2-0-0	2-0-6+	2-3-0+	2-6-5+	2-11-4
HALF-BREADTHS							
℄ TO KEEL HALF-SIDING	0-0-4	0-0-4	0-2-4+	0-4-1+	0-3-5	0-2-1	0-1-0
" " 20" W.L.	—	—	0-5-0+	1-2-1+	1-2-0+	0-9-1	0-3-6
" " 28" W.L.	—	—	1-11-3+	2-8-3+	2-5-7+	1-9-1	0-10-1+
" " 36" W.L.	—	1-6-6	3-0-7+	3-4-2	3-0-7	2-4-2	1-3-4
" " 44" W.L.	—	2-9-1	3-4-4	3-5-5+	3-3-3+	2-8-0	1-6-7
" " 52" W.L.	1-11-6	2-11-3+	3-4-4+	3-6-3+	3-5-0	2-10-5-	1-9-3+
" " SHEER	2-0-2-	2-11-5+	3-4-6+	3-6-4+	3-5-6+	3-1-4-	2-2-4+
DIAGONALS							
℄ TO D-A	—	0-5-1-	3-3-3-	3-6-0+	3-3-7+	2-8-4+	1-8-6
" " D-B	—	1-4-1	2-3-2-	2-8-0	2-7-2+	2-2-4	1-5-5+
" " D-C	—	0-6-6	1-4-2+	1-9-2+	1-9-1+	1-6-5+	1-1-2-
" " D-D	—	—	0-4-6+	0-7-4+	0-7-6+	0-5-7	0-3-2+

SET FLUSH OUTSIDE
10"
10"
TRANSOM TO HAVE 5/8" ROD VERTICAL FRAMES LOCATED AS SHOWN — SET FLUSH WITH OUTSIDE OF TRANSOM FRAME TO HOLD CANVAS & COVER INSIDE WITH 3" FLAP OF MESH
DIAGONALS:
D-A
D-B
D-C
D-D
6
5
4
3
2
1
B
NOTES:
LINES MUST BE LOFTED FULL SIZE — DO NOT SCALE PRINTS.
LINES & OFFSETS ARE TO THE OUTSIDE OF THE SHELL, DEDUCT 5/8" FOR SHELL THICKNESS & STRUCTURE.
OFFSETS IN FEET-INCHES-EIGHTHS + OR - A SIXTEENTH.
BOOTTOP IS 2" WIDE STRIPE OFFSETS GIVEN TO UPPER EDGE.
ANY ALTERATION FROM THESE PLANS RELIEVES THE DESIGNERS FROM FURTHER RESPONSIBILITY.
THESE PLANS ARE THE PROPERTY OF THE DESIGNERS & MAY BE USED ONLY AS AUTHORIZED. IT IS UNDERSTOOD THAT NO MORE THAN ONE BOAT WILL BE BUILT FROM THESE PLANS WITHOUT PRIOR ARRANGEMENT WITH THE DESIGNER.
5/16" x 1/2" F.B. SCREED
AFTER SHELL IS TIED UP COMPLETELY, CUT OFF PIPES BELOW SHEER AS SHOWN & RUN THE EXTRA LAYER OF MESH THAT COVERS THE PIPE UP TO THE SCREED
2"
EXPANDED TRANSOM:
NOTE: OFFSETS GIVEN TO OUTSIDE OF FRAME — 5/8" SHELL DEDUCTION ALL READY TAKEN.
B1
B2
10 5/8"
11 3/4"
BULWARK
DECK PIPE
KNEE
6" = 1'-0"
4 TO 6" (ON HULL & DECK FRAME) FOR KNEE LOCATION
SHEER
SHEER
TOP OF TRANSOM
8 7/8"
B3
16 9/16"
19 3/4"
B2
TANGENT @ ℄
6
5
SHEER TO TRANSOM TRANSITION:
REVISED: 6/3/93
14' TUGBOAT
FOR: RICHARD THOMPSON, ESQ.
DATE 10/2/92
SCALE: 1 1/2" = 1'-0"
OFFSETS
LOA 14'-0"
LWL 13'-0"
BEAM 7'-0"
DRAFT 3'-0"
FREEBOARD:
FWD. 3'-6"
LEAST 2'-0"
AFT 2'-4 1/4"
JAY R. BENFORD
P.O. BOX 447
ST. MICHAELS, MD 21663
(410) 745-3235
98-3

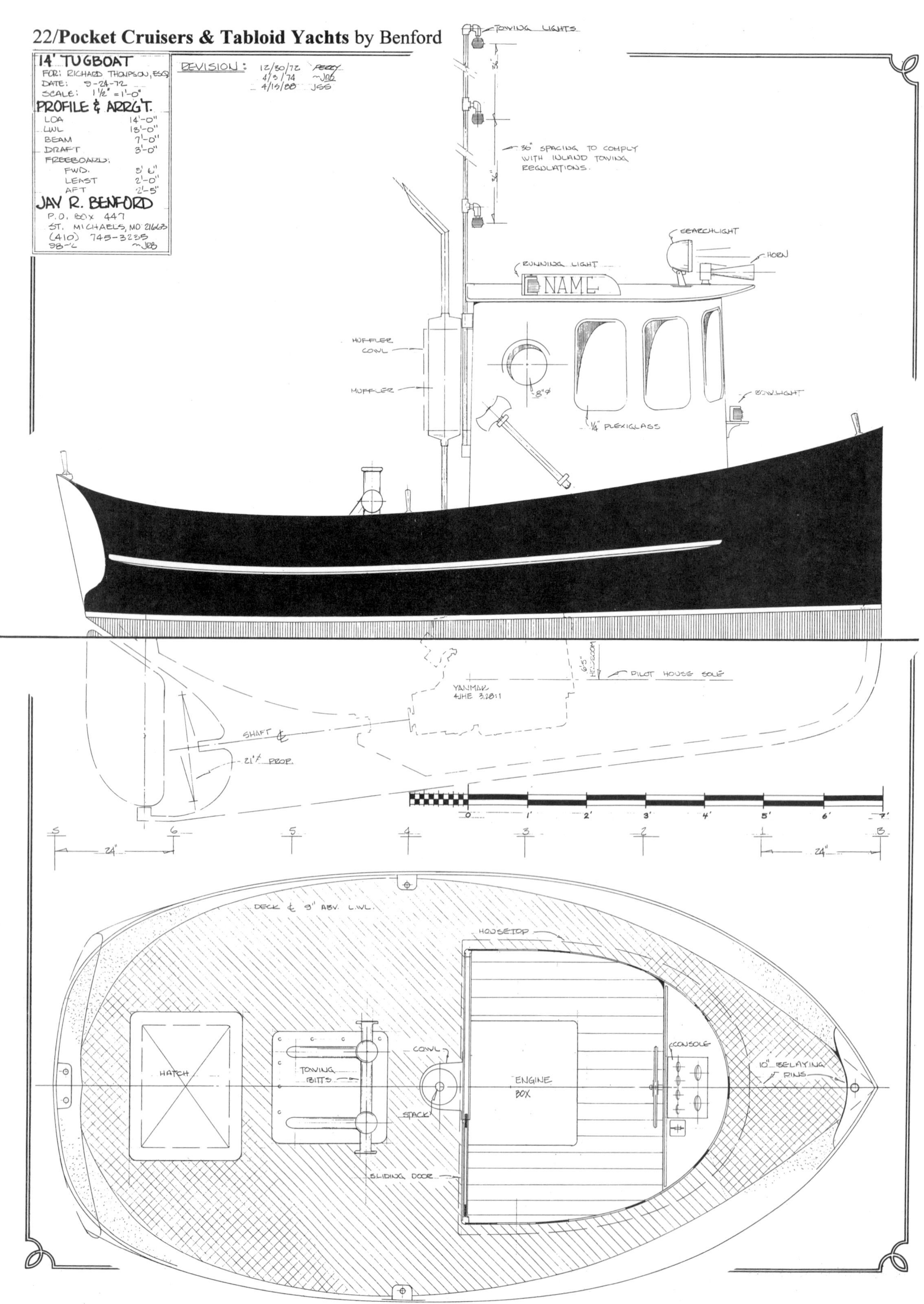

14' TUGBOAT
FOR: RICHARD THOMPSON, ESQ.
DATE: 9-24-72
SCALE: 1½" = 1'-0"
PROFILE & ARRG'T.
LOA 14'-0"
LWL 13'-0"
BEAM 7'-0"
DRAFT 3'-0"
FREEBOARD:
FWD. 3' 6"
LEAST 2'-0"
AFT 2'-5"
JAY R. BENFORD
P.O. BOX 447
ST. MICHAELS, MD 21663
(410) 745-3235
REVISION: 12/30/72 4/3/74 4/15/88
TOWING LIGHTS
36" SPACING TO COMPLY WITH INLAND TOWING REGULATIONS.
SEARCHLIGHT
HORN
RUNNING LIGHT
NAME
MUFFLER COWL
MUFFLER
8"⌀
¼" PLEXIGLASS
BOW LIGHT
HEADROOM
PILOT HOUSE SOLE
YANMAR 4JHE 3.28:1
SHAFT ℄
21"⌀ PROP.
0' 1' 2' 3' 4' 5' 6' 7'
24"
DECK ℄ 9" ABV. L.W.L.
HOUSETOP
HATCH
TOWING BITTS
COWL
STACK
ENGINE BOX
CONSOLE
10" BELAYING PINS
SLIDING DOOR

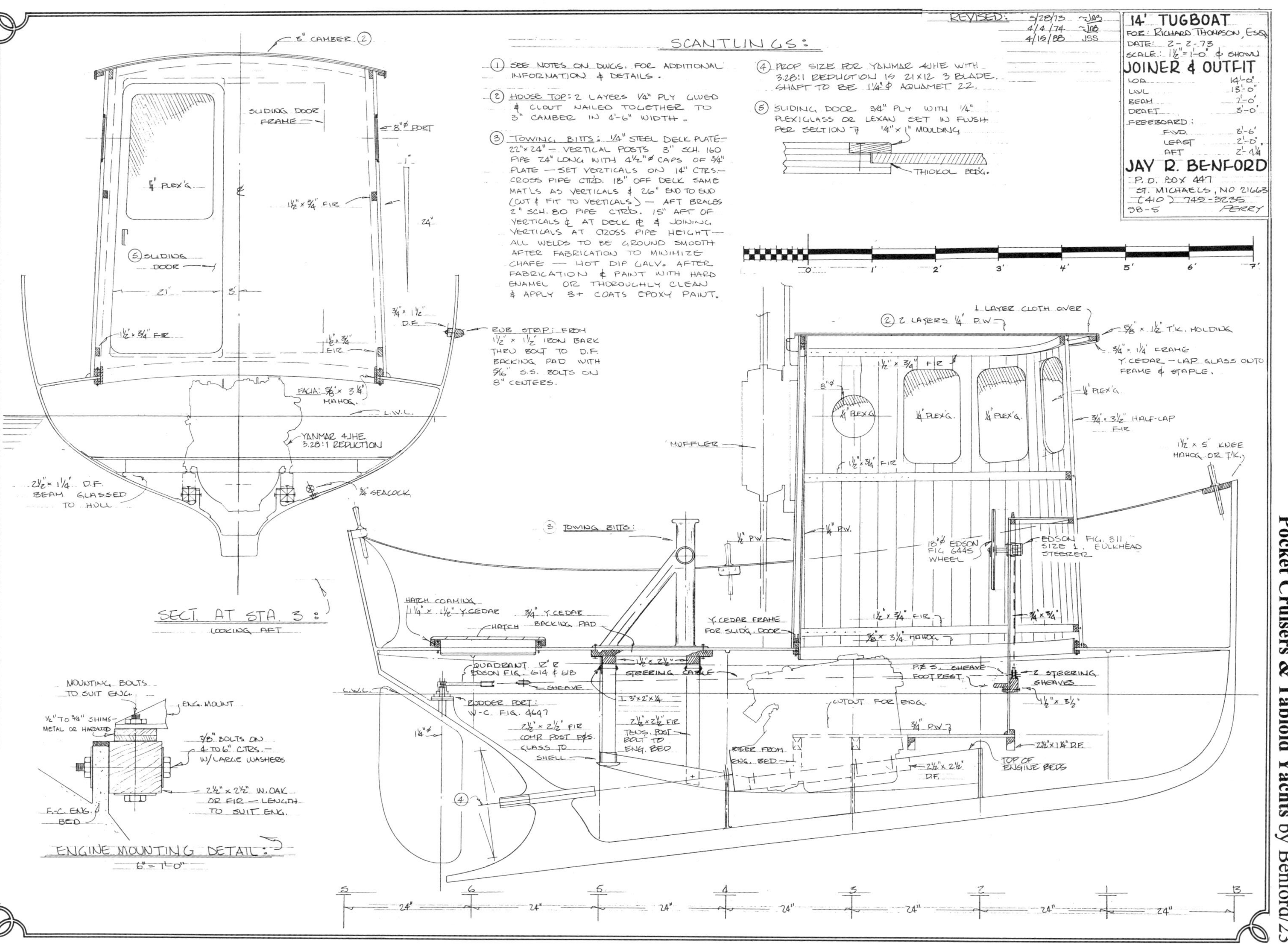
14' TUGBOAT
FOR: RICHARD THOMPSON, ESQ.
DATE: 2-2-73
SCALE: 1½" = 1'-0" & SHOWN
JOINER & OUTFIT
LOA 14'-0"
LWL 13'-0"
BEAM 7'-0"
DRAFT 3'-0"
FREEBOARD:
FWD. 3'-6"
LEAST 2'-0"
AFT 2'-1¼"
JAY R. BENFORD
P.O. BOX 447
ST. MICHAELS, MD 21663
(410) 745-3235
98-5 PERRY
REVISED: 5/28/73 JRB 4/4/74 JRB 4/15/88 JSS
SCANTLINGS:
① SEE NOTES ON DWGS. FOR ADDITIONAL INFORMATION & DETAILS.
② HOUSE TOP: 2 LAYERS ¼" PLY GLUED & CLOUT NAILED TOGETHER TO 3" CAMBER IN 4'-6" WIDTH.
③ TOWING BITTS: ¼" STEEL DECK PLATE 22"×24" — VERTICAL POSTS 3" SCH. 160 PIPE 24" LONG WITH 4½"Ø CAPS OF ¾" PLATE — SET VERTICALS ON 14" CTRS. — CROSS PIPE CTRD. 18" OFF DECK SAME MAT'LS AS VERTICALS & 26" END TO END (CUT & FIT TO VERTICALS) — AFT BRACES 2" SCH. 80 PIPE CTRD. 15" AFT OF VERTICALS ℄ AT DECK ℄ & JOINING VERTICALS AT CROSS PIPE HEIGHT — ALL WELDS TO BE GROUND SMOOTH AFTER FABRICATION TO MINIMIZE CHAFE — HOT DIP GALV. AFTER FABRICATION & PAINT WITH HARD ENAMEL OR THOROUGHLY CLEAN & APPLY 3+ COATS EPOXY PAINT.
④ PROP SIZE FOR YANMAR 4JHE WITH 3.28:1 REDUCTION IS 21X12 3 BLADE. SHAFT TO BE 1¼"Ø AQUAMET 22.
⑤ SLIDING DOOR ¾" PLY WITH ¼" PLEXIGLASS OR LEXAN SET IN FLUSH PER SECTION ⑦ ¼"×1" MOULDING
THIOKOL BED'G.
0' 1' 2' 3' 4' 5' 6' 7'
3" CAMBER ②
SLIDING DOOR FRAME
8"Ø PORT
¼" PLEX'G.
1½"×¾" FIR
24"
⑤ SLIDING DOOR
21" 3'
1½"×¾" FIR
¾"×1½" D.F.
RUB STRIP: FROM 1½"×1½" IRON BARK THRU BOLT TO D.F. BACKING PAD WITH 5/16" S.S. BOLTS ON 8" CENTERS.
FACIA: ⅝"×3¼" MAHOG.
L.W.L.
YANMAR 4JHE 3.28:1 REDUCTION
2½"×1¼" D.F. BEAM GLASSED TO HULL
¾" SEACOCK
SECT. AT STA. 3: LOOKING AFT
② 2 LAYERS ¼" P.W.
1 LAYER CLOTH OVER
⅝"×1½" T.K. HOLDING
¾"×1¼" FRAME Y. CEDAR — LAP GLASS ONTO FRAME & STAPLE.
8"Ø
¼" PLEX'G.
¾"×3½" HALF-LAP FIR
1½"×5" KNEE MAHOG. OR T.K.
MUFFLER
③ TOWING BITTS:
½" P.W.
18"Ø EDSON FIG. 644S WHEEL
EDSON FIG. 311 SIZE 1 BULKHEAD STEERER
HATCH COAMING 1¼"×1½" Y. CEDAR
¾" Y. CEDAR BACKING PAD
HATCH
Y. CEDAR FRAME FOR SLID'G. DOOR
1½"×¾" FIR
¾"×¾"
⅝"×3¼" MAHOG.
QUADRANT 12" R EDSON FIG. 614 & 618
SHEAVE
1½"×2½"
STEERING CABLE
P.&S. SHEAVE
FOOT REST
2 STEERING SHEAVES
1½"×3½"
L.W.L.
RUDDER PORT: W-C. FIG. 4647
I 3"×2"×¼
CUTOUT FOR ENG.
1¼"Ø
2½"×2½" FIR COMP. POST P&S. GLASS TO SHELL
2½"×2½" FIR TENS. POST BOLT TO ENG. BED
RISER FROM ENG. BED
¾ P.W.
2⅞"×1¾" D.F.
2½"×2½" D.F.
TOP OF ENGINE BEDS
④
MOUNTING BOLTS TO SUIT ENG.
ENG. MOUNT
½" TO ¾" SHIMS — METAL OR HARDWD.
⅜" BOLTS ON 4 TO 6" CTRS. — W/LARGE WASHERS
2½"×2½" W. OAK OR FIR — LENGTH TO SUIT ENG.
F.-C. ENG. BED
ENGINE MOUNTING DETAIL: 6" = 1'-0"
5 6 5 4 3 2 1 B
24" 24" 24" 24" 24" 24" 24"

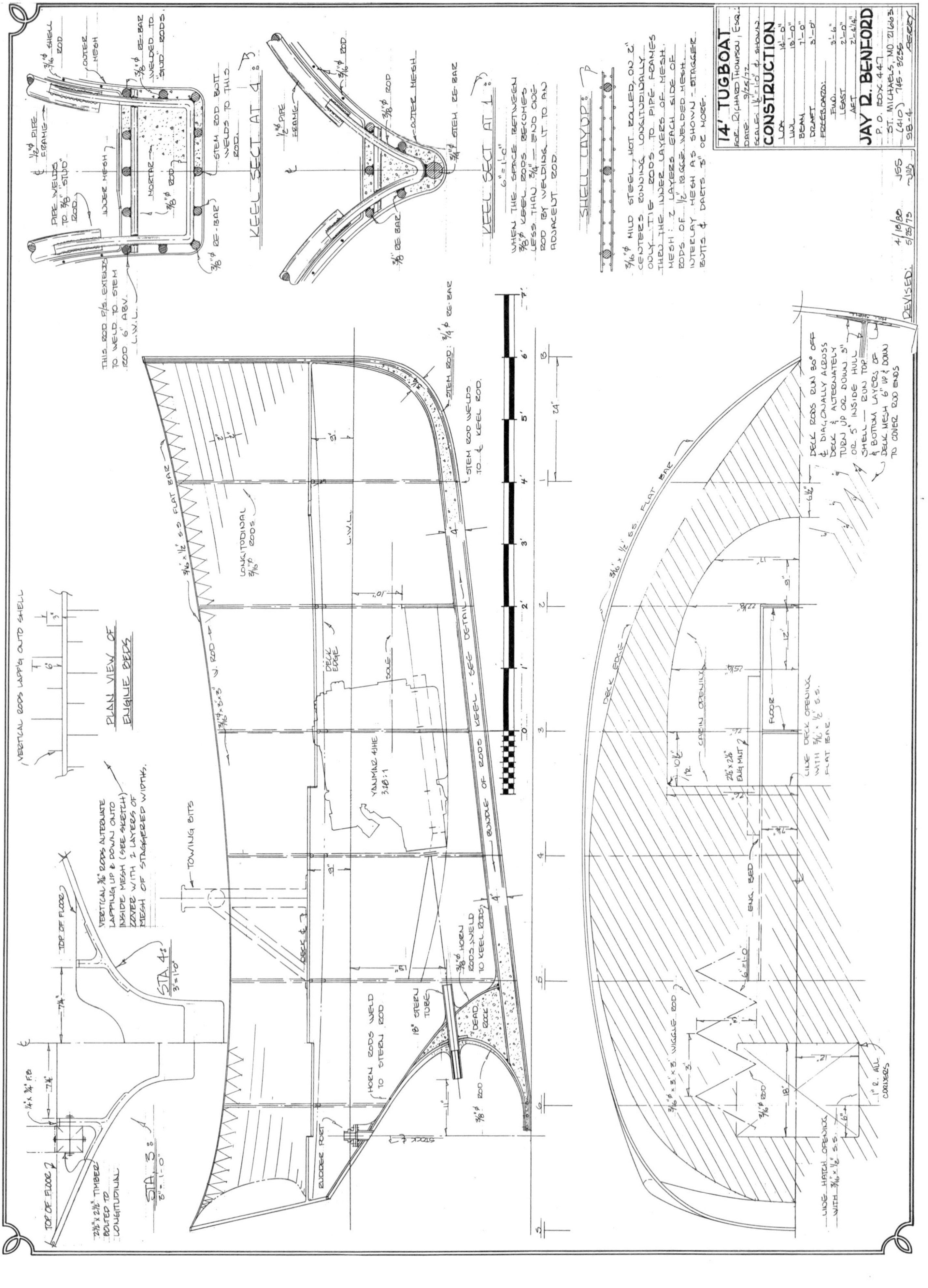

14' TUGBOAT

FOR RICHARD THOMPSON, ESQ.
DATE: 9/25/72
SCALE: 1½" = 1'-0" & SHOWN

CONSTRUCTION

LOA	14'-0"
LWL	13'-0"
BEAM	7'-0"
DRAFT	3'-0"
FREEBOARD:	
FWD.	3'-6"
LEAST	2'-0"
AFT	2'-6¼"

JAY R. BENFORD
P. O. BOX 447
ST. MICHAELS, MD 21663
(410) 745-3235

98-4 PERRY

REVISED: 4/18/88 JSS; 5/25/73 JRB

KEEL SECT AT 4: B

THIS ROD P/S. EXTENDS TO WELD TO STEM ROD 6" ABV. L.W.L.

½"ϕ PIPE FRAME

PIPE WELDS TO ⅜" "STUD" ROD

3/16"ϕ SHELL ROD

OUTER MESH

INNER MESH

⅜"ϕ RE-BAR WELDED TO "STUD" RODS.

MORTAR

⅜"ϕ ROD

⅜"ϕ RE-BAR

STEM ROD BOTT WELDS TO THIS ROD.

KEEL SECT AT 1: C

6" = 1'-0"

½"ϕ PIPE FRAME

3/16"ϕ ROD

⅜"ϕ ROD

⅜" RE BAR

OUTER MESH

¾"ϕ STEM RE-BAR

WHEN THE SPACE BETWEEN ⅜"ϕ KEEL RODS BECOMES LESS THAN ¾" — END ONE ROD BY WELDING IT TO AN ADJACENT ROD.

SHELL LAYUP: D

3/16"ϕ MILD STEEL, HOT ROLLED, ON 2" CENTERS RUNNING LONGITUDINALLY ONLY. TIE RODS TO PIPE FRAMES THRU THE INNER LAYERS OF MESH. MESH: 2 LAYERS EACH SIDE OF RODS OF ½" 19GGE. WELDED MESH. INTERLAY MESH AS SHOWN - STAGGER BUTTS & DARTS 3" OR MORE.

STA. 3: A

3" = 1'-0"

TOP OF FLOOR

¼" x ¾" F.B.

7¼"

2½" x 2½" TIMBER BOLTED TO LONGITUDINAL

STA. 4:

3" = 1'-0"

TOP OF FLOOR

VERTICAL 3/16" RODS ALTERNATE LAPPING UP & DOWN ONTO INSIDE MESH (SEE SKETCH) COVER WITH 2 LAYERS OF MESH OF STAGGERED WIDTHS.

PLAN VIEW OF ENGINE BEDS

VERTICAL RODS LAPP'G ONTO SHELL

6"

3"

Profile

TOWING BITS

3/16" x ½" S.S. FLAT BAR

3/16"ϕ x 3" x 3" W. ROD

LONGITUDINAL 3/16"ϕ RODS

DECK ℄

RUDDER PORT

DECK EDGE

L.W.L.

YANMAR 4JHE 3.28:1

SOLE

HORN RODS WELD TO STERN ROD

18" STERN TUBE

⅜"ϕ HORN RODS WELD TO KEEL RODS

DEAD ROCK

⅜"ϕ ROD

STOCK ℄

BUNDLE OF RODS KEEL - SEE DETAIL

STEM ROD: ¾"ϕ RE-BAR

STEM ROD WELDS TO ℄ KEEL ROD.

0' 1' 2' 3' 4' 5' 6' 7'

5 6 5 4 3 2 1 B

24"

Deck plan

DECK EDGE

3/16" x ½" S.S. FLAT BAR

3/16"ϕ x 3" x 3" WIGGLE ROD

3/16"ϕ ROD

6" = 1'-0"

ENG. BED

2½" x 2½" ENG MNT

CABIN OPENING

FLOOR

WIDE HATCH OPENING WITH 3/16" x ½" S.S.

1" R. ALL CORNERS

WIDE DECK OPENING WITH 3/16" x ½" S.S. FLAT BAR

DECK RODS RUN 30° OFF ℄ DIAGONALLY ACROSS DECK & ALTERNATELY TURN UP OR DOWN 3" OR 5" INSIDE HULL SHELL — RUN TOP & BOTTOM LAYERS OF DECK MESH 6" UP & DOWN TO COVER ROD ENDS

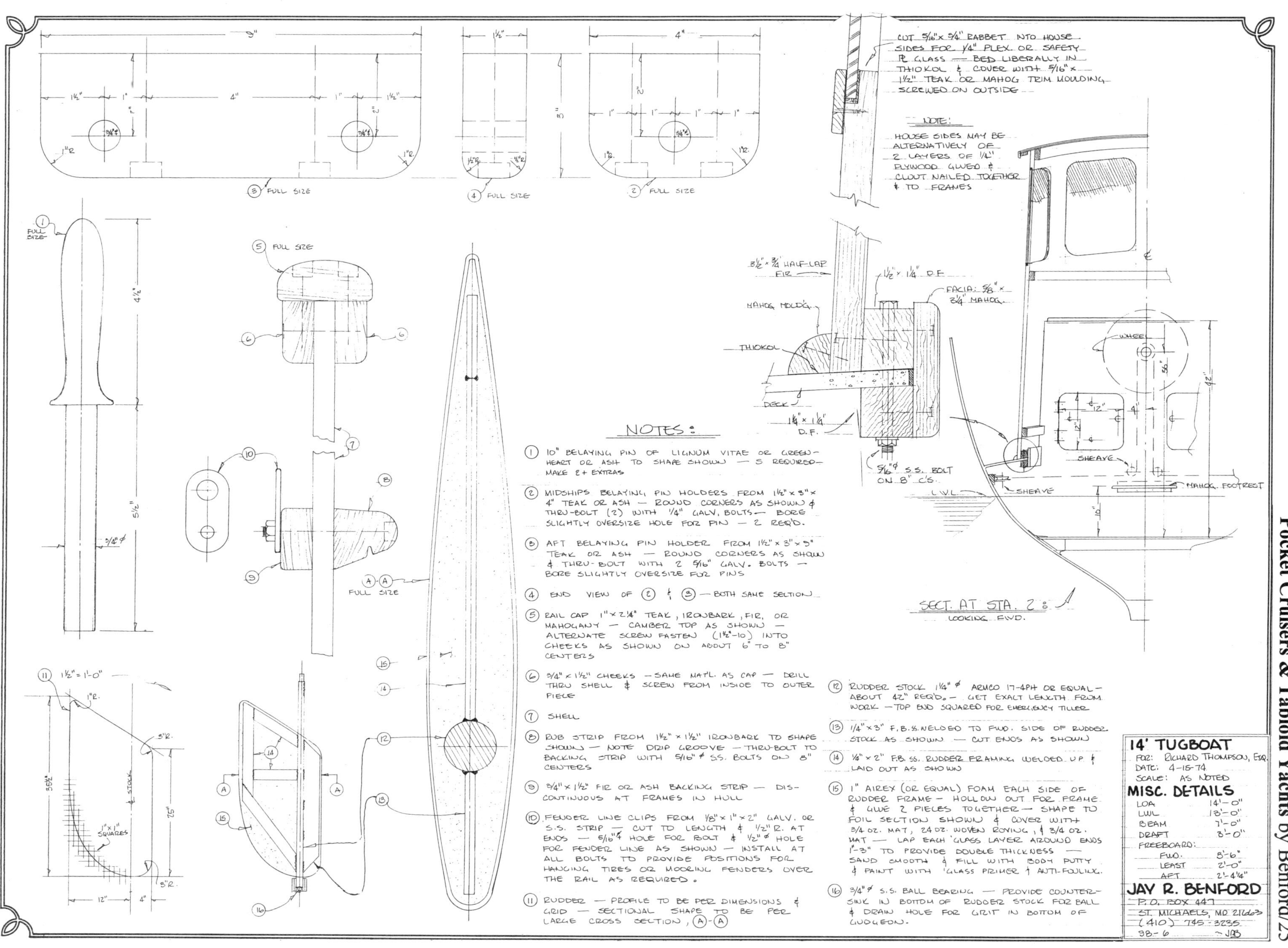

CUT 5/16" x 3/4" RABBET INTO HOUSE SIDES FOR 1/4" PLEX. OR SAFETY PL GLASS — BED LIBERALLY IN THIOKOL & COVER WITH 5/16" x 1 1/2" TEAK OR MAHOG TRIM MOULDING SCREWED ON OUTSIDE
NOTE:
HOUSE SIDES MAY BE ALTERNATIVELY OF 2 LAYERS OF 1/4" PLYWOOD GLUED & CLOUT NAILED TOGETHER & TO FRAMES
3 1/2" x 3/4" HALF-LAP FIR
1 1/2" x 1 1/4" D.F.
FACIA: 5/8" x 3/4" MAHOG.
MAHOG. MOLD'G.
THIOKOL
DECK
1 1/4" x 1 1/4" D.F.
5/16" ø S.S. BOLT ON 8" C'S.
WHEEL
SHEAVE
SHEAVE
MAHOG. FOOTREST
L.W.L.
SECT. AT STA. 2 :
LOOKING FWD.
3 FULL SIZE
4 FULL SIZE
2 FULL SIZE
1 FULL SIZE
5 FULL SIZE
A-A FULL SIZE
11 1 1/2" = 1'-0"
1"x1" SQUARES
STOCK
NOTES:
1 10" BELAYING PIN OF LIGNUM VITAE OR GREENHEART OR ASH TO SHAPE SHOWN — 5 REQUIRED — MAKE 2+ EXTRAS
2 MIDSHIPS BELAYING PIN HOLDERS FROM 1 1/2" x 3" x 4" TEAK OR ASH — ROUND CORNERS AS SHOWN & THRU-BOLT (2) WITH 1/4" GALV. BOLTS — BORE SLIGHTLY OVERSIZE HOLE FOR PIN — 2 REQ'D.
3 AFT BELAYING PIN HOLDER FROM 1 1/2" x 3" x 5" TEAK OR ASH — ROUND CORNERS AS SHOWN & THRU-BOLT WITH 2 5/16" GALV. BOLTS — BORE SLIGHTLY OVERSIZE FOR PINS
4 END VIEW OF 2 & 3 — BOTH SAME SECTION
5 RAIL CAP 1" x 2 1/4" TEAK, IRONBARK, FIR, OR MAHOGANY — CAMBER TOP AS SHOWN — ALTERNATE SCREW FASTEN (1 1/2"-10) INTO CHEEKS AS SHOWN ON ABOUT 6" TO 8" CENTERS
6 3/4" x 1 1/2" CHEEKS — SAME MAT'L. AS CAP — DRILL THRU SHELL & SCREW FROM INSIDE TO OUTER PIECE
7 SHELL
8 RUB STRIP FROM 1 1/2" x 1 1/2" IRONBARK TO SHAPE SHOWN — NOTE DRIP GROOVE — THRU-BOLT TO BACKING STRIP WITH 5/16" ø S.S. BOLTS ON 8" CENTERS
9 3/4" x 1 1/2" FIR OR ASH BACKING STRIP — DISCONTINUOUS AT FRAMES IN HULL
10 FENDER LINE CLIPS FROM 1/8" x 1" x 2" GALV. OR S.S. STRIP — CUT TO LENGTH & 1/2" R. AT ENDS — 5/16" ø HOLE FOR BOLT & 1/2" ø HOLE FOR FENDER LINE AS SHOWN — INSTALL AT ALL BOLTS TO PROVIDE POSITIONS FOR HANGING TIRES OR MOORING FENDERS OVER THE RAIL AS REQUIRED.
11 RUDDER — PROFILE TO BE PER DIMENSIONS & GRID — SECTIONAL SHAPE TO BE PER LARGE CROSS SECTION, A-A
12 RUDDER STOCK 1 1/4" ø ARMCO 17-4PH OR EQUAL — ABOUT 42" REQ'D. — GET EXACT LENGTH FROM WORK — TOP END SQUARED FOR EMERGENCY TILLER
13 1/4" x 3" F.B.S.S. WELDED TO FWD. SIDE OF RUDDER STOCK AS SHOWN — CUT ENDS AS SHOWN
14 1/8" x 2" F.B. S.S. RUDDER FRAMING WELDED UP & LAID OUT AS SHOWN
15 1" AIREX (OR EQUAL) FOAM EACH SIDE OF RUDDER FRAME — HOLLOW OUT FOR FRAME & GLUE 2 PIECES TOGETHER — SHAPE TO FOIL SECTION SHOWN & COVER WITH 3/4 OZ. MAT, 24 OZ. WOVEN ROVING, & 3/4 OZ. MAT — LAP EACH GLASS LAYER AROUND ENDS 1"-3" TO PROVIDE DOUBLE THICKNESS — SAND SMOOTH & FILL WITH BODY PUTTY & PAINT WITH GLASS PRIMER & ANTI-FOULING.
16 3/4" ø S.S. BALL BEARING — PROVIDE COUNTERSINK IN BOTTOM OF RUDDER STOCK FOR BALL & DRAIN HOLE FOR GRIT IN BOTTOM OF GUDGEON.
14' TUGBOAT
FOR: RICHARD THOMPSON, ESQ.
DATE: 4-15-74
SCALE: AS NOTED
MISC. DETAILS
LOA 14'-0"
LWL 13'-0"
BEAM 7'-0"
DRAFT 3'-0"
FREEBOARD:
FWD. 3'-6"
LEAST 2'-0"
AFT 2'-4 1/4"
JAY R. BENFORD
P.O. BOX 447
ST. MICHAELS, MD 21663
(410) 745-3235
38-6 ~JRB

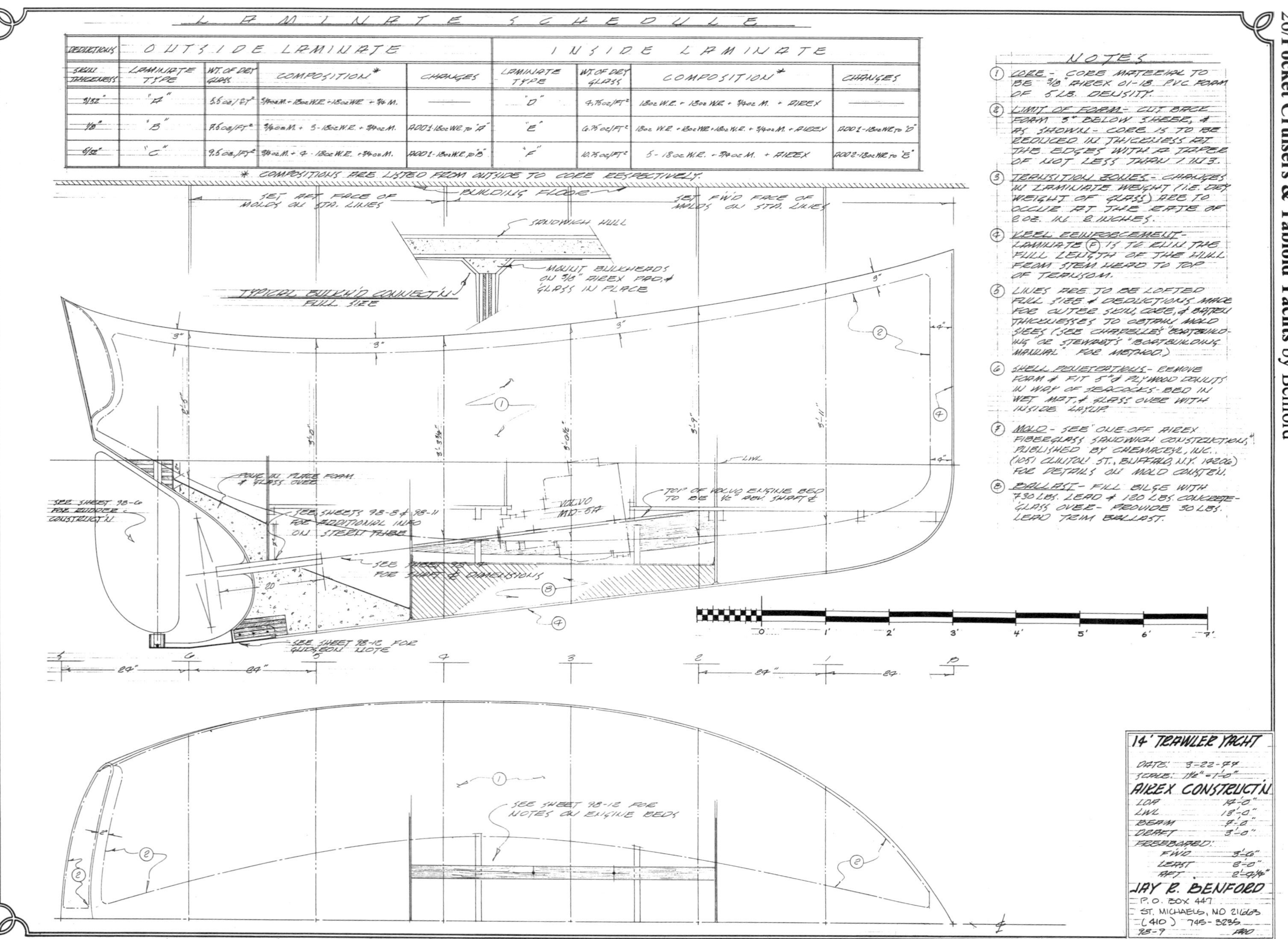
LAMINATE SCHEDULE
DEDUCTIONS
OUTSIDE LAMINATE
INSIDE LAMINATE
SKIN THICKNESS | LAMINATE TYPE | WT. OF DRY GLASS | COMPOSITION* | CHANGES | LAMINATE TYPE | WT. OF DRY GLASS | COMPOSITION* | CHANGES
3/32" | "A" | 5.5 oz/FT² | 3/4 oz M. + 18 oz W.R. + 18 oz W.R. + 3/4 M. | — | "D" | 4.75 oz/FT² | 18 oz W.R. + 18 oz W.R. + 3/4 oz M. + AIREX | —
1/8" | "B" | 7.5 oz/FT² | 3/4 oz M. + 3-18 oz W.R. + 3/4 oz M. | ADD 1-18 oz W.R. to "A" | "E" | 6.75 oz/FT² | 18 oz W.R. + 18 oz W.R. + 18 oz W.R. + 3/4 oz M. + AIREX | ADD 1-18 oz W.R. to "D"
5/32" | "C" | 9.5 oz/FT² | 3/4 oz M. + 4-18 oz W.R. + 3/4 oz M. | ADD 1-18 oz W.R. to "B" | "F" | 10.75 oz/FT² | 5-18 oz W.R. + 3/4 oz M. + AIREX | ADD 2-18 oz W.R. to "E"
* COMPOSITIONS ARE LISTED FROM OUTSIDE TO CORE RESPECTIVELY.
NOTES
① CORE - CORE MATERIAL TO BE 3/8" AIREX 01-18 PVC FOAM OF 5 LB. DENSITY.
② LIMIT OF FOAM - CUT BACK FOAM 3" BELOW SHEER, & AS SHOWN - CORE IS TO BE REDUCED IN THICKNESS AT THE EDGES WITH A TAPER OF NOT LESS THAN 1 IN 3.
③ TRANSITION ZONES - CHANGES IN LAMINATE WEIGHT (I.E. DRY WEIGHT OF GLASS) ARE TO OCCUR AT THE RATE OF 2 OZ. IN 2 INCHES.
④ KEEL REINFORCEMENT - LAMINATE (F) IS TO RUN THE FULL LENGTH OF THE HULL FROM STEM HEAD TO TOP OF TRANSOM.
⑤ LINES ARE TO BE LOFTED FULL SIZE & DEDUCTIONS MADE FOR OUTER SKIN, CORE, & BATEN THICKNESSES TO OBTAIN MOLD SIZES (SEE CHAPELLE'S "BOATBUILDING" OR STEWART'S "BOATBUILDING MANUAL" FOR METHOD.)
⑥ SHELL PENETRATIONS - REMOVE FOAM & FIT 5" Ø PLYWOOD DONUTS IN WAY OF SEACOCKS - BED IN WET MAT & GLASS OVER WITH INSIDE LAYUP.
⑦ MOLD - SEE "ONE-OFF AIREX FIBERGLASS SANDWICH CONSTRUCTION," PUBLISHED BY CHEMACRYL, INC., (1051 CLINTON ST., BUFFALO, N.Y. 14206) FOR DETAILS ON MOLD CONSTR.
⑧ BALLAST - FILL BILGE WITH 730 LBS. LEAD & 120 LBS. CONCRETE - GLASS OVER - PROVIDE 30 LBS. LEAD TRIM BALLAST.
BUILDING FLOOR
SET AFT FACE OF MOLDS ON STA. LINES
SET FWD FACE OF MOLDS ON STA. LINES
SANDWICH HULL
MOUNT BULKHEADS ON 3/8" AIREX PAD, & GLASS IN PLACE
TYPICAL BULKH'D CONNECT'N FULL SIZE
LWL
VOLVO MD-5A
TOP OF VOLVO ENGINE BED TO BE 1/2" ABV. SHAFT ℄
POUR IN PLACE FOAM & GLASS OVER
SEE SHEET 98-6 FOR RUDDER CONSTRUCT'N
SEE SHEETS 98-8 & 98-11 FOR ADDITIONAL INFO ON STERN TUBE
SEE SHEET 98-11 FOR SHAFT & DIMENSIONS
SEE SHEET 98-12 FOR GUDGEON NOTE
SEE SHEET 98-12 FOR NOTES ON ENGINE BEDS
0' 1' 2' 3' 4' 5' 6' 7'
14' TRAWLER YACHT
DATE: 3-22-94
SCALE: 1½" = 1'-0"
AIREX CONSTRUCT'N
LOA 14'-0"
LWL 13'-0"
BEAM 7'-0"
DRAFT 3'-0"
FREEBOARD:
FWD 3'-6"
LEAST 2'-0"
AFT 2'-9¼"
JAY R. BENFORD
P.O. BOX 447
ST. MICHAELS, MD 21663
(410) 745-3235
98-9

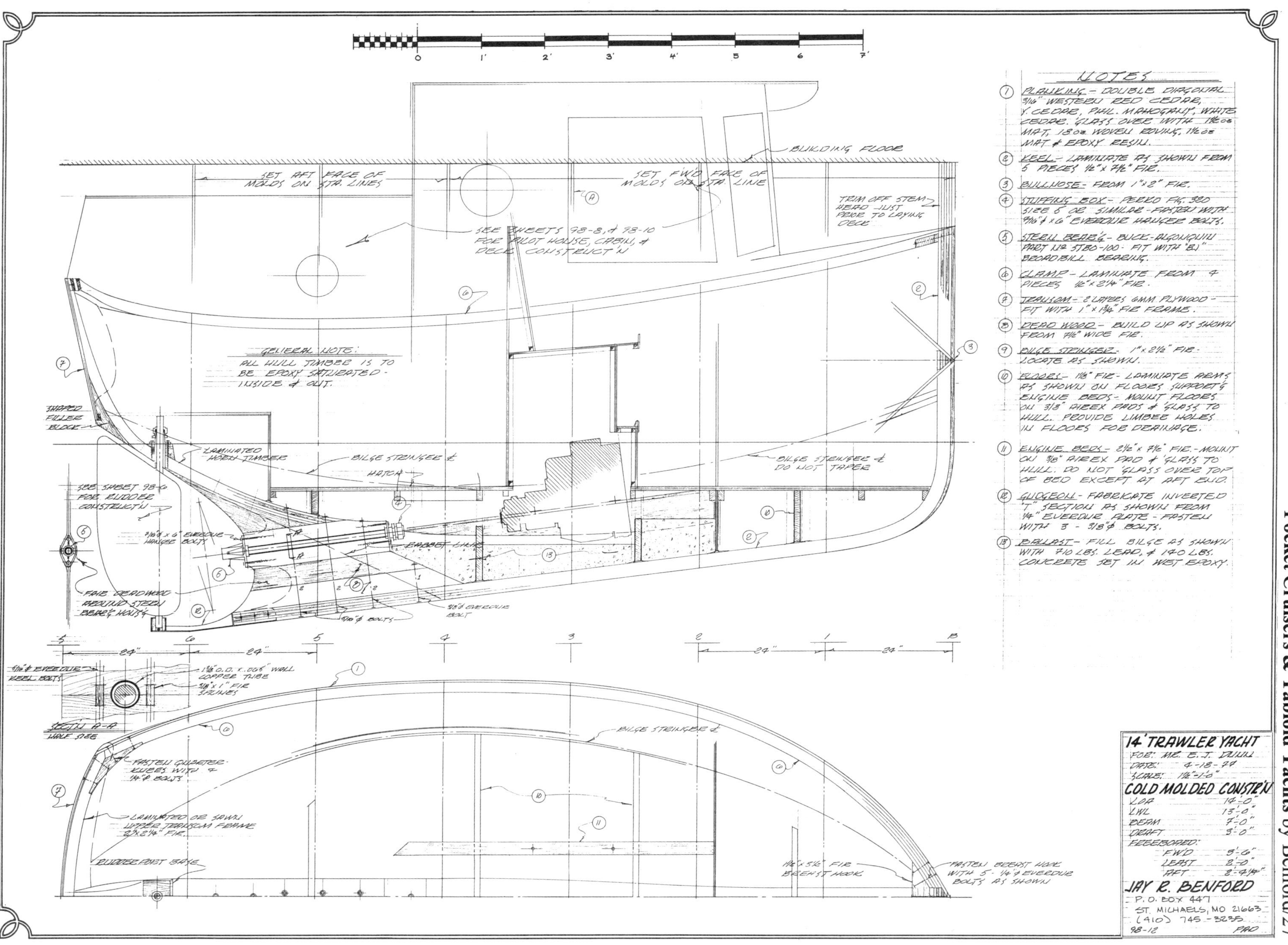
NOTES
1 PLANKING - DOUBLE DIAGONAL 3/16" WESTERN RED CEDAR, Y. CEDAR, PHIL. MAHOGANY, WHITE CEDAR. 'GLASS OVER WITH 1½oz MAT, 18oz WOVEN ROVING, 1½oz MAT & EPOXY RESIN.
2 KEEL - LAMINATE AS SHOWN FROM 5 PIECES ½" x 7⅛" FIR.
3 BULLNOSE - FROM 1" x 2" FIR.
4 STUFFING BOX - PERKO FIG. 380 SIZE 5 OR SIMILAR - FASTEN WITH 5/16" ø x 6" EVERDUR HANGER BOLTS.
5 STERN BEAR'G - BUCK-ALGONQUIN PART 12 STBO-100 - FIT WITH "BJ" BROADBILL BEARING.
6 CLAMP - LAMINATE FROM 4 PIECES ½" x 2¼" FIR.
7 TRANSOM - 2 LAYERS 6MM PLYWOOD - FIT WITH 1" x 1¾" FIR FRAME.
8 DEAD WOOD - BUILD UP AS SHOWN FROM 7⅛" WIDE FIR.
9 BILGE STRINGER - 1" x 2½" FIR. LOCATE AS SHOWN.
10 FLOORS - 1⅛" FIR - LAMINATE ARMS AS SHOWN ON FLOORS SUPPORT'G ENGINE BEDS - MOUNT FLOORS ON 3/8" AIREX PADS & 'GLASS TO HULL. PROVIDE LIMBER HOLES IN FLOORS FOR DRAINAGE.
11 ENGINE BEDS - 2⅛" x 7⅛" FIR - MOUNT ON 3/8" AIREX PAD & 'GLASS TO HULL. DO NOT 'GLASS OVER TOP OF BED EXCEPT AT AFT END.
12 GUDGEON - FABRICATE INVERTED "T" SECTION AS SHOWN FROM ¼" EVERDUR PLATE - FASTEN WITH 3 - 3/8" ø BOLTS.
13 BALLAST - FILL BILGE AS SHOWN WITH 710 LBS. LEAD, & 140 LBS. CONCRETE SET IN WET EPOXY.
14' TRAWLER YACHT
FOR: MR. E.J. DUNN
DATE: 4-18-97
SCALE: 1½"=1'-0"
COLD MOLDED CONSTR'N
LOA 14'-0"
LWL 13'-0"
BEAM 7'-0"
DRAFT 3'-0"
FREEBOARD:
FWD 3'-6"
LEAST 2'-0"
AFT 2'-9¾"
JAY R. BENFORD
P. O. BOX 447
ST. MICHAELS, MD 21663
(410) 745-3235
98-12
PRO
BUILDING FLOOR
SET AFT FACE OF MOLDS ON STA. LINES
SET FWD FACE OF MOLDS ON STA. LINE
TRIM OFF STEM HEAD JUST PRIOR TO LAYING DECK
SEE SHEETS 98-8, & 98-10 FOR PILOT HOUSE, CABIN, & DECK CONSTRUCT'N
GENERAL NOTE: ALL HULL TIMBER IS TO BE EPOXY SATURATED - INSIDE & OUT.
SHAPED FILLER BLOCK
LAMINATED HORN TIMBER
BILGE STRINGER & HATCH
BILGE STRINGER ℄ DO NOT TAPER
SEE SHEET 98-4 FOR RUDDER CONSTRUCT'N
5/16" ø x 6" EVERDUR HANGER BOLTS
RABBET LINE
FAIR DEADWOOD AROUND STERN BEAR'G HOUS'G
3/8" ø EVERDUR BOLT
5/16" ø BOLTS
5/16" ø EVERDUR KEEL BOLTS
1⅜" O.D. x .008" WALL COPPER TUBE
3/8" x 1" FIR SPLINES
SECT'N A-A HALF SIZE
BILGE STRINGER ℄
FASTEN QUARTER KNEES WITH 4 ¼" ø BOLTS
LAMINATED OR SAWN UPPER TRANSOM FRAME 2⅝" x 2¼" FIR.
RUDDER PORT BASE
1⅛" x 5⅛" FIR BREAST HOOK
FASTEN BREAST HOOK WITH 5 - ¼" ø EVERDUR BOLTS AS SHOWN

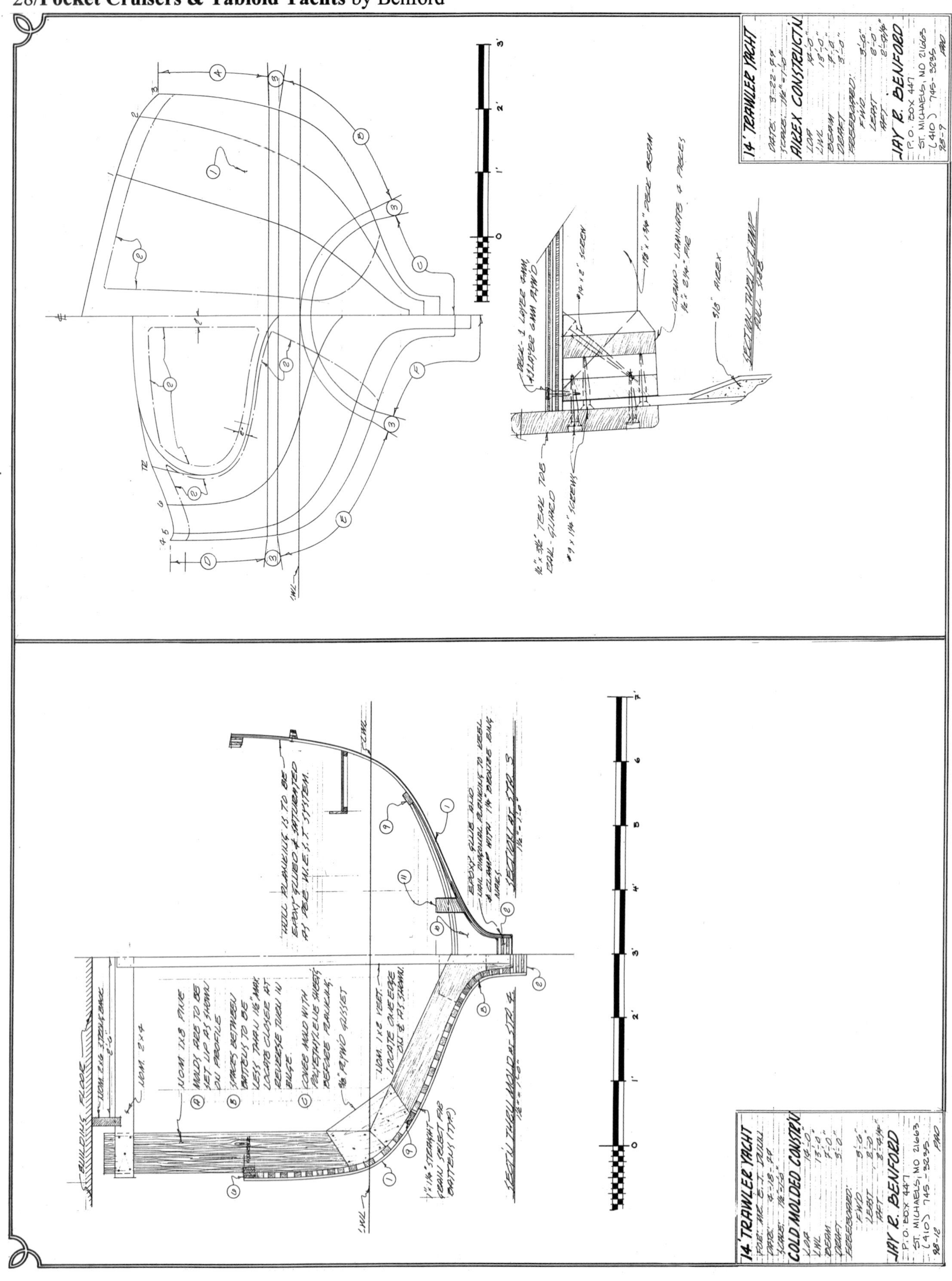
14' TRAWLER YACHT
AIREX CONSTRUCT'N
JAY R. BENFORD
14' TRAWLER YACHT
COLD MOLDED CONSTR'N
JAY R. BENFORD

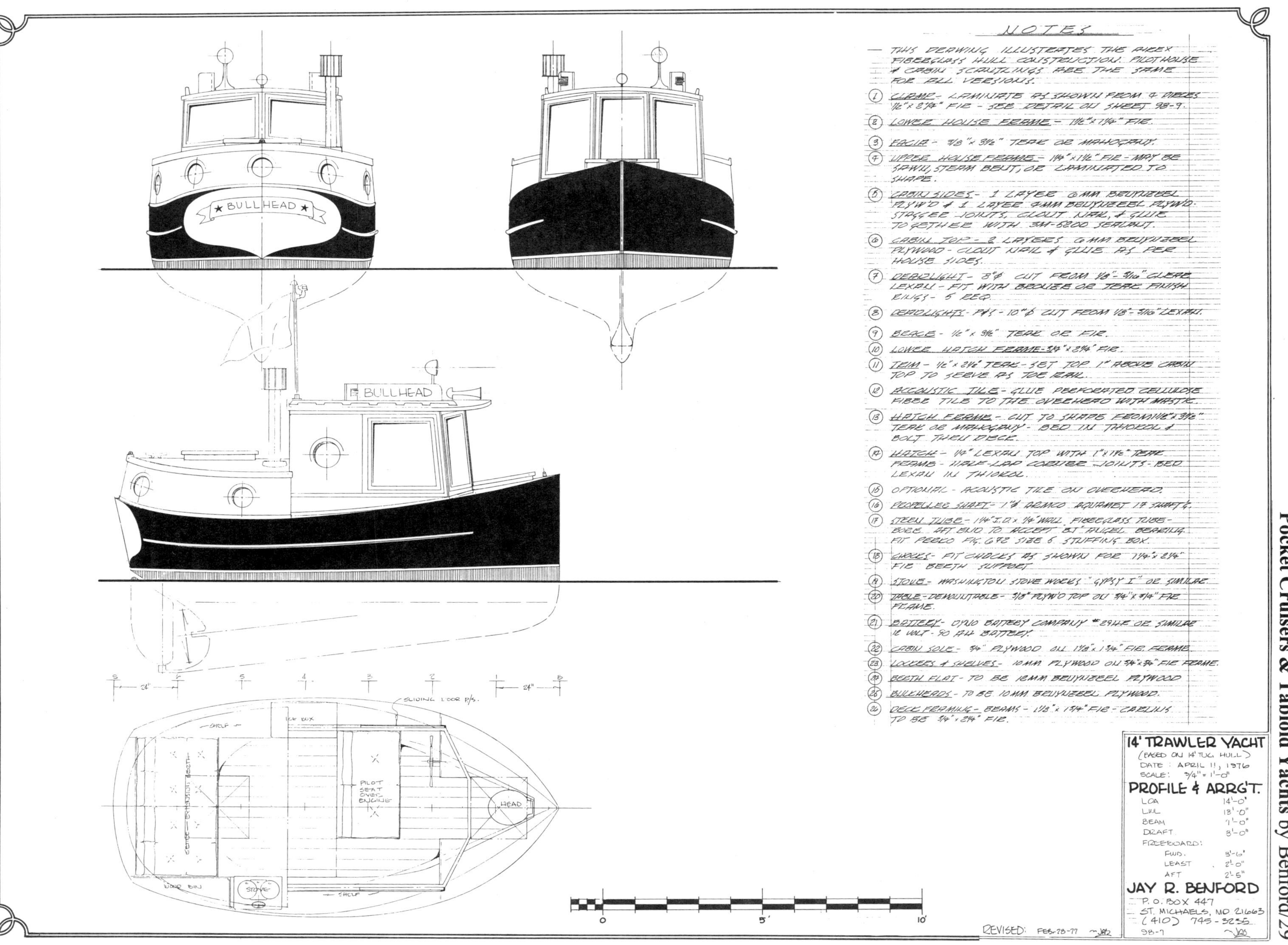
NOTES
— THIS DRAWING ILLUSTRATES THE AIREX FIBERGLASS HULL CONSTRUCTION. PILOTHOUSE & CABIN SCANTLINGS ARE THE SAME FOR ALL VERSIONS.
(1) CLAMP - LAMINATE AS SHOWN FROM 4 PIECES 1/2" x 2 1/4" FIR - SEE DETAIL ON SHEET 98-9.
(2) LOWER HOUSE FRAME - 1 1/2" x 1 1/4" FIR.
(3) FACIA - 3/8" x 3 1/2" TEAK OR MAHOGANY.
(4) UPPER HOUSE FRAME - 1 1/4" x 1 1/2" FIR - MAY BE SAWN, STEAM BENT, OR LAMINATED TO SHAPE.
(5) CABIN SIDES - 1 LAYER 6MM BRUYNZEEL PLYW'D & 1 LAYER 4MM BRUYNZEEL PLYW'D. STAGGER JOINTS, CLOUT NAIL, & GLUE TOGETHER WITH 3M-5200 SEALANT.
(6) CABIN TOP - 2 LAYERS 6MM BRUYNZEEL PLYWOOD - CLOUT NAIL & GLUE AS PER HOUSE SIDES.
(7) DEADLIGHT - 8"Ø CUT FROM 1/8" - 3/16" CLEAR LEXAN - FIT WITH BRONZE OR TEAK FINISH RINGS - 5 REQ.
(8) DEADLIGHTS - P&S - 10"Ø CUT FROM 1/8" - 3/16" LEXAN.
(9) BRACE - 1/2" x 3 1/2" TEAK OR FIR.
(10) LOWER HATCH FRAME - 3/4" x 2 1/4" FIR.
(11) TRIM - 1/2" x 2 1/2" TEAK - SET TOP 1" ABOVE CABIN TOP TO SERVE AS TOE RAIL.
(12) ACCOUSTIC TILE - GLUE PERFORATED CELLULOSE FIBER TILE TO THE OVERHEAD WITH MASTIC.
(13) HATCH FRAME - CUT TO SHAPE FROM 1 1/2" x 3 1/2" TEAK OR MAHOGANY - BED IN THIOKOL & BOLT THRU DECK.
(14) HATCH - 1/4" LEXAN TOP WITH 1" x 1 1/2" TEAK FRAME - HALF-LAP CORNER JOINTS - BED LEXAN IN THIOKOL.
(15) OPTIONAL - ACOUSTIC TILE ON OVERHEAD.
(16) PROPELLER SHAFT - 1"Ø ARMCO AQUAMET 17 SHAFTG.
(17) STERN TUBE - 1 1/4" I.D. x 1/4" WALL FIBERGLASS TUBE - BORE AFT END TO ACCEPT "BJ" AUGEL BEARING. FIT PERKO FIG. 672 SIZE 6 STUFFING BOX.
(18) CHOCKS - FIT CHOCKS AS SHOWN FOR 1 1/4" x 2 1/4" FIR BERTH SUPPORT.
(19) STOVE - WASHINGTON STOVE WORKS "GYPSY I" OR SIMILAR.
(20) TABLE - DEMOUNTABLE - 3/8" PLYW'D TOP ON 3/4" x 3/4" FIR FRAME.
(21) BATTERY - DYNO BATTERY COMPANY #29HE OR SIMILAR 12 VOLT - 90 AH BATTERY.
(22) CABIN SOLE - 3/4" PLYWOOD ON 1 1/8" x 1 3/4" FIR FRAME.
(23) LOCKERS & SHELVES - 10MM PLYWOOD ON 3/4" x 3/4" FIR FRAME.
(24) BERTH FLAT - TO BE 12MM BRUYNZEEL PLYWOOD.
(25) BULKHEADS - TO BE 10MM BRUYNZEEL PLYWOOD.
(26) DECK FRAMING - BEAMS - 1 1/8" x 1 3/4" FIR - CARLINS TO BE 3/4" x 2 1/4" FIR.
BULLHEAD
★ BULLHEAD ★
SLIDING DOOR P/S.
ICE BOX
SHELF
PILOT SEAT OVER ENGINE
HEAD
STOVE
WOOD BIN
24"
0
5'
10'
14' TRAWLER YACHT
(BASED ON 14' TUG HULL)
DATE : APRIL 11, 1976
SCALE: 3/4" = 1'-0"
PROFILE & ARRG'T.
LOA 14'-0"
LWL 13'-0"
BEAM 7'-0"
DRAFT 3'-0"
FREEBOARD:
FWD. 3'-6"
LEAST 2'-0"
AFT 2'-5"
JAY R. BENFORD
P. O. BOX 447
ST. MICHAELS, MD 21663
(410) 745-3235
98-7
REVISED: FEB-28-77

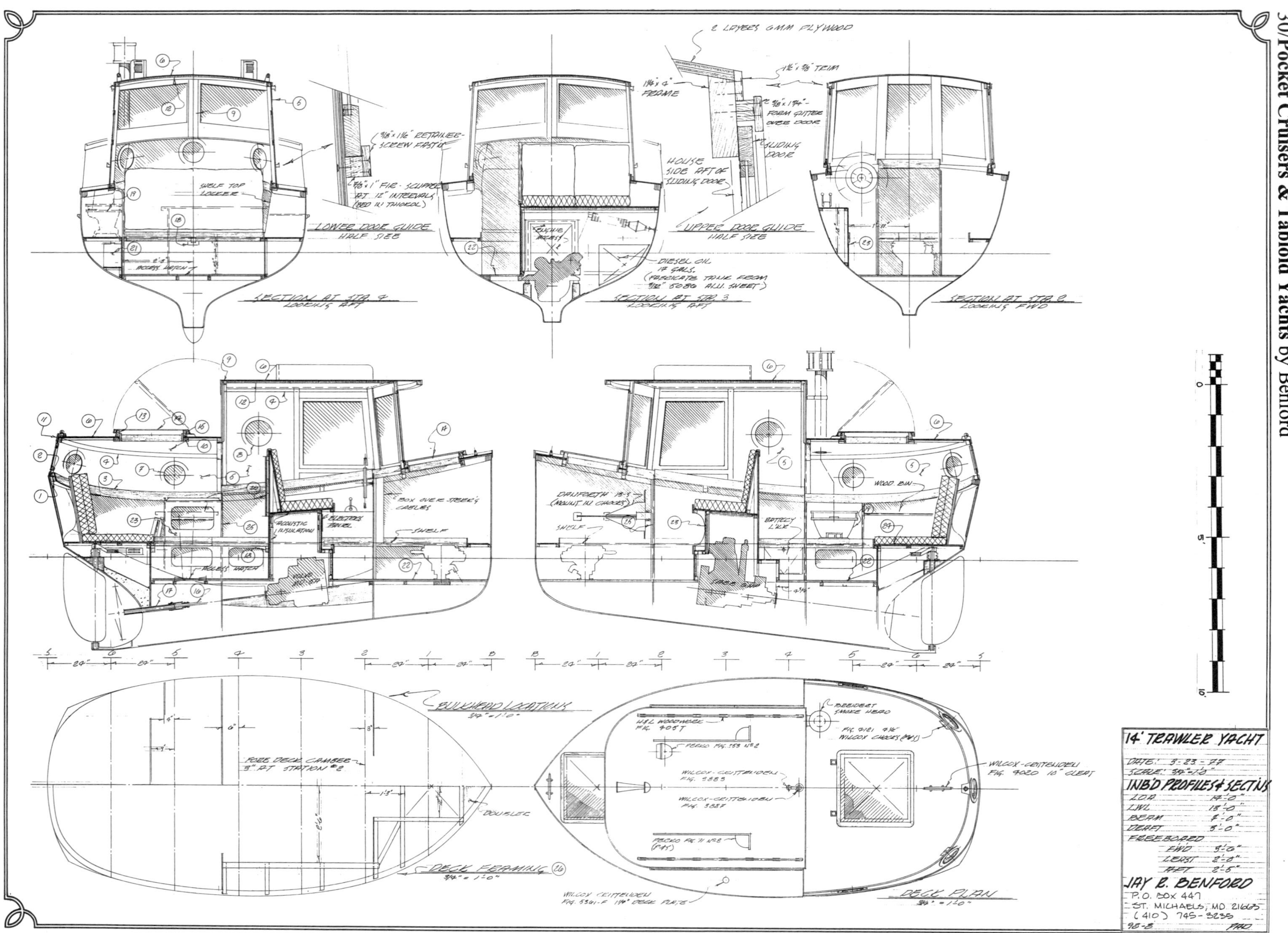

14' TRAWLER YACHT
DATE: 3-23-77
SCALE: 3/4"=1'0"
INB'D PROFILES & SECT'NS
LOA 14'-0"
LWL 13'-0"
BEAM 7'-0"
DRAFT 3'-0"
FREEBOARD
FWD 3'-0"
LEAST 2'-0"
AFT 2'-5"
JAY R. BENFORD
P.O. BOX 447
ST. MICHAELS, MD 21663
(410) 745-3235
SECTION AT STA 4
LOOKING AFT
SECTION AT STA 3
LOOKING AFT
SECTION AT STA 2
LOOKING FWD
LOWER DOOR GUIDE
HALF SIZE
UPPER DOOR GUIDE
HALF SIZE
2 LAYERS 6MM PLYWOOD
1 3/4" x 4" FRAME
HOUSE SIDE AFT OF SLIDING DOOR
SLIDING DOOR
SHELF TOP LOCKER
ACCESS HATCH
DIESEL OIL
17 GALS.
BOX OVER STEERS CABLES
SHELF
ACOUSTIC INSULATION
ELECTRIC PANEL
WOOD BIN
BATTERY L'KR
DANFORTH 13-S (MOUNT IN CHOCKS)
BULKHEAD LOCATIONS
3/4" = 1'-0"
FORE DECK CAMBER 3" AT STATION #2
DOUBLER
DECK FRAMING
3/4" = 1'-0"
DECK PLAN
3/4" = 1'-0"
WILCOX-CRITTENDEN FIG. 4020 10" CLEAT
WILCOX-CRITTENDEN FIG. 3883
WILCOX-CRITTENDEN FIG. 3887
WILCOX CRITTENDEN FIG. 5341-F 1 1/4" DECK PLATE
FIG. 4181 4 1/2" WILCOX CHOCKS (P&S)
H&L WOODWORK FIG. 405T
PERKO FIG. 11 NO. 2 (P&S)

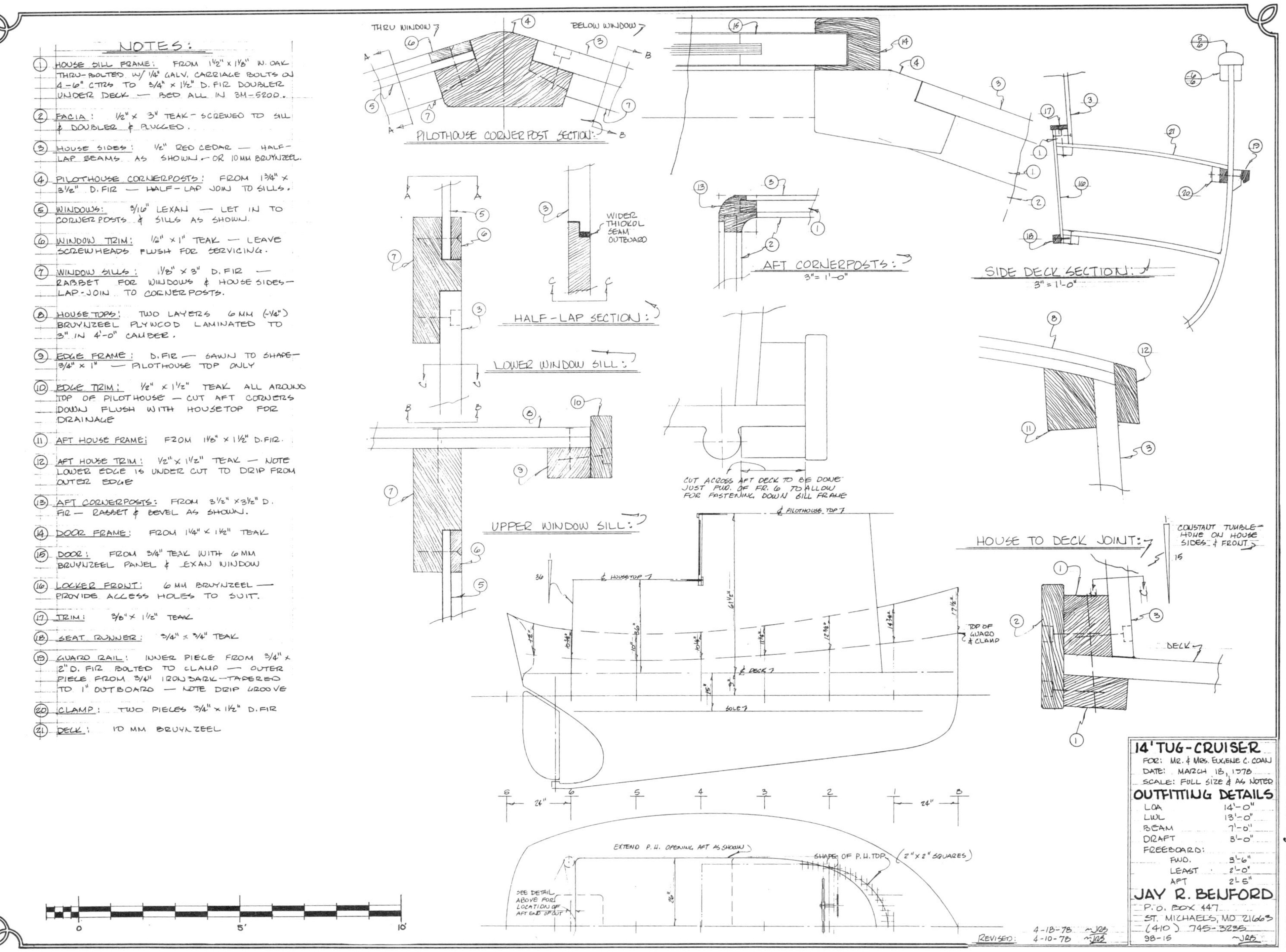
NOTES:
1 HOUSE SILL FRAME: FROM 1½" x 1⅛" W. OAK THRU-BOLTED W/ ¼" GALV. CARRIAGE BOLTS ON 4-6" CTRS TO ¾" x 1½" D. FIR DOUBLER UNDER DECK — BED ALL IN 3M-5200.
2 FACIA: ½" x 3" TEAK - SCREWED TO SILL & DOUBLER & PLUGGED.
3 HOUSE SIDES: ½" RED CEDAR — HALF-LAP SEAMS AS SHOWN - OR 10MM BRUYNZEEL.
4 PILOTHOUSE CORNERPOSTS: FROM 1¾" x 3½" D. FIR — HALF-LAP JOIN TO SILLS.
5 WINDOWS: 3/16" LEXAN — LET IN TO CORNER POSTS & SILLS AS SHOWN.
6 WINDOW TRIM: ½" x 1" TEAK — LEAVE SCREWHEADS FLUSH FOR SERVICING.
7 WINDOW SILLS: 1⅛" x 3" D. FIR — RABBET FOR WINDOWS & HOUSE SIDES - LAP-JOIN TO CORNER POSTS.
8 HOUSE TOPS: TWO LAYERS 6MM (~¼") BRUYNZEEL PLYWOOD LAMINATED TO 3" IN 4'-0" CAMBER.
9 EDGE FRAME: D. FIR — SAWN TO SHAPE - ¾" x 1" — PILOTHOUSE TOP ONLY
10 EDGE TRIM: ½" x 1½" TEAK ALL AROUND TOP OF PILOTHOUSE — CUT AFT CORNERS DOWN FLUSH WITH HOUSETOP FOR DRAINAGE
11 AFT HOUSE FRAME: FROM 1⅛" x 1½" D. FIR.
12 AFT HOUSE TRIM: ½" x 1½" TEAK — NOTE LOWER EDGE IS UNDER CUT TO DRIP FROM OUTER EDGE
13 AFT CORNERPOSTS: FROM 3½" x 3½" D. FIR — RABBET & BEVEL AS SHOWN.
14 DOOR FRAME: FROM 1¼" x 1½" TEAK
15 DOOR: FROM ¾" TEAK WITH 6MM BRUYNZEEL PANEL & LEXAN WINDOW
16 LOCKER FRONT: 6MM BRUYNZEEL — PROVIDE ACCESS HOLES TO SUIT.
17 TRIM: ⅜" x 1½" TEAK
18 SEAT RUNNER: ¾" x ¾" TEAK
19 GUARD RAIL: INNER PIECE FROM ¾" x 2" D. FIR BOLTED TO CLAMP — OUTER PIECE FROM ¾" IRONBARK - TAPERED TO 1" OUTBOARD — NOTE DRIP GROOVE
20 CLAMP: TWO PIECES ¾" x 1½" D. FIR
21 DECK: 10 MM BRUYNZEEL
THRU WINDOW
BELOW WINDOW
PILOTHOUSE CORNER POST SECTION:
HALF-LAP SECTION:
WIDER THIOKOL SEAM OUTBOARD
LOWER WINDOW SILL:
UPPER WINDOW SILL:
AFT CORNERPOSTS:
3" = 1'-0"
SIDE DECK SECTION:
3" = 1'-0"
CUT ACROSS AFT DECK TO BE DONE JUST FWD. OF FR. 6 TO ALLOW FOR FASTENING DOWN SILL FRAME
℄ PILOTHOUSE TOP
℄ HOUSETOP
℄ DECK
SOLE
TOP OF GUARD & CLAMP
HOUSE TO DECK JOINT:
CONSTANT TUMBLEHOME ON HOUSE SIDES & FRONT
DECK
EXTEND P.H. OPENING AFT AS SHOWN
SHAPE OF P.H. TOP (2" x 2" SQUARES)
SEE DETAIL ABOVE FOR LOCATION OF AFT END OF CUT
24"
0
5'
10'
14' TUG-CRUISER
FOR: MR. & MRS. EUGENE C. COAN
DATE: MARCH 18, 1978
SCALE: FULL SIZE & AS NOTED
OUTFITTING DETAILS
LOA 14'-0"
LWL 13'-0"
BEAM 7'-0"
DRAFT 3'-0"
FREEBOARD:
FWD. 3'-6"
LEAST 2'-0"
AFT 2'-5"
JAY R. BENFORD
P.O. BOX 447
ST. MICHAELS, MD 21663
(410) 745-3235
98-15
REVISED: 4-18-78 4-10-78

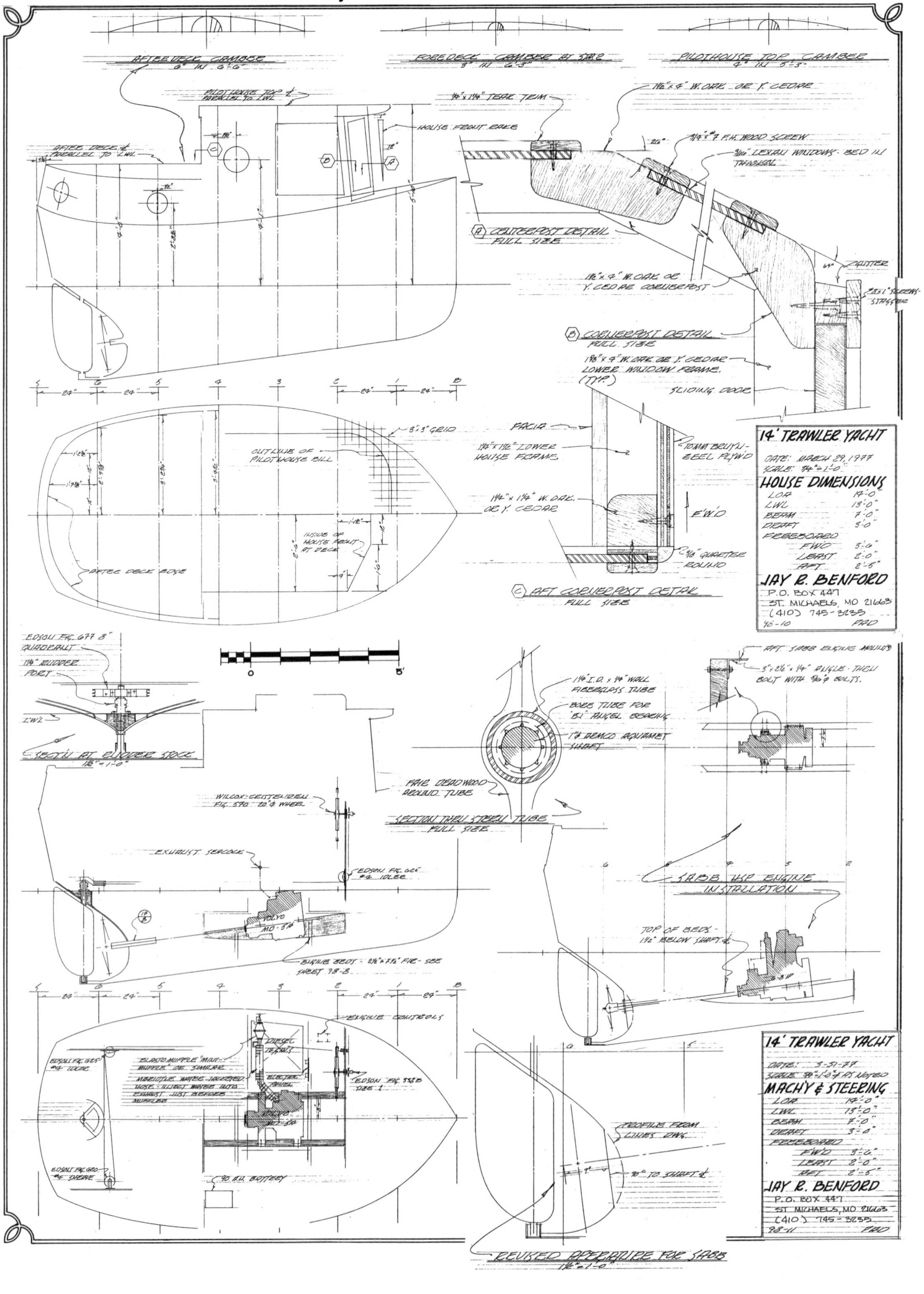

AFTER DECK CAMBER 6" IN 6'-6"

FOREDECK CAMBER AT STA. 2 3" IN 6'-3"

PILOTHOUSE TOP CAMBER 4" IN 5'-3"

PILOT HOUSE TOP ℄ PARALLEL TO LWL

AFTER DECK ℄ PARALLEL TO LWL

HOUSE FRONT RAKE

1¼" x 1¼" TEAK TRIM

1½" x 4" W. OAK OR Y. CEDAR

¼" x 1" F.H. WOOD SCREW

3/16" LEXAN WINDOWS - BED IN THIOKOL

(A) CENTERPOST DETAIL FULL SIZE

1½" x 4" W. OAK OR Y. CEDAR CORNERPOST

GUTTER

(B) CORNERPOST DETAIL FULL SIZE

1⅜" x 4" W. OAK OR Y. CEDAR LOWER WINDOW FRAME. (TYP.)

SLIDING DOOR

FACIA

1½" x 1½" LOWER HOUSE FRAME

TOMA BRUYNZEEL PLYW'D

1¼" x 1¼" W. OAK. OR Y. CEDAR

E.W.O.

⅜" QUARTER ROUND

(C) AFT CORNERPOST DETAIL FULL SIZE

3" x 3" GRID

OUTLINE OF PILOTHOUSE SILL

INSIDE OF HOUSE FRONT AT DECK

AFTER DECK EDGE

14' TRAWLER YACHT

DATE: MARCH 29, 1977
SCALE: ¾" = 1'-0"

HOUSE DIMENSIONS

LOA	14'-0"
LWL	13'-0"
BEAM	7'-0"
DRAFT	3'-0"
FREEBOARD	
FWD	5'-6"
LEAST	2'-0"
AFT	2'-5"

JAY R. BENFORD
P.O. BOX 447
ST. MICHAELS, MD 21663
(410) 745-3235
98-10 FAD

EDSON FIG. 677 8" QUADRANT

1¼" RUDDER PORT

LWL

SECT'N AT RUDDER STOCK 1½" = 1'-0"

1¼" I.D. x ¼" WALL FIBERGLASS TUBE

BORE TUBE FOR "B" ANGEL BEARING

1" ⌀ ARMCO AQUAMET SHAFT

FAIR DEADWOOD AROUND TUBE

SECTION THRU STERN TUBE FULL SIZE

AFT SABB ENGINE MOUNTS

3" x 2½" x ¼" ANGLE - THRU BOLT WITH 5/16" ⌀ BOLTS.

WILCOX-CRITTENDEN FIG. 590 20" ⌀ WHEEL

EXHAUST SEACOCK

EDSON FIG. 606 #4 IDLER

VOLVO MD-5A

ENGINE BEDS - 2⅛" x 3½" FIR - SEE SHEET 98-8

SABB 10HP ENGINE INSTALLATION

TOP OF BEDS 1½" BELOW SHAFT ℄

ENGINE CONTROLS

EDSON FIG. 625 #4 IDLER

BLASTO MUFFLE "MINI-MUFFLE" OR SIMILAR.

MANIFOLD WATER JACKETED HOSE - INJECT WATER INTO EXHAUST JUST BEFORE MUFFLER

DIESEL TANK

EDSON FIG. 358B SIZE 1

EDSON FIG. 680 #4 SHEAVE

90 A.H. BATTERY

PROFILE FROM LINES DWG.

90° TO SHAFT ℄

REVISED APERATURE FOR SABB 1½" = 1'-0"

14' TRAWLER YACHT

DATE: 3-31-77
SCALE: ¾" = 1'-0" & AS NOTED

MACHY & STEERING

LOA	14'-0"
LWL	13'-0"
BEAM	7'-0"
DRAFT	3'-0"
FREEBOARD	
FWD	3'-0"
LEAST	2'-0"
AFT	2'-5"

JAY R. BENFORD
P.O. BOX 447
ST. MICHAELS, MD 21663
(410) 745-3235
98-11 FAD

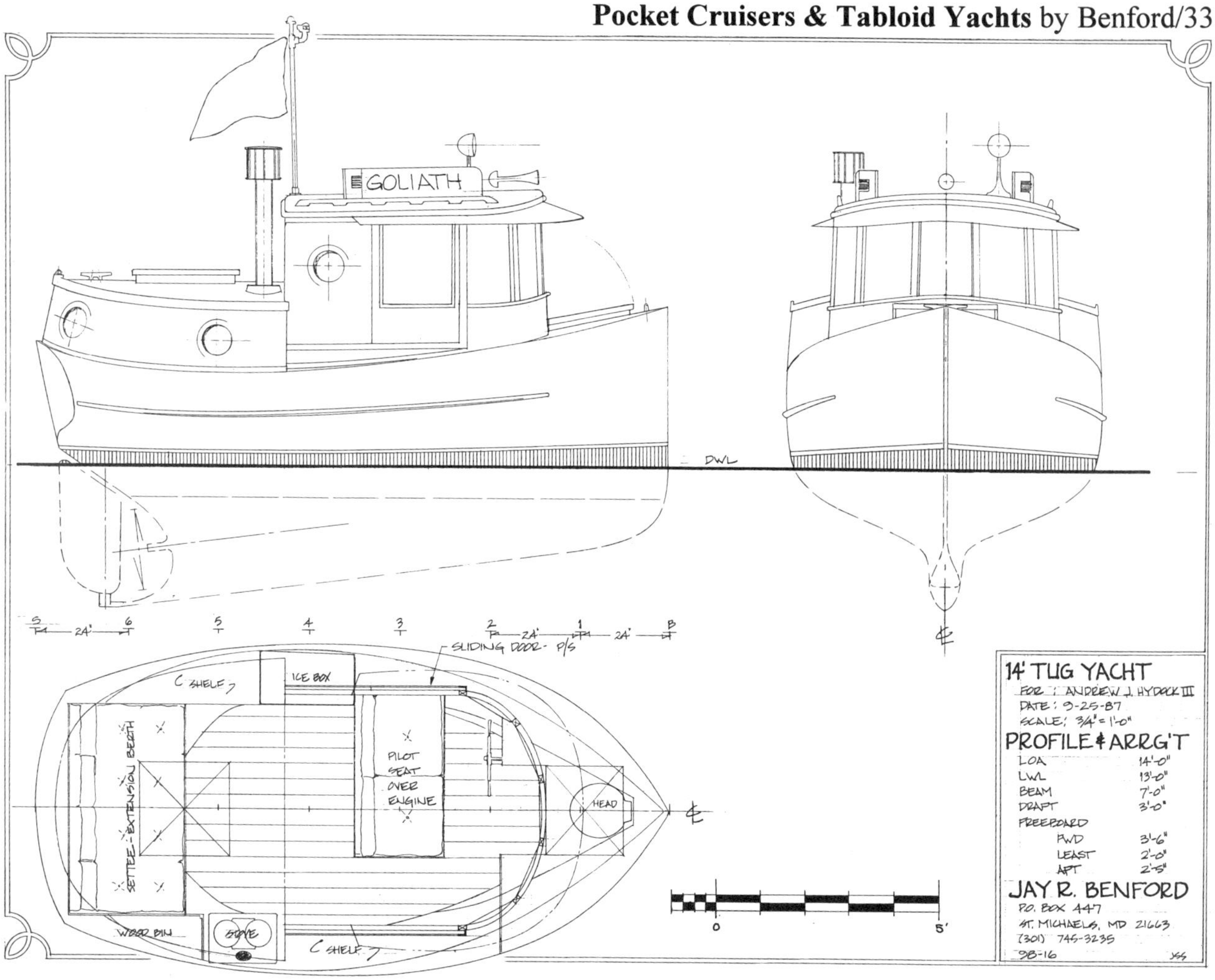

GOLIATH

DWL

SLIDING DOOR- P/S

ICE BOX

C SHELF

SETTEE-EXTENSION BERTH

PILOT SEAT OVER ENGINE

HEAD

WOOD BIN

STOVE

C SHELF

14' TUG YACHT

FOR : ANDREW J. HYDOCK III
DATE : 9-25-87
SCALE: 3/4" = 1'-0"

PROFILE & ARRG'T

LOA	14'-0"
LWL	13'-0"
BEAM	7'-0"
DRAFT	3'-0"
FREEBOARD	
FWD	3'-6"
LEAST	2'-0"
AFT	2'-5"

JAY R. BENFORD
P.O. BOX 447
ST. MICHAELS, MD 21663
(301) 745-3235
98-16

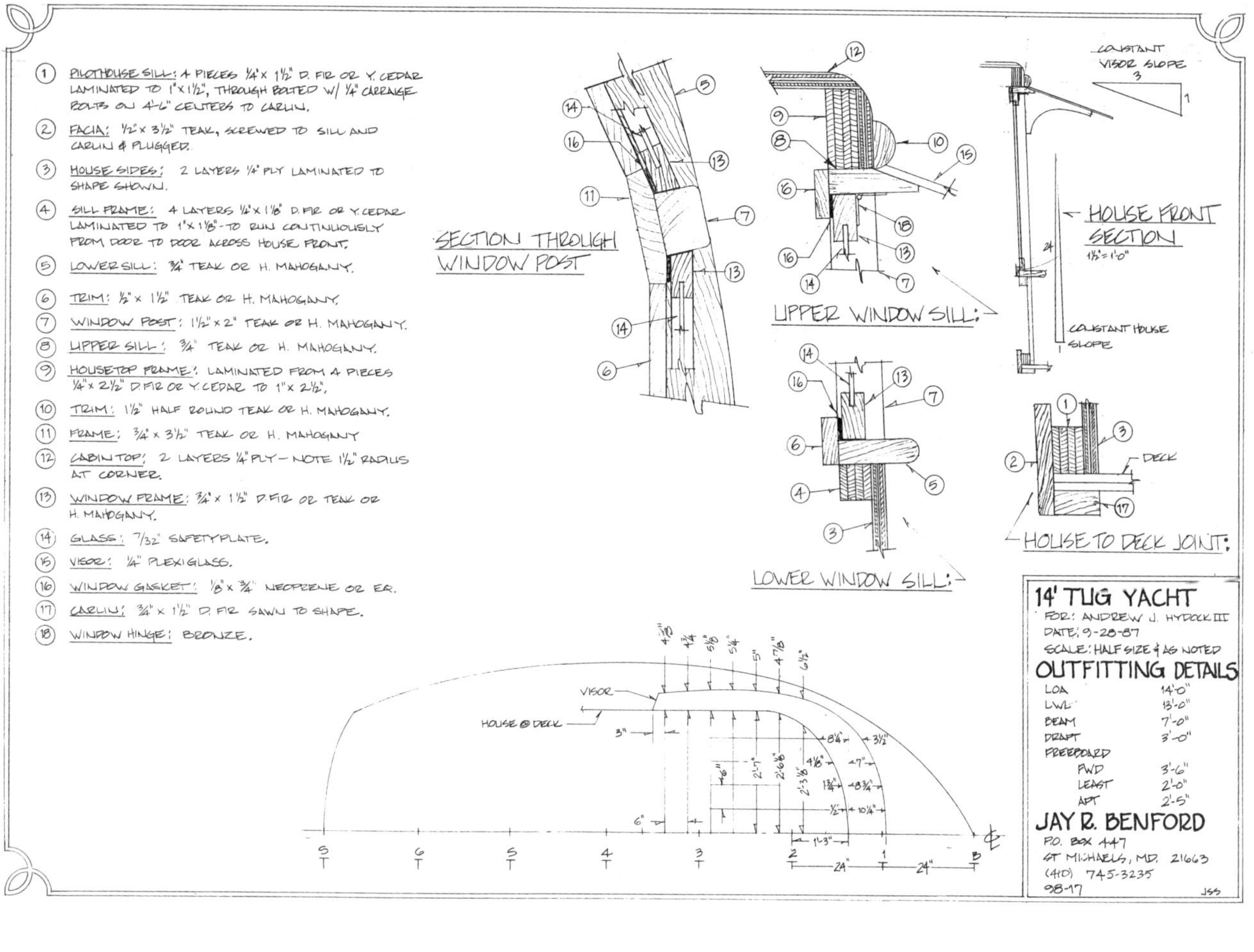

1. PILOTHOUSE SILL: 4 PIECES 1/4" x 1 1/2" D. FIR OR Y. CEDAR LAMINATED TO 1" x 1 1/2", THROUGH BOLTED W/ 1/4" CARRAIGE BOLTS ON 4'-6" CENTERS TO CARLIN.
2. FACIA: 1/2" x 3 1/2" TEAK, SCREWED TO SILL AND CARLIN & PLUGGED.
3. HOUSE SIDES: 2 LAYERS 1/4" PLY LAMINATED TO SHAPE SHOWN.
4. SILL FRAME: 4 LAYERS 1/4" x 1 1/8" D. FIR OR Y. CEDAR LAMINATED TO 1" x 1 1/8" - TO RUN CONTINUOUSLY FROM DOOR TO DOOR ACROSS HOUSE FRONT.
5. LOWER SILL: 3/4" TEAK OR H. MAHOGANY.
6. TRIM: 1/2" x 1 1/2" TEAK OR H. MAHOGANY.
7. WINDOW POST: 1 1/2" x 2" TEAK OR H. MAHOGANY.
8. UPPER SILL: 3/4" TEAK OR H. MAHOGANY.
9. HOUSETOP FRAME: LAMINATED FROM 4 PIECES 1/4" x 2 1/2" D. FIR OR Y. CEDAR TO 1" x 2 1/2".
10. TRIM: 1 1/2" HALF ROUND TEAK OR H. MAHOGANY.
11. FRAME: 3/4" x 3 1/2" TEAK OR H. MAHOGANY
12. CABIN TOP: 2 LAYERS 1/4" PLY — NOTE 1 1/2" RADIUS AT CORNER.
13. WINDOW FRAME: 3/4" x 1 1/2" D. FIR OR TEAK OR H. MAHOGANY.
14. GLASS: 7/32" SAFETYPLATE.
15. VISOR: 1/4" PLEXIGLASS.
16. WINDOW GASKET: 1/8" x 3/4" NEOPRENE OR EQ.
17. CARLIN: 3/4" x 1 1/2" D. FIR SAWN TO SHAPE.
18. WINDOW HINGE: BRONZE.

SECTION THROUGH WINDOW POST

UPPER WINDOW SILL

LOWER WINDOW SILL

CONSTANT VISOR SLOPE

HOUSE FRONT SECTION
1 1/2" = 1'-0"

CONSTANT HOUSE SLOPE

DECK

HOUSE TO DECK JOINT

VISOR

HOUSE @ DECK

14' TUG YACHT

FOR: ANDREW J. HYDOCK III
DATE: 9-28-87
SCALE: HALF SIZE & AS NOTED

OUTFITTING DETAILS

LOA	14'-0"
LWL	13'-0"
BEAM	7'-0"
DRAFT	3'-0"
FREEBOARD	
FWD	3'-6"
LEAST	2'-0"
AFT	2'-5"

JAY R. BENFORD
P.O. BOX 447
ST MICHAELS, MD. 21663
(410) 745-3235
98-17

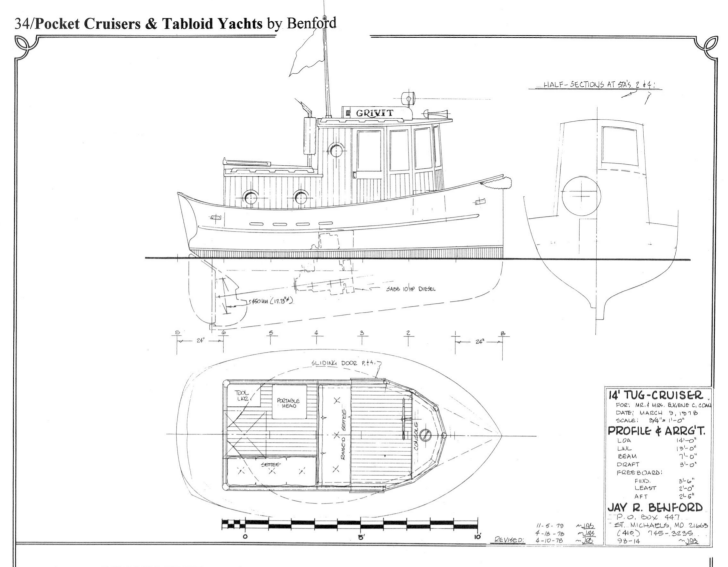

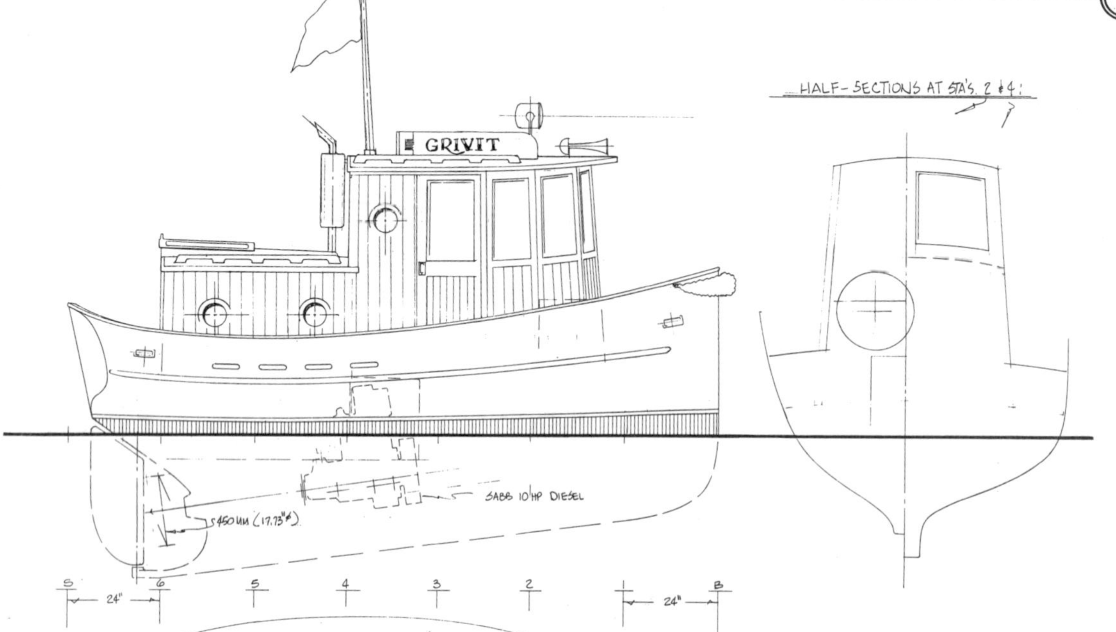

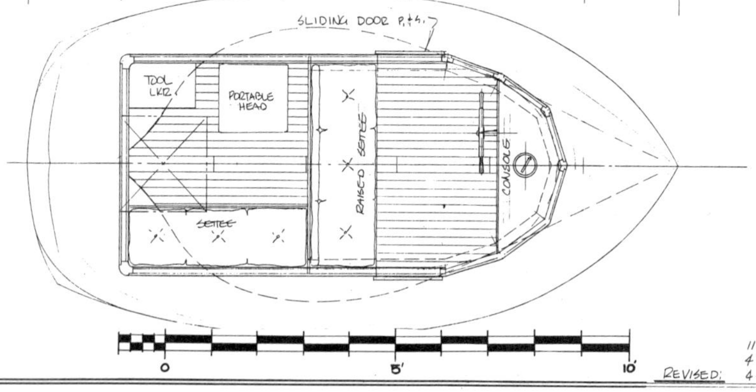

HALF-SECTIONS AT STA'S. 2 & 4:

GRIVIT

SABB 10 HP DIESEL

450 MM (17.73")

5 6 5 4 3 2 B

24" 24"

SLIDING DOOR P. & S.

TOOL LKR.

PORTABLE HEAD

RAISED SETTEE

CONSOLE

SETTEE

0 5' 10'

14' TUG-CRUISER

FOR: MR. & MRS. EUGENE C. COAN

DATE: MARCH 9, 1978

SCALE: 3/4" = 1'-0"

PROFILE & ARRG'T.

LOA	14'-0"
LWL	13'-0"
BEAM	7'-0"
DRAFT	3'-0"
FREEBOARD:	
FWD.	3'-6"
LEAST	2'-0"
AFT	2'-5"

REVISED: 11-5-79 JRB; 4-18-78 JRB; 4-10-78 JRB

JAY R. BENFORD

P.O. BOX 447

ST. MICHAELS, MD 21663

(410) 745-3235

98-14 JRB

NOTES:

1. THIS PATTERN SET CONSISTS OF 5 SHEETS LAID OUT AS SHOWN. APPROXIMATELY 2" OVERLAP BETWEEN SHEETS WAS ALLOWED IN TRACING OUR LOFT FLOOR, TO ALLOW FOR VARIANCES IN PRINTING.
2. PATTERNS SHOULD BE LAID OUT ON A SMOOTH FLOOR (WOOD/PLYWOOD PREFERRED) & ALIGNED SO THE BASELINE & WL'S ALL LINE UP & SO THAT THE 24" STATION SPACING IS CORRECT.
3. ONCE SHEETS ARE ALL PROPERLY POSITIONED, THEY MAY BE GLUED (WALLPAPERED, OR PAINTED) IN PLACE TO MINIMIZE DISTORTION DUE TO HUMIDITY EFFECTS ON THE PAPER SIZE.
4. DECK CAMBER CURVE IS SHOWN IN PLACE OF UNDERSIDE OF 3/8" THICK DECK ON TUG VERSION — USE THIS SHAPE AT SHEER LEVEL FOR FOREDECK & SIDE DECKS ON TRAWLER
5. RADIUS CURVE FOR PUTTING CAMBER IN TRANSOM
6. EXPANDED TRANSOM SHAPE — THIS IS THE TRUE SHAPE OF THE TRANSOM WHEN FLATTENED — CURVE PER NOTE 5
7. SHELL THICKNESS SHOWN ON TEMPLATES IS FOR FERRO VERSIONS — MAKE A DISC AS SHOWN AT RIGHT & SLIDE ALONG BATTEN TO GET OTHER SHELL THICKNESS DEDUCTIONS — RADIUS OF DISC TO EQUAL SHELL DEDUCTION.

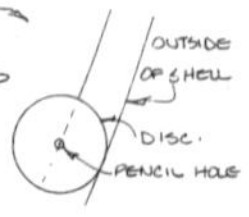

OUTSIDE OF SHELL

DISC.

PENCIL HOLE

8. DO NOT LEAVE PATTERNS & PRINTS EXPOSED TO EXTENDED SUNLIGHT, AS THIS QUICKLY FADES THE BLUE LINES.
9. THE PRINTING PAPER IS ALSO TEMPERATURE & HUMIDITY SENSITIVE, CAUSING IT TO CHANGE SIZE. THUS FOLLOW NOTE 3 DIRECTIONS. BUILDER MUST CHECK PRINTED PATTERNS FOR DISTORTIONS BEFORE USING.

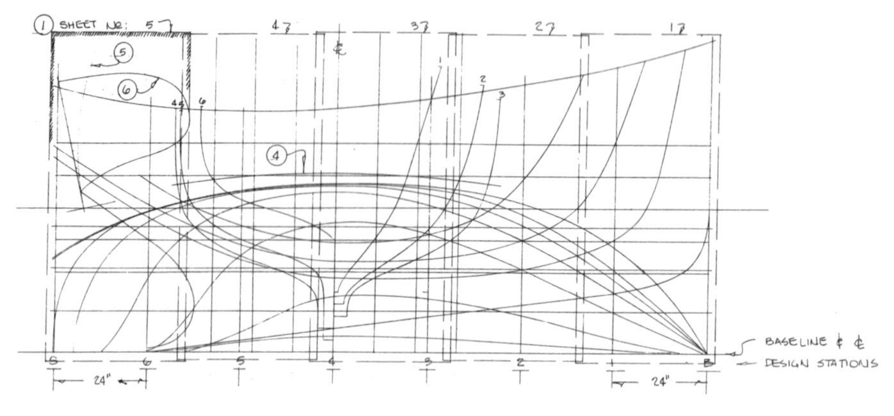

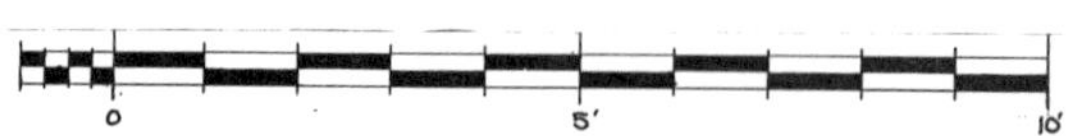

14' TUG/TRAWLER

FOR: R. THOMPSON, ESQ.

DATE: 3-26-77

SCALE: 3/4" = 1'-0"

PATTERNS-NOTES

LOA	14'-0"
LWL	13'-0"
BEAM	7'-0"
DRAFT	3'-0"
FREEBOARD:	
FWD.	3'-6"
LEAST	2'-0"
AFT	2'-4 1/4"

JAY R. BENFORD

P.O. BOX 447

ST. MICHAELS, MD 21663

(410) 745-3235

98-13 JRB

Chapter Three

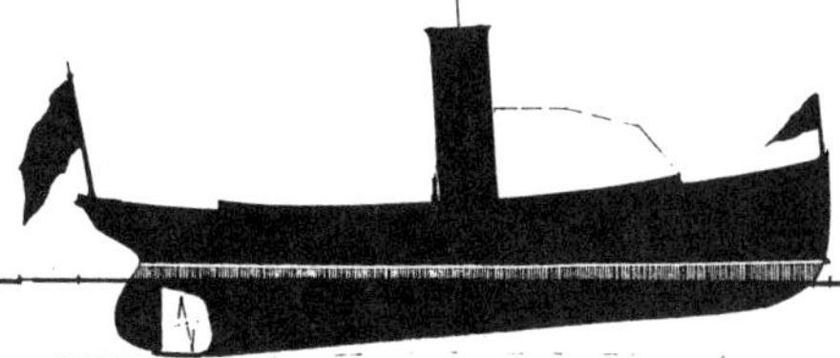

17' Fantail Steam Launch *Myf*

Design Number 217
1984

My work on this design began with a discussion with Rob Denny, whose clients wanted him to build a small fantail steam launch. They had seen our larger 34' Fantail Motor Yacht and liked the style of the design. We took that successful boat and created a smaller version of it for this launch.

The 17' steam launch **Myf** was built in Rob Denny's shop in Victoria, B.C. in 1985 and her wood fired machinery was built by her owner, Blayney Scott.

She's built of traditional wood construction with modern adhesives to facilitate building, aid longevity, and reduce maintenance. Since she is often trailer-sailed, it was decided to seal all the structure with epoxy, so that she would not dry out and change size while out of the water. This has worked out well and she's a delight to behold.

In fact, she is so well done that she's been awarded a prize at the Victoria Classic Boat Festival. There's often a good contingent of the local steamboat group there, and these little steamers are very popular with the visitors.

Her cockpit provides comfortable seating for the crew and is open enough to provide easy access to the engine and controls.

Myf's hull form is quite easily driven and has good form stability. She can also be fitted with the smallest of inboard engines to make a diesel launch too.

As Blayney often tells me, "She's just like a duck on the water." One of the photos on the back cover of this book shows her with four adults aboard and this is a comfortable crew for her to carry. She is quite buoyant and seems to ride over the swells instead of plowing through them.

Alternative Power

Alternative power would be a small inboard engine. She only needs a few horsepower to mover her along, so the smallest of the marine diesel engines would be plenty of power for her.

Alternative Construction

This boat would lend itself well to strip-planking with a covering of a couple of diagonal cold-molded veneers. The strips might be three-eighths of an inch and the veneers one-eighth each.

Pattern Set

We were fortunate in being able to get Rob Denny to make up a set of patterns from the loft floor used to build **Myf**. The layout shown below is what these patterns look like. The three views of the lines plan have been overlaid on each other to conserve space, as is traditional in doing lofting work. The edges of the sheets overlap so that we can allow for variations in the patterns being printed all the way to the edges of the paper. While it is best for each builder to do their own lofting work, to familiarize them with the work at hand, use of patterns like these can speed up the work for those unfamiliar with doing the work.

Particulars:		English	Metric
Length overall		17'-0"	5.18 m
Length designed waterline		15'-6"	4.72 m
Beam		5'-3"	1.60 m
Draft		1'-8"	0.51 m
Freeboard:	Forward	2'-7½"	0.80 m
	Least	1'-4½"	0.42 m
	Aft	1'-9"	0.53 m
Displacement, cruising trim		1,160 lbs.	526 kg.
Displacement-length ratio		139	
Prismatic coefficient		.605	
Pounds per inch immersion		330	59 kg/cm
Entrance half angle		20°	

***CAUTION:** The displacement quoted here is for the boat in cruising trim. That is, with the fuel and water tanks filled, the crew on board, as well as the crews' gear and stores in the lockers. This should not be confused with the "shipping weight" often quoted as "displacement" by some manufacturers. This should be taken into account when comparing figures and ratios between this and other designs.

17' FANTAIL STEAMER
FOR: BLAYNEY SCOTT
10/21/97 3/4"=1'-0"
PATTERN LAYOUT

JAY R. BENFORD
P. O. BOX 447
ST. MICHAELS, MD 21663
(410) 745-3235

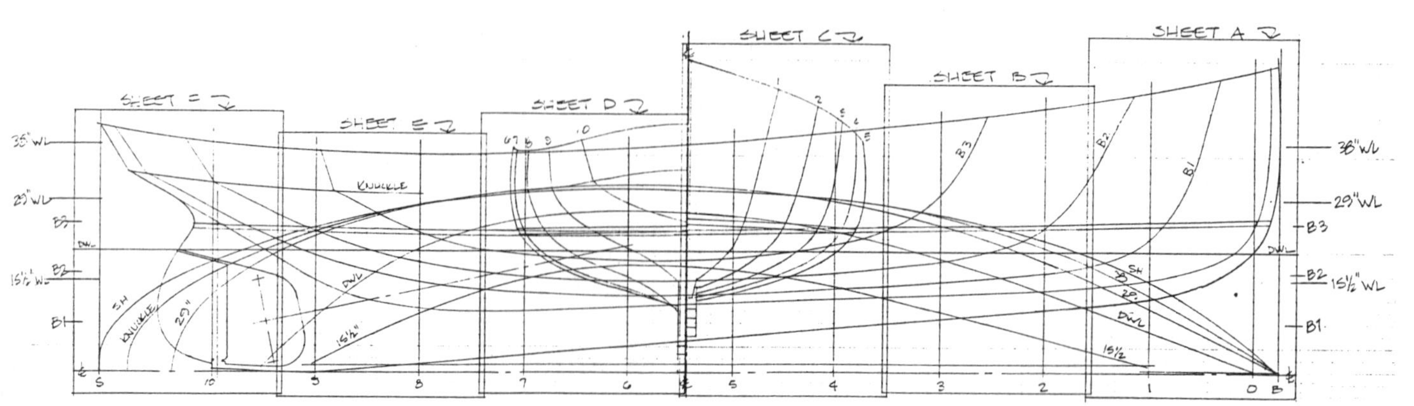

217-6

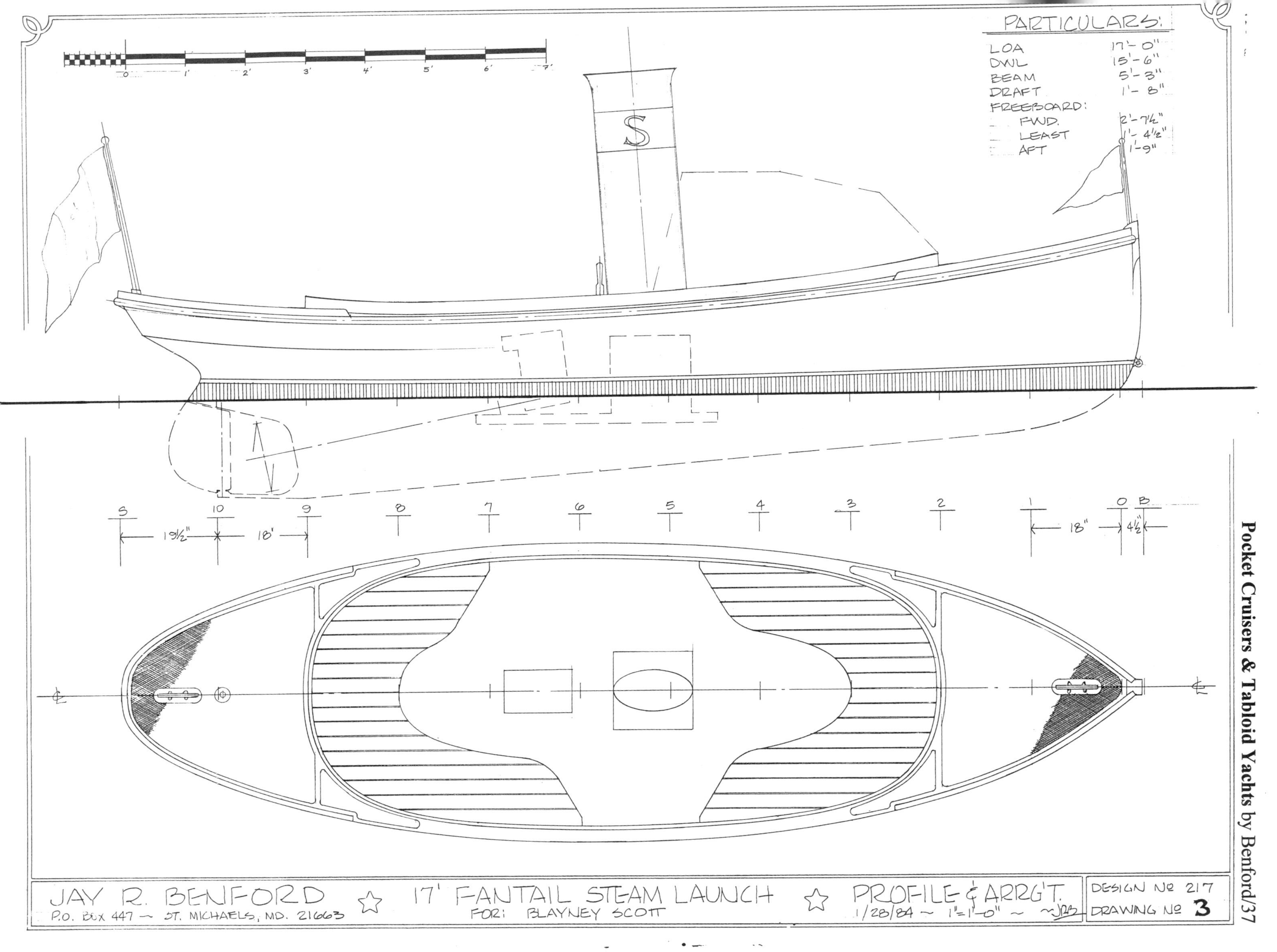
PARTICULARS:
LOA 17'-0"
DWL 15'-6"
BEAM 5'-3"
DRAFT 1'-8"
FREEBOARD:
FWD. 2'-7½"
LEAST 1'-4½"
AFT 1'-9"
0 1' 2' 3' 4' 5' 6' 7'
S
5 10 9 8 7 6 5 4 3 2 1 0 B
19½" 18" 18" 4½"
JAY R. BENFORD ☆ 17' FANTAIL STEAM LAUNCH ☆ PROFILE & ARRG'T.
P.O. BOX 447 ~ ST. MICHAELS, MD. 21663
FOR: BLAYNEY SCOTT
1/28/84 ~ 1"=1'-0" ~ ~JRB
DESIGN No 217
DRAWING No 3

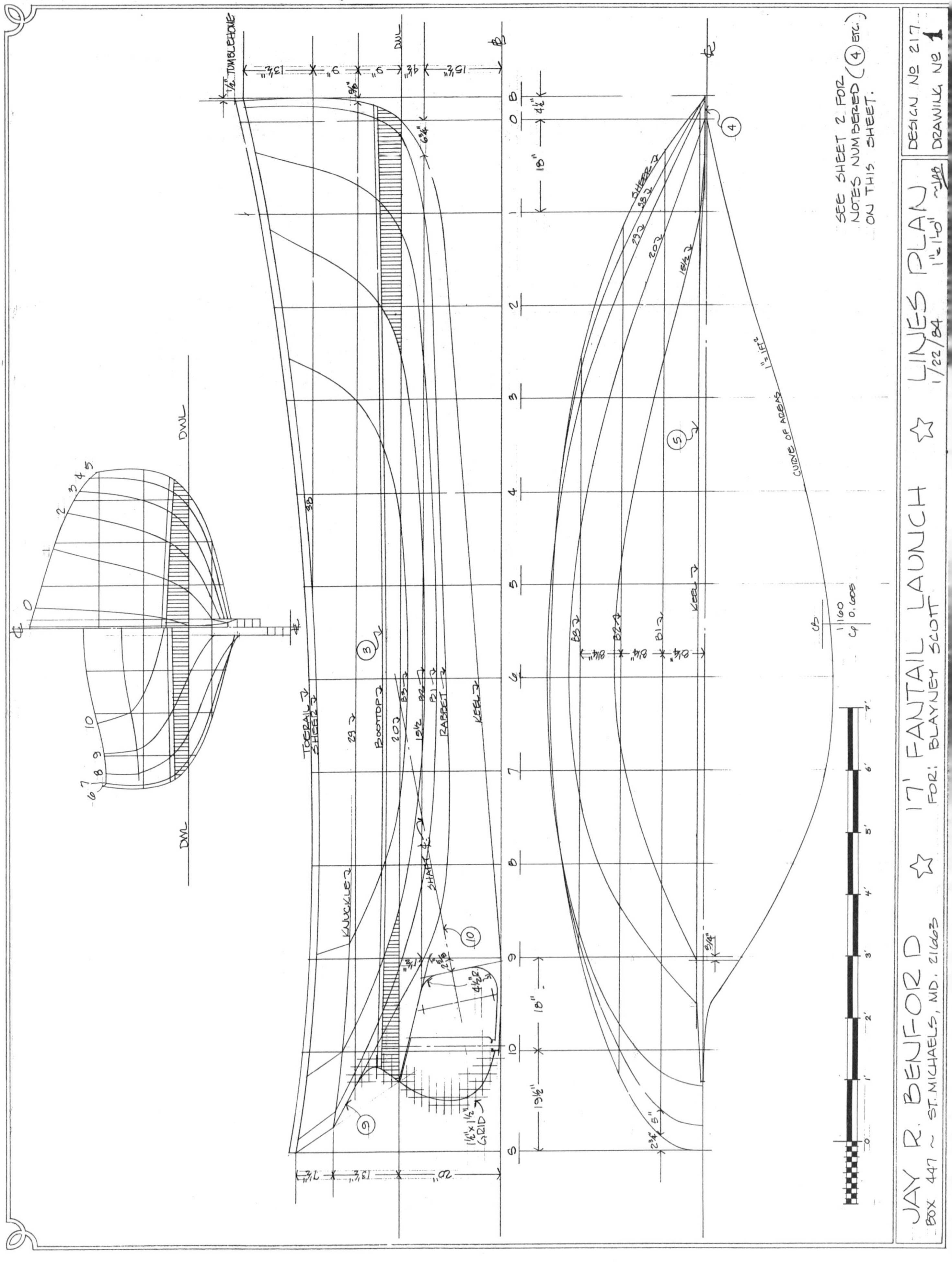

DWL

DWL

1/2" TUMBLEHOME

TOERAIL

SHEER

KNUCKLE

29

BOOTTOP

20

15 1/2

B3

B2

B1

RABBET

KEEL

SHAFT ℄

1 1/2" x 1 1/2" GRID

4 1/2" R.

CURVE OF AREAS 1" = 1 FT²

CB

1.160

Cp 0.605

SEE SHEET 2 FOR NOTES NUMBERED (4) ETC. ON THIS SHEET.

JAY R. BENFORD ☆ 17' FANTAIL LAUNCH ☆ LINES PLAN

BOX 447 ~ ST. MICHAELS, MD. 21663

FOR: BLAYNEY SCOTT

1/22/84 1" = 1'-0" ~JRB

DESIGN № 217

DRAWING № 1

STATION	10	9	8	7	6	5	4	3	2	1	0
	HEIGHTS										
℄ TO KEEL	0-0-0	0-0-0	0-1-4	0-3-0	0-4-4	0-6-0	0-7-4	0-9-0	0-10-4	1-0-2	1-8-0
" " RABBET	(9)	1-3-0	0-10-5	0-10-1	0-10-7	0-11-5	1-0-3	1-1-1	1-1-7	1-3-0	(11)
" " B1	2-2-7	1-7-7	1-2-6	1-1-1	1-0-6	1-1-1	1-1-7	1-2-7	1-4-1	1-10-4	—
" " B2	2-7-6	1-11-2	1-6-2	1-3-7	1-3-1	1-3-3	1-4-4	1-6-4	2-0-1	(4-3-1)	—
" " B3	—	—	1-11-2	1-7-3	1-6-5	1-7-1	1-9-1	2-5-0	—	—	—
DWL TO BOOTTOP	0-4-2	0-3-7	0-3-5+	0-3-5	0-3-5	0-3-6	0-4-0	0-4-3	0-4-6	0-5-2	0-5-6
" " KNUCKLE	0-11-6	0-10-3	0-10-0	(0-10-1)	—	—	—	—	—	—	—
" " SHEER	1-6-3	1-4-7	1-4-4+	1-4-5+	1-5-2	1-6-1	1-7-5	1-9-5	2-0-0	2-2-7+	2-6-4+
	HALF-BREADTHS										
15½" WL	—	0-1-7	0-9-7	1-3-5	1-5-7	1-5-1	1-2-1	0-10-1	0-5-4	0-1-4	—
20" WL (DWL)	—	0-9-4	1-8-7	2-1-5	2-3-0	2-2-1	1-11-3	1-7-1	1-1-3	0-6-7	0-0-3
29" WL	1-0-7	1-11-0	2-4-0	2-6-4	2-7-3	2-6-5	2-4-4	2-0-6	1-6-4	0-10-7	0-2-2
38" WL	—	—	—	—	—	2-6-2	2-5-0	2-2-0	1-8-7	1-0-7	0-3-1
KNUCKLE	1-4-4	1-11-7	2-4-2	(2-6-4)	—	—	—	—	—	—	—
SHEER	1-6-5	2-0-4	2-4-2	2-6-2	2-6-6	2-6-2	2-5-0	2-2-3	1-10-0	1-3-1	0-3-7

NOTES:

1. LINES & OFFSETS IN FEET-INCHES-EIGHTHS TO OUTSIDE OF PLANKING. DEDUCT FOR MOLD FRAMES AS REQUIRED.
2. LINES MUST BE LOFTED & FAIRED FULL-SIZE — DO NOT SCALE PRINTS.
3. BOOTTOP OFFSETS TO TOP EDGE OF STRIPE — STRIPE IS 1½" HIGH IN PROFILE FULL LENGTH.
4. HALF-SIDING OF STEM IS 0-0-3.
5. HALF-SIDING OF KEEL IS 0-1-4.
6. THESE PLANS ARE THE PROPERTY OF THE DESIGNER & MAY BE USED ONLY AS AUTHORIZED BY THE DESIGNER IN WRITING.
7. ANY ALTERATION FROM THESE PLANS RELIEVES THE DESIGNER FROM ANY FURTHER RESPONSIBILITY.
8. IT IS UNDERSTOOD THAT NO MORE THAN ONE BOAT WILL BE BUILT FROM THESE PLANS WITHOUT WRITTEN PERMISSION FROM THE DESIGNER.
9. RABBET IS STRAIGHT LINE IN PROFILE FROM INTERSECTION WITH KNUCKLE AT STERN DOWN TO 15½" WL.
10. SHAFT ℄ IS 1" ABOVE DWL AT STA. 6 & 10" BELOW DWL AT STA. 9.
11. DEVELOP RABBET POSITION ON STEM PER DETAIL! →
12. OFFSETS IN BRACKETS (0-0-0) FOR FAIRING PURPOSES ONLY.

STEM SECTION:

FULL SIZE

3/4"

3/8"

1"

1/2"

BRZ. 3/4" HALF-OVAL

JAY R. BENFORD ☆ 17' FANTAIL LAUNCH ☆ OFFSETS & NOTES

BOX 447 ~ ST. MICHAELS, MD. 21663

FOR: BLAYNEY SCOTT

1/24/84 ~JRB

DESIGN NR 217

DRAWING NR 2

REV'D.: 3-8-89

NOTES:

1. KEEL: SIDED 3" D. FIR.
2. WORMSHOE: 3/4" x 3" GUM OR IRONBARK.
3. FRAMES: 3/4" x 3/4" W. OAK ON 9" CENTERS.
4. PLANKING: 1/2" R. CEDAR OR 7/16" H. MAHOG. W/GLUED SEAMS.
5. CLAMP: 1 1/8" x 2" D. FIR.
6. TOERAIL: FROM 1 1/2" x 1 1/8" TEAK OR H. MAHOG. — TAPER TO 3/4" AT TOP.
7. GUARD: 1 1/2" TEAK OR H. MAHOG HALF-ROUND.
8. SHEER STRAKE: H. MAHOG. OR TEAK.
9. APRON: 1 1/8" x 5" D. FIR.
10. FLOORS: 3/4" x 3 1/2" Y. CEDAR.
11. ENGINE BEDS: 2 1/2" x 2 1/2" D. FIR OR Y. CEDAR.
12. COAMING: 3/4" x 5" TEAK OR H. MAHOG.
13. DECK: 10 MM (3/8") BRUYNZEEL PLY.
14. LONG'L DECK BEAMS: 3/4" x 2" Y. CEDAR ON 9" CTRS. — BUTT TO CLAMP
15. COAMING CARLIN: 1" x 2" Y. CEDAR SAWN TO SHAPE
16.

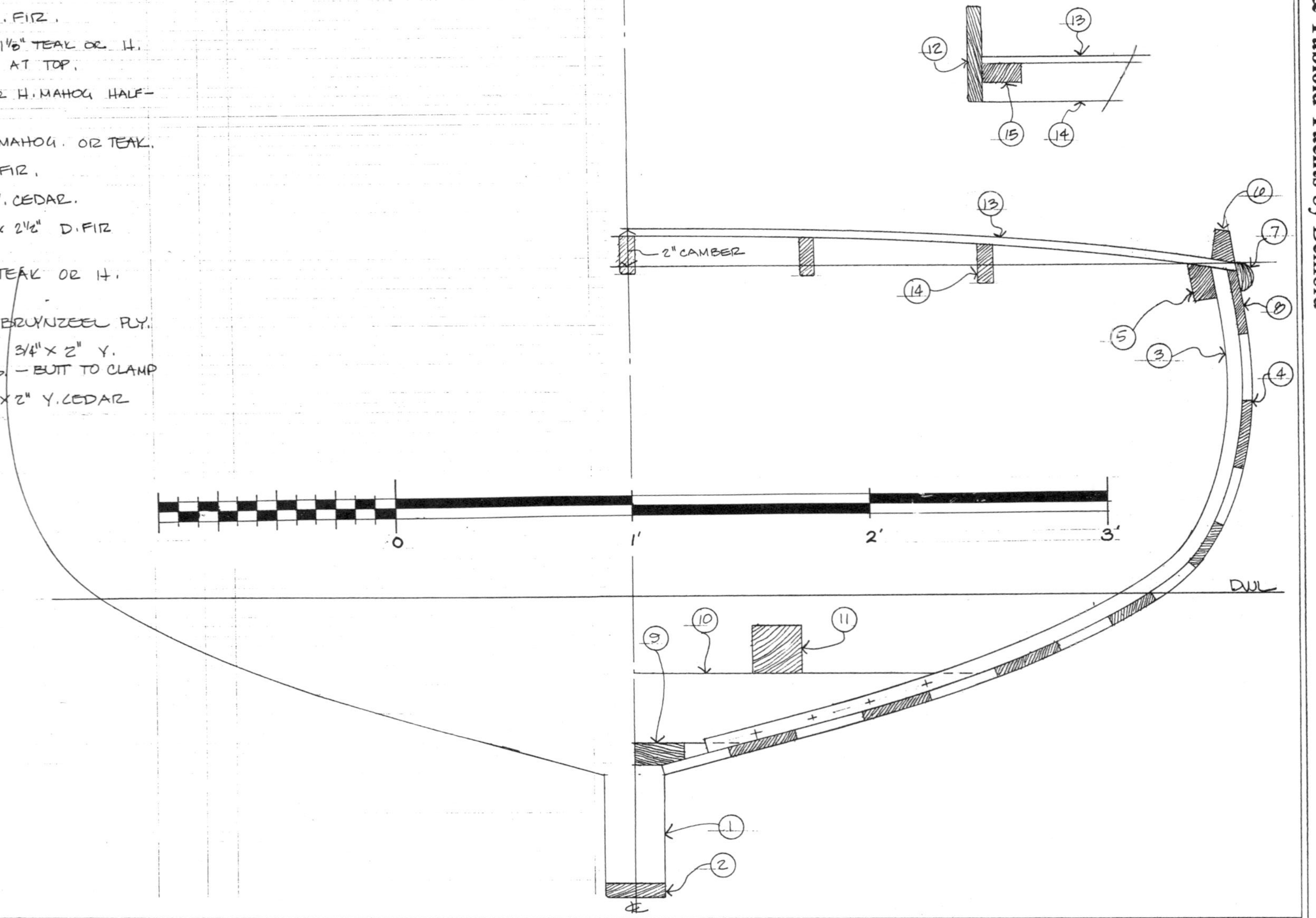

JAY R. BENFORD ☆ 17' FANTAIL LAUNCH ☆ SCANTLING SECTION

BOX 447 ~ ST. MICHAELS, MD 21663

FOR: BLAYNEY SCOTT 1/28/84 3" = 1'-0" ~JRB

DESIGN Nº 217

DRAWING Nº 4

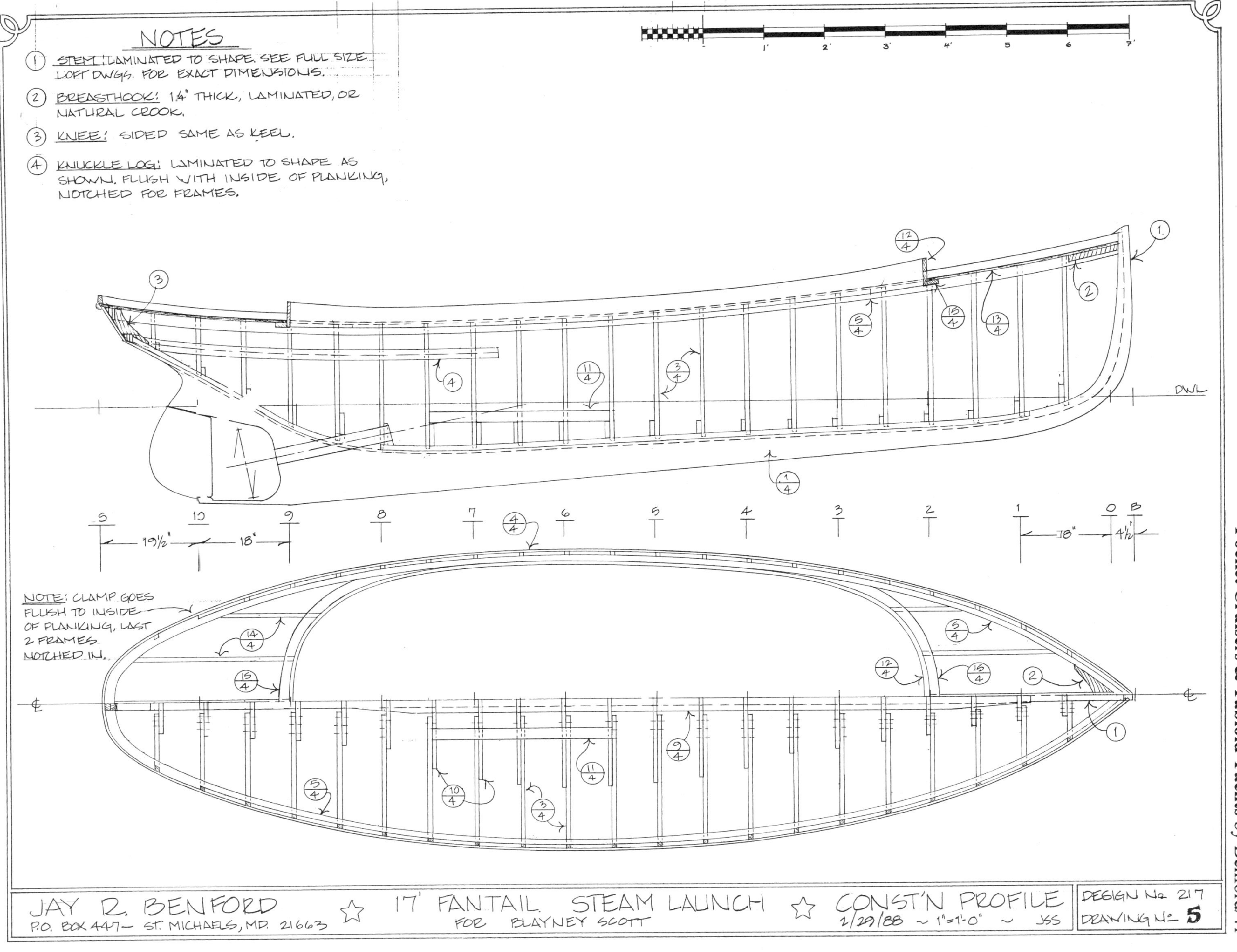
NOTES
1 STEM: LAMINATED TO SHAPE. SEE FULL SIZE LOFT DWGS. FOR EXACT DIMENSIONS.
2 BREASTHOOK: 1¼" THICK, LAMINATED, OR NATURAL CROOK.
3 KNEE: SIDED SAME AS KEEL.
4 KNUCKLE LOG: LAMINATED TO SHAPE AS SHOWN. FLUSH WITH INSIDE OF PLANKING, NOTCHED FOR FRAMES.
DWL
S
10
9
8
7
6
5
4
3
2
1
0
B
19½"
18"
18"
4½"
NOTE: CLAMP GOES FLUSH TO INSIDE OF PLANKING, LAST 2 FRAMES NOTCHED IN.
JAY R. BENFORD
P.O. BOX 447 – ST. MICHAELS, MD. 21663
17' FANTAIL STEAM LAUNCH
FOR BLAYNEY SCOTT
CONST'N PROFILE
2/29/88 ~ 1"=1'-0" ~ JSS
DESIGN No 217
DRAWING No 5

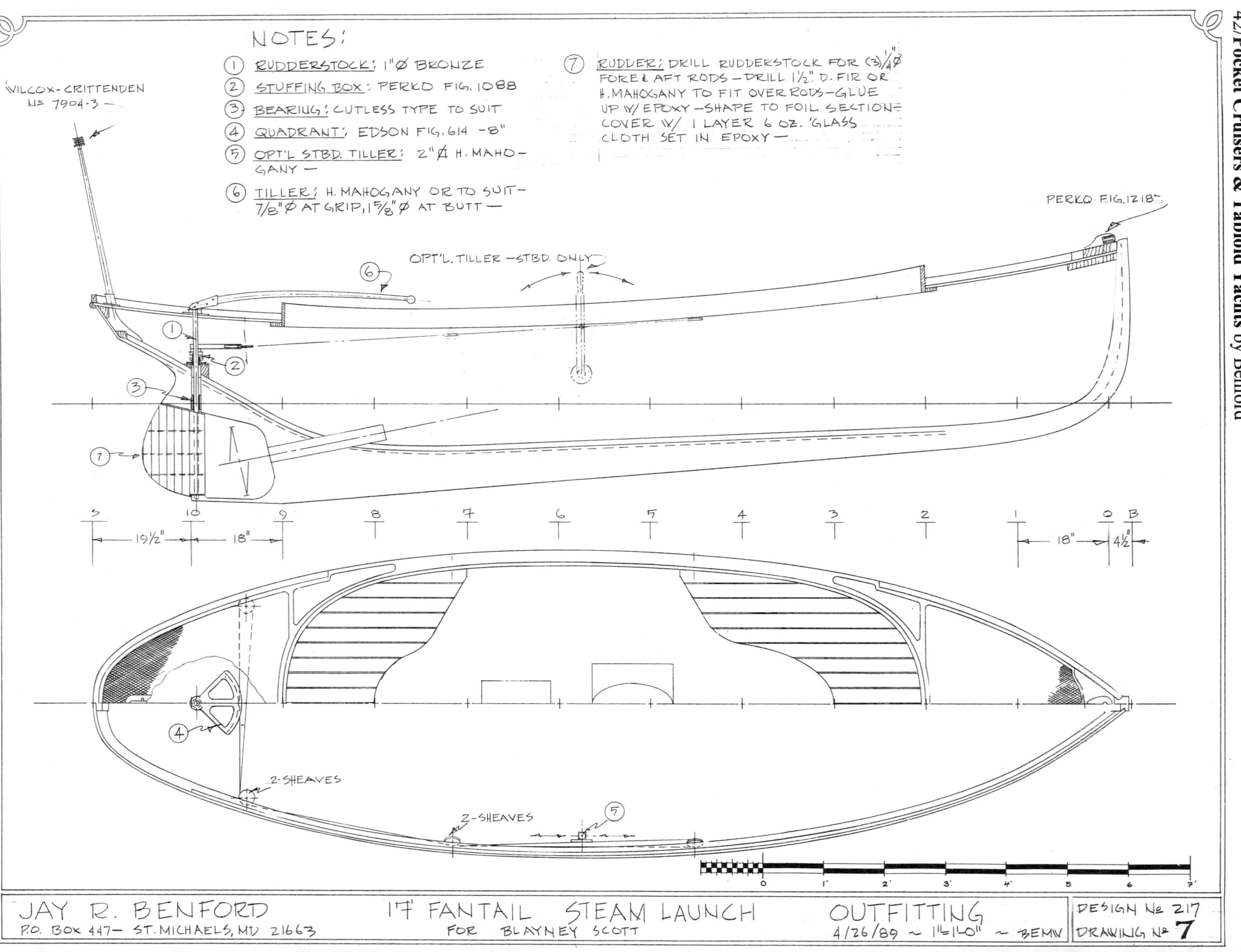
NOTES:
1 RUDDERSTOCK: 1"Ø BRONZE
2 STUFFING BOX: PERKO FIG. 1088
3 BEARING: CUTLESS TYPE TO SUIT
4 QUADRANT: EDSON FIG. 614 -8"
5 OPT'L STBD. TILLER: 2"Ø H. MAHOGANY —
6 TILLER: H. MAHOGANY OR TO SUIT — 7/8"Ø AT GRIP, 1 5/8"Ø AT BUTT —
7 RUDDER: DRILL RUDDERSTOCK FOR (3) 1/4"Ø FORE & AFT RODS — DRILL 1 1/2" D. FIR OR H. MAHOGANY TO FIT OVER RODS — GLUE UP W/ EPOXY — SHAPE TO FOIL SECTION — COVER W/ 1 LAYER 6 OZ. 'GLASS CLOTH SET IN EPOXY —
WILCOX-CRITTENDEN No 7904-3 —
PERKO FIG. 1218
OPT'L. TILLER — STBD. ONLY
2-SHEAVES
2-SHEAVES
JAY R. BENFORD
P.O. BOX 447 — ST. MICHAELS, MD 21663
17' FANTAIL STEAM LAUNCH
FOR BLAYNEY SCOTT
OUTFITTING
4/26/89 ~ 1"=1'-0" ~ BEMW
DESIGN No 217
DRAWING No 7

These photos show Rob Denny's well ordered shop during the construction of **Myf**. The mold frames and ribbands with the steam bent frames over them can be readily seen. Note also the way the framing for the knuckle at the fantail is laminated and carved to shape.

The photos on the following page show more of the construction and some of the finished boat. For more photos of her in color, see the front and back cover of this book.

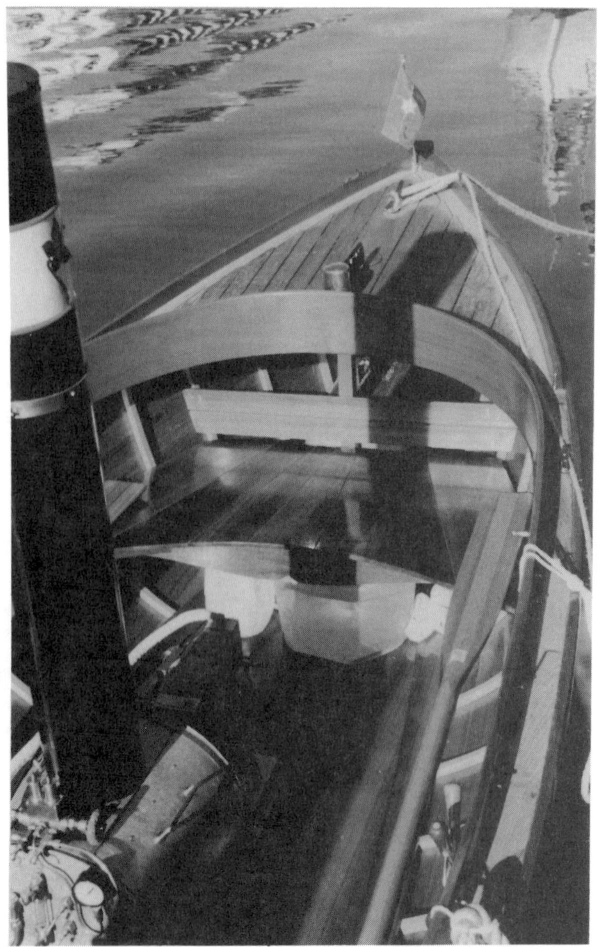

Chapter Four

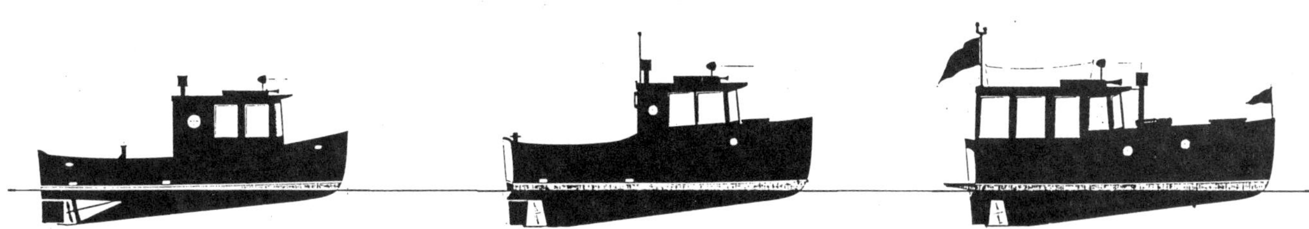

20' Supply Boat *Båten* & Lake Union Cruiser

Design Number 132

1975

Supply Boat *Båten*

In the fall of 1975, Marilyn Anderson and Rachel Adams came to see me in my office in Seattle. They had retired to Crane Island and were in need of a better boat to serve as their supply boat and year 'round commuter. They had but a short run from the Crane Island Association (CIA) floating docks on Crane over to the CIA Orcas Island floats.

The primary restriction on the design was that it had to fit within the 20' length overall limit in force at the CIA floats. This limit was an effort by the CIA to be sure that every property owner would have enough space to keep a boat at the community floats. The effect for us as designers was to immediately suggest a very short ended boat, to maximize the waterline length, since this is the one of the prime determinants in setting the speed of a displacement hull. The primary use of the new boat is these short runs, and we wanted to be sure the boat was one that would be easily driven at modest speeds. The beam was chosen as being one that would permit trailering if there was a need to move her overland.

We did two construction plans and the boat was bid in both Airex® cored fiberglass and in carvel planked wood. Jensen Shipyards in Friday Harbor was awarded the contract to build her and Bill Ryerson did a very nice job of putting her together there.

Over the years, I've had quite a number of trips with **Båten**, both short trips aboard and longer cruises in company with her. She's proven to be a very capable supply boat and general utility pickup vessel. She's ideally suited to the Pacific Northwest climate, with shelter and heat for the crew in the stand-up pilothouse and a generous open cockpit. For making close quarters landings or operating in fair weather, there is another helm and set of engine controls in the cockpit.

The cockpit has a full width seat aft, covering the batteries, fuel tankage, and steering gear. Her bulwarks are deep enough to make you feel that you are **in** the boat instead of **on** it.

Another part of the design brief was for us to provide for the boat being useful and usable for their geriatric years. Towards this end, we've added steps at the forward corners of the cockpit and handgrabs off the aft corners of the house right above the steps. Also, some boarding and offloading can be done by an adult sitting on the cockpit coaming cap and swinging their legs over onto the float or cockpit sole, depending on whether departing or loading.

With sliding windows on either side at the forward end of the pilothouse, there is an additional way to look over the side without getting too wet or cold.

The v-berths forward make a pleasant place to relax underway as well as one for sleeping aboard. Having had a chance to try them out, I can say that she's both comfortable and cozy. There is room to sit up and read on the bunks too.

The pilothouse has 6'-2" headroom and room for several adults to stay snug near the stove and enjoy the view underway. ***Båten*** has a little cast iron wood burning stove installed and this has much to recommend it. On her longer passages, such as the run of almost an hour when they would come over to Friday Harbor to visit us, there was plenty of time to get some good heat going and make hot drinks too.

As sometimes happens, a very pleasant friendship arose with the owners of this delightful boat, so I've had plenty of chances to see her in action and keep track of her evolution. She has survived well and gracefully, giving good service year 'round in all sorts of weather.

Alternate Version

This design went through several iterations before we got to the final version. Two are shown in this chapter, one with the final choice of the raised deck section forward and one without it. Construction for either one would be done in a similar manner, and the details shown here can be used for whichever one best suits your use.

Lake Union Cruiser Version

The Lake Union Cruiser version was done in the style of Lake Union Drydock's classic Dreamboats. On this one, we've slid the pilothouse of ***Båten*** further aft and made it longer, fully enclosing the cockpit. This can be enclosed with curtains or the windows shown, depending on your climate. The addition of a built-in head in lieu of the portable used on ***Båten***'s cruising and more lockers and galley facilities will make longer cruises go easier.

The original ***Båten*** was fitted with an eighteen horsepower Sabb diesel with a feathering propeller. The Lake Union Cruiser version has a four cylinder Yanmar diesel indicated, which is rated at fifty horsepower. Her hull form has a flat enough run to make use of more power like this, getting her up into the semi-displacement speed range.

Particulars:		**English**	**Metric**
Length overall		19'-11½"	6.08 m
Length designed waterline		19'-0"	5.79 m
Beam		7'-11½"	2.43 m
Draft (2'-3" light)		2'-6"	0.76 m
Freeboard:	Forward	4'-6"	1.37 m
	Least	2'-9½"	0.85 m
	Aft	3'-0"	0.91 m
Displacement, light version		3,100 lbs.	1,406 kg.
Displacement, cruising trim		4,600 lbs.	2,086 kg.
Displacement-length ratio		202/299	
Prismatic coefficient		.68	
Pounds per inch immersion		550	249 kg/cm
Fuel tankage		30 Gals.	
Headroom		6'-2"	1.88 m

***CAUTION:** The displacement quoted here is for the boat in cruising trim. That is, with the fuel and water tanks filled, the crew on board, as well as the crews' gear and stores in the lockers. This should not be confused with the "shipping weight" often quoted as "displacement" by some manufacturers. This should be taken into account when comparing figures and ratios between this and other designs.

Clockwise from upper left: **Båten** at the Crane Island floats, her dual helm setup, underway and coming in for a landing at Friday Harbor.

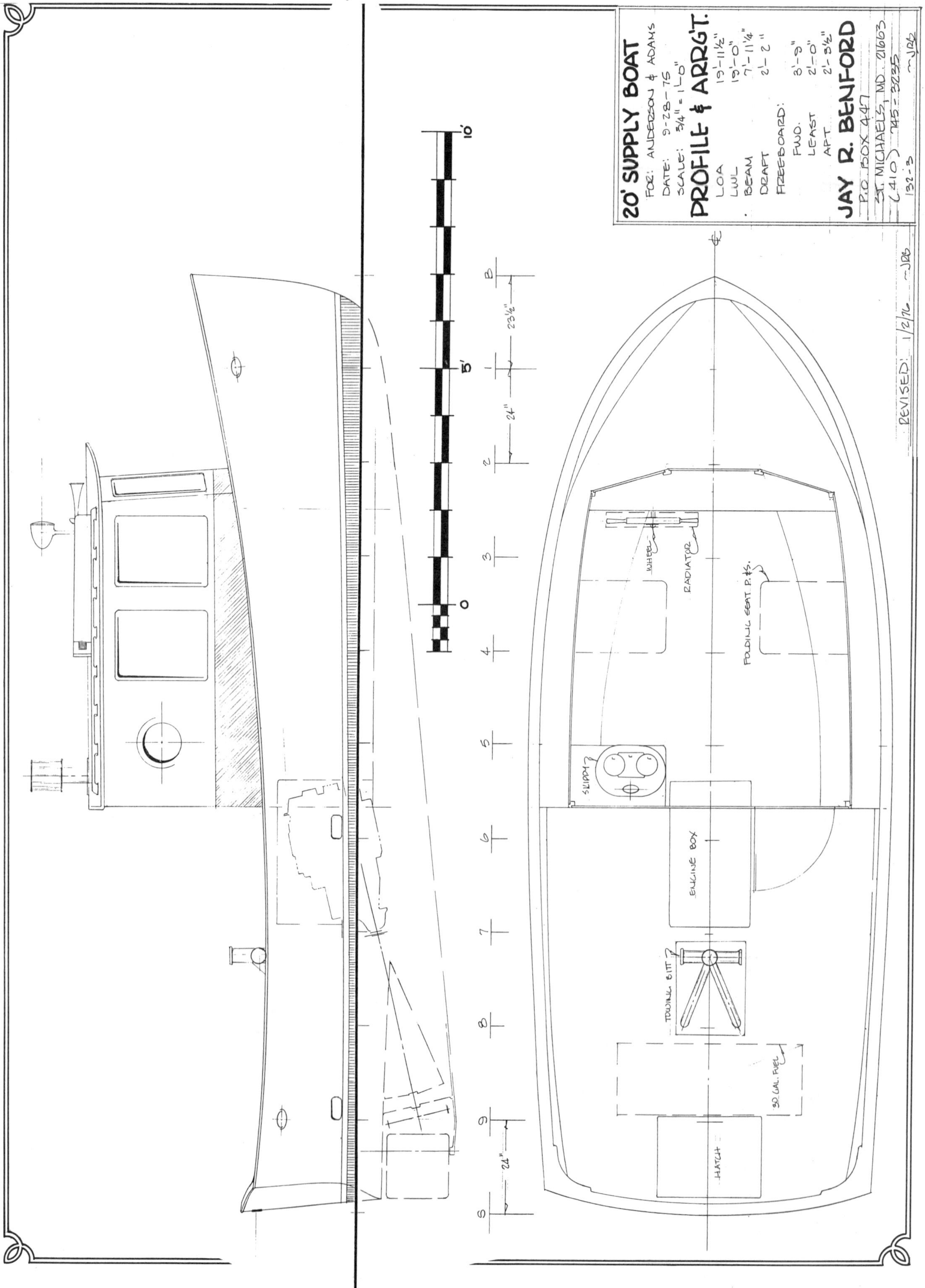

0 5' 10'

S 9 8 7 6 5 4 3 2 1 B

24" 24" 23½"

SKIPPY

TOWING BITT

ENGINE BOX

WHEEL

RADIATOR

HATCH

30 GAL. FUEL

FOLDING SEAT P. & S.

℄

20' SUPPLY BOAT

FOR: ANDERSON & ADAMS

DATE: 9-28-75

SCALE: 3/4" = 1'-0"

PROFILE & ARRG'T.

LOA	19'-11½"
LWL	19'-0"
BEAM	7'-11¼"
DRAFT	2'-2"
FREEBOARD:	
FWD.	3'-9"
LEAST	2'-0"
AFT	2'-3½"

JAY R. BENFORD

P.O. BOX 447

ST. MICHAELS, MD. 21663

(410) 745-3235

132-3 ~JRB

REVISED: 1/2/76 ~JRB

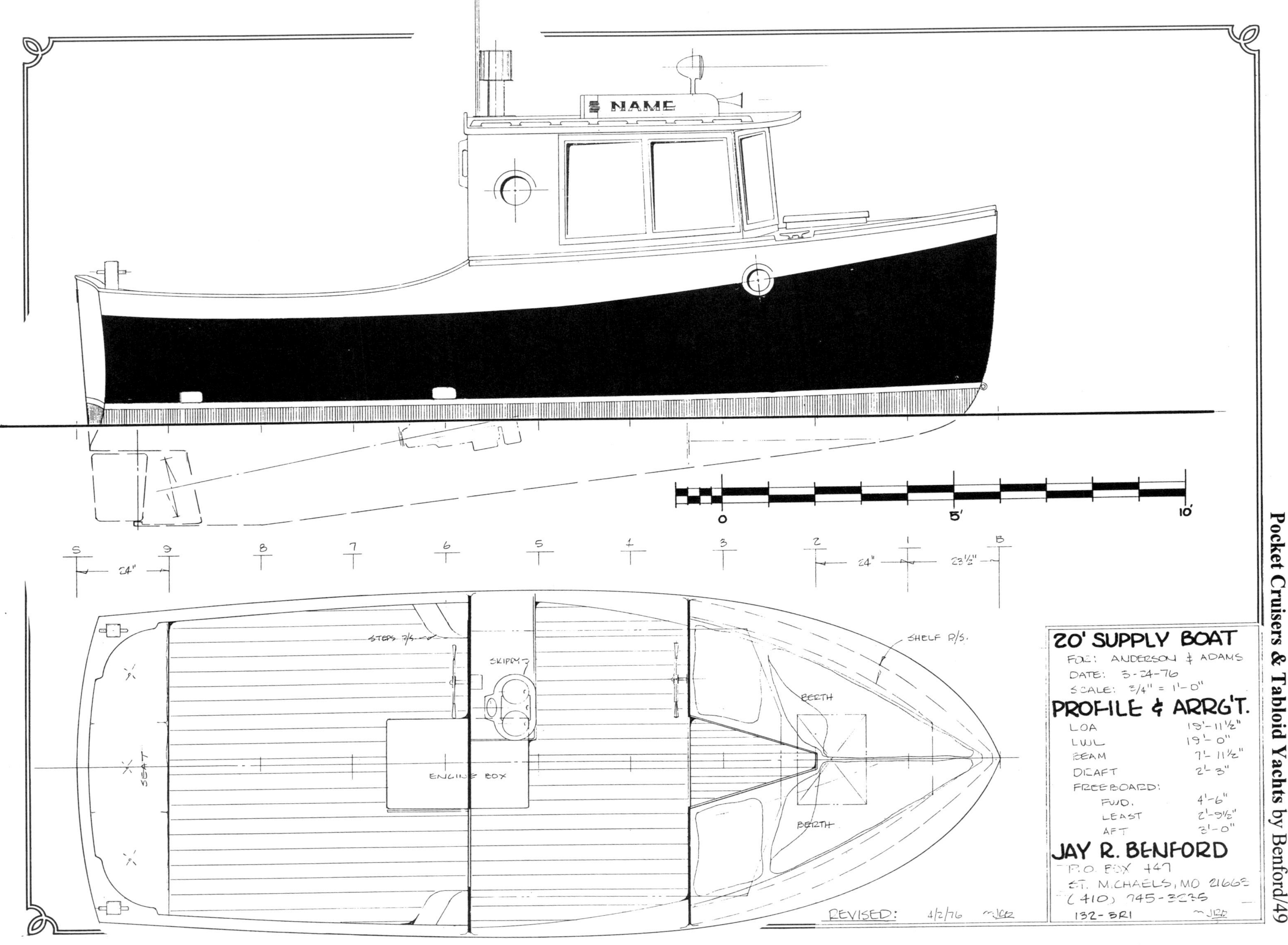

NAME
0
5'
10'
S
9
8
7
6
5
4
3
2
1
B
24"
24"
23½"
STEPS 7/S
SKIPPY?
ENGINE BOX
SEAT
SHELF P/S.
BERTH
BERTH
REVISED: 4/2/76 JRB
20' SUPPLY BOAT
FOR: ANDERSON & ADAMS
DATE: 5-24-76
SCALE: 3/4" = 1'-0"
PROFILE & ARRG'T.
LOA 19'-11½"
LWL 19'-0"
BEAM 7'-11½"
DRAFT 2'-3"
FREEBOARD:
FWD. 4'-6"
LEAST 2'-9½"
AFT 3'-0"
JAY R. BENFORD
P.O. BOX 447
ST. MICHAELS, MD 21663
(410) 745-3235
132-BR1
JRB

STATION	S	9	8	7	6	5	4	3	2	1
	HEIGHTS									
℄ TO KEEL	—	0-3-0	0-3-0	0-6-0	0-9-0	1-0-0	1-3-0	1-6-0	1-9-0	2-0-1
" " FAIRBODY	1-11-3	1-11-1	1-10-2	1-9-2	1-8-3	1-7-5	1-7-2	1-7-5	1-9-0	2-0-1
" " B1	2-1-4	2-0-6	1-11-6	1-10-7	1-10-2	1-9-5	1-9-4	1-10-5	2-1-2	2-11-6
" " B2	2-4-1	2-2-7	2-1-6	2-1-0	2-0-3	2-0-2	2-0-6	2-2-6	2-11-2	5-7-4
" " B3	2-9-0	2-6-7	2-5-3	2-4-2	2-4-0	2-4-3	2-6-7	3-2-3	5-7-1	—
30"WL TO BOOTTOP	0-6-1	0-6-0	0-5-7	0-5-7	0-6-0	0-6-2	0-6-5	0-7-0	0-7-5	0-8-2
" " WALE	2-6-1	2-4-6	2-4-0	2-4-0	2-4-5	2-5-6	2-8-2	2-11-2	3-3-1	3-7-3
" " SHEER	3-0-2	2-10-5	2-9-6	2-10-1	3-2-6	3-6-6	3-8-1	3-9-6	3-11-6	4-2-5
	HALF-BREADTHS									
℄ TO KEEL BOTTOM	—	—	0-1-1	0-1-5	0-1-7	0-2-0	0-2-0	0-1-5	0-0-4	0-0-4
" " " TOP TRACE	—	—	0-3-0	0-3-0	0-3-0	0-2-6	0-2-3	0-1-6	0-0-4	—
" " 30" WL	2-6-0	2-10-2	3-1-4	3-3-5	3-4-0	3-2-5	2-10-7	2-4-5	1-7-4	0-8-2
" " 39" "	3-3-2	3-5-6	3-7-4	3-8-6	3-9-2	3-8-6	3-5-5	3-0-4	2-3-3	1-1-3
" " 48" "	3-5-6	3-7-5	3-9-2	3-10-3	3-11-2	3-11-0	3-8-6	3-3-7	2-7-0	1-5-4
" " 57" "	3-6-1	3-7-7	3-9-5	3-10-6	3-11-5	3-11-6	3-10-2	3-6-2	2-9-7	1-8-3
" " WALE	3-5-6	3-7-5	3-9-4	3-10-6	3-11-4	3-11-5	3-10-2	3-6-6	3-0-3	2-1-3
" " SHEER	3-5-0	3-6-6	3-8-3	3-9-6	3-10-4	3-10-6	3-10-2	3-7-5	3-2-0	2-3-2

NOTES:

1. THESE PLANS ARE THE PROPERTY OF THE DESIGNERS & MAY BE USED ONLY AS AUTHORIZED BY THE DESIGNERS IN WRITING.
2. NO MORE THAN ONE BOAT MAY BE BUILT FROM THESE PLANS WITHOUT PRIOR WRITTEN PERMISSION FROM THE DESIGNERS.
3. ANY ALTERATION FROM THESE PLANS RELIEVES THE DESIGNERS FROM ANY FURTHER RESPONSIBILITY.
4. LINES MUST BE LOFTED & FAIRED FULL SIZE — DO NOT SCALE PRINTS!
5. LINES & OFFSETS TO OUTSIDE OF SHELL IN FEET-INCHES-EIGHTHS — MAKE SHELL THICKNESS DEDUCTIONS FOR MOLDS AS DIRECTED.

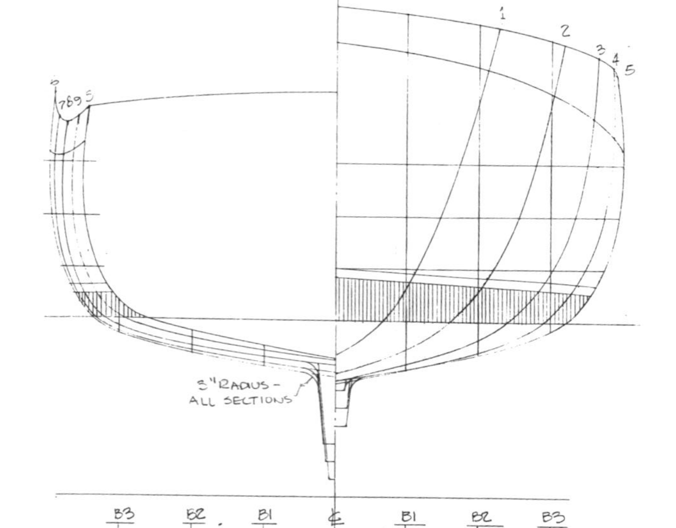

SYMBOLS USED FOR DETAILS

VERTICAL SECTION — DETAIL NUMBER / SHEET NUMBER

HORIZONTAL SECTION — DETAIL NUMBER / SHEET NUMBER

20' POWERBOAT

FOR: ANDERSON & ADAMS
DATE: 3-23-76
SCALE: AS NOTED

OFFSETS

LOA	19'-11½"
LWL	19'-0"
BEAM	7'-11"
DRAFT	2'-3"
FREEBOARD:	
FWD.	4'-6"
LEAST	2'-9½"
AFT	3'-0"

JAY R. BENFORD
P.O. BOX 447
ST. MICHAELS, MD 21663
(410) 745-3235

32-2R JRB

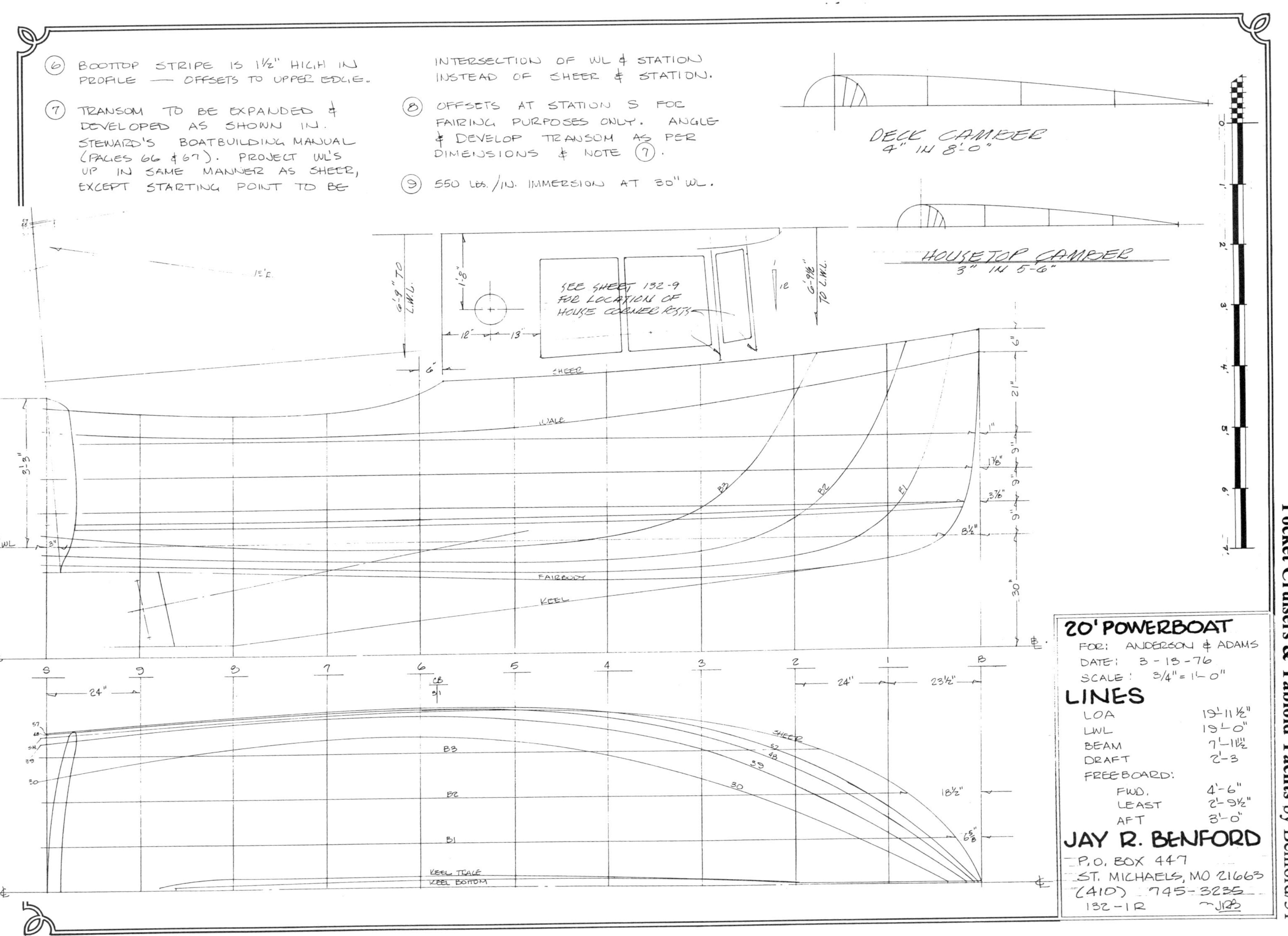
⑥ BOOTTOP STRIPE IS 1 1/2" HIGH IN PROFILE — OFFSETS TO UPPER EDGE.
⑦ TRANSOM TO BE EXPANDED & DEVELOPED AS SHOWN IN STEWARD'S BOATBUILDING MANUAL (PAGES 66 & 67). PROJECT WL'S UP IN SAME MANNER AS SHEER, EXCEPT STARTING POINT TO BE INTERSECTION OF WL & STATION INSTEAD OF SHEER & STATION.
⑧ OFFSETS AT STATION 5 FOR FAIRING PURPOSES ONLY. ANGLE & DEVELOP TRANSOM AS PER DIMENSIONS & NOTE ⑦.
⑨ 550 LBS./IN. IMMERSION AT 30" WL.
DECK CAMBER 4" IN 8'-0"
HOUSETOP CAMBER 3" IN 5'-6"
SEE SHEET 132-9 FOR LOCATION OF HOUSE CORNER POSTS
6'-9" TO L.W.L.
6'-9 1/16" TO L.W.L.
SHEER
WALE
FAIRBODY
KEEL
30" WL
KEEL TRACE
KEEL BOTTOM
20' POWERBOAT
FOR: ANDERSON & ADAMS
DATE: 3-15-76
SCALE: 3/4" = 1'-0"
LINES
LOA 19'-11 1/2"
LWL 19'-0"
BEAM 7'-11 1/2"
DRAFT 2'-3
FREEBOARD:
FWD. 4'-6"
LEAST 2'-9 1/2"
AFT 3'-0"
JAY R. BENFORD
P.O. BOX 447
ST. MICHAELS, MD 21663
(410) 745-3235
132-1R

STATION	S	9	8	7	6	5	4	3	2	1
	HEIGHTS									
℄ TO KEEL										—
" " FAIRBODY	1-11-3	1-11-1	1-10-2	1-9-2	1-8-3	1-7-5	1-7-2	1-7-5	1-9-0	2-0-1
" " B1	2-1-4	2-0-6	1-11-6	1-10-7	1-10-2	1-9-5	1-9-4	1-10-5	2-1-2	2-11-6
" " B2	2-4-1	2-2-7	2-1-6	2-1-0	2-0-3	2-0-2	2-0-6	2-2-6	2-11-3	5-2-2
" " B3	2-9-0	2-6-7	2-5-3	2-4-2	2-4-0	2-4-3	2-6-7	3-4-2	4-10-1	—
LWL TO BOOTTOP	0-3-7	0-3-6	0-3-6	0-3-6	0-3-7	0-4-1	0-4-3	0-4-7	0-5-5	0-6-4
" " SHEER	2-4-0	2-1-3	2-0-2	2-0-0	2-0-4	2-1-7	2-3-7	2-6-7	2-10-6	3-3-4
	HALF-BREADTHS									
℄ TO 30" WL	2-6-0	2-10-2	3-1-4	3-3-5	3-4-0	3-2-5	2-10-7	2-4-5	1-7-4	0-8-2
" " 39" WL	3-3-2	3-5-6	3-7-4	3-8-6	3-9-2	3-8-4	3-4-6	2-11-2	2-2-1	1-1-3
" " 48" WL	3-5-3	3-7-2	3-8-6	3-10-0	3-10-6	3-10-6	3-8-6	3-3-7	2-6-7	1-5-2
" " 57" WL	—	—	—	—	—	—	3-10-6	3-7-2	2-11-3	1-9-1
" " SHEER	3-6-0	3-7-7	3-9-3	3-10-4	3-11-2	3-11-5	3-10-7	3-8-4	3-2-7	2-3-7

NOTES:

1. THESE PLANS ARE THE PROPERTY OF THE DESIGNERS & MAY BE USED ONLY AS AUTHORIZED BY THE DESIGNERS IN WRITING.
2. NO MORE THAN ONE BOAT MAY BE BUILT FROM THESE PLANS WITHOUT PRIOR WRITTEN PERMISSION FROM THE DESIGNERS.
3. ANY ALTERATION FROM THESE PLANS RELIEVES THE DESIGNERS FROM ANY FURTHER RESPONSIBILITY.
4. LINES MUST BE LOFTED & FAIRED FULL SIZE — DO NOT SCALE PRINTS!
5. LINES & OFFSETS TO OUTSIDE OF SHELL IN FEET — INCHES — EIGHTHS — MAKE SHELL THICKNESS DEDUCTIONS FOR MOLDS AS DIRECTED.
6. BOOTTOP STRIPE IS 1½" HIGH IN PROFILE — OFFSETS TO UPPER EDGE.

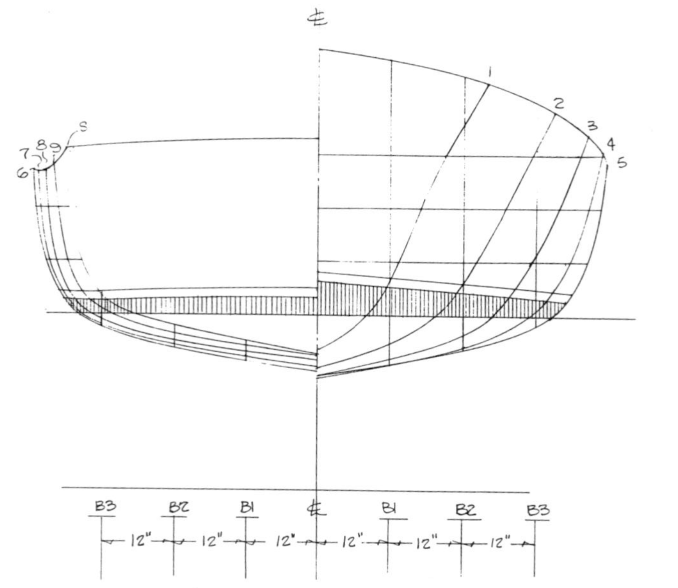

20' POWERBOAT

FOR: ANDERSON & ADAMS
DATE: 9-24-75
SCALE: AS NOTED

OFFSETS

LOA	19'-11½"
LWL	19'-0"
BEAM	7'-11"
DRAFT	2'-0"
FREEBOARD:	
FWD.	3'-9"
LEAST	2'-0"
AFT	2'-3½"

JAY R. BENFORD
P.O. BOX 447
ST. MICHAELS, MD 21663
(410) 745-3235
132-2
~JRB

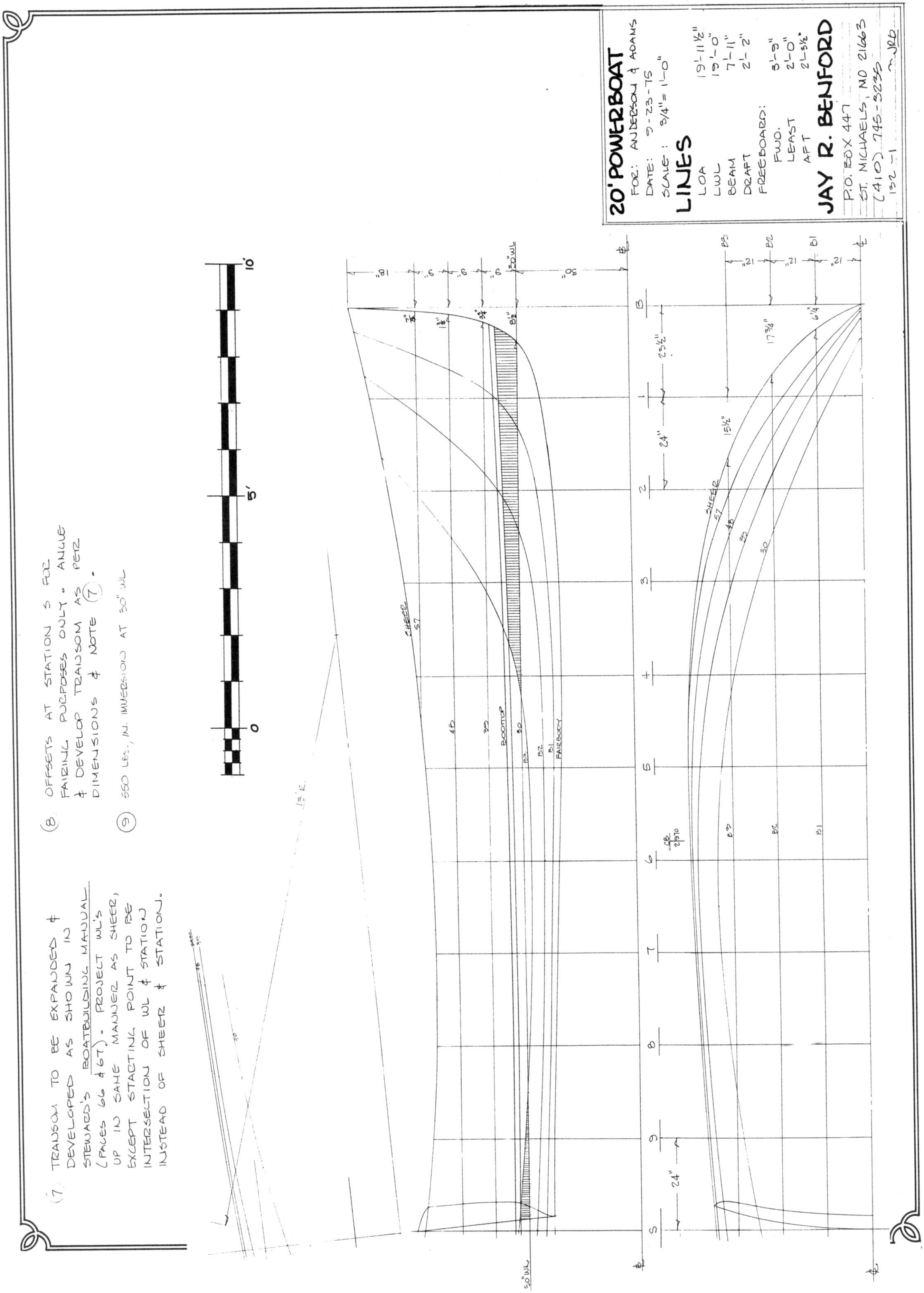

(7) TRANSOM TO BE EXPANDED & DEVELOPED AS SHOWN IN STEWARD'S BOATBUILDING MANUAL (PAGES 66 & 67). PROJECT WL'S UP IN SAME MANNER AS SHEER, EXCEPT STARTING POINT TO BE INTERSECTION OF WL & STATION INSTEAD OF SHEER & STATION.

(8) OFFSETS AT STATION S FOR FAIRING PURPOSES ONLY. ANGLE & DEVELOP TRANSOM AS PER DIMENSIONS & NOTE (7).

(9) 550 LBS./IN. IMMERSION AT 30" WL

20' POWERBOAT

FOR: ANDERSON & ADAMS
DATE: 9-23-75
SCALE: 3/4" = 1'-0"

LINES

LOA	19'-11½"
LWL	19'-0"
BEAM	7'-11"
DRAFT	2'-2"
FREEBOARD:	
FWD.	3'-9"
LEAST	2'-0"
AFT	2'-3½"

JAY R. BENFORD
P.O. BOX 447
ST. MICHAELS, MD 21663
(410) 745-3235

132-1 JRB

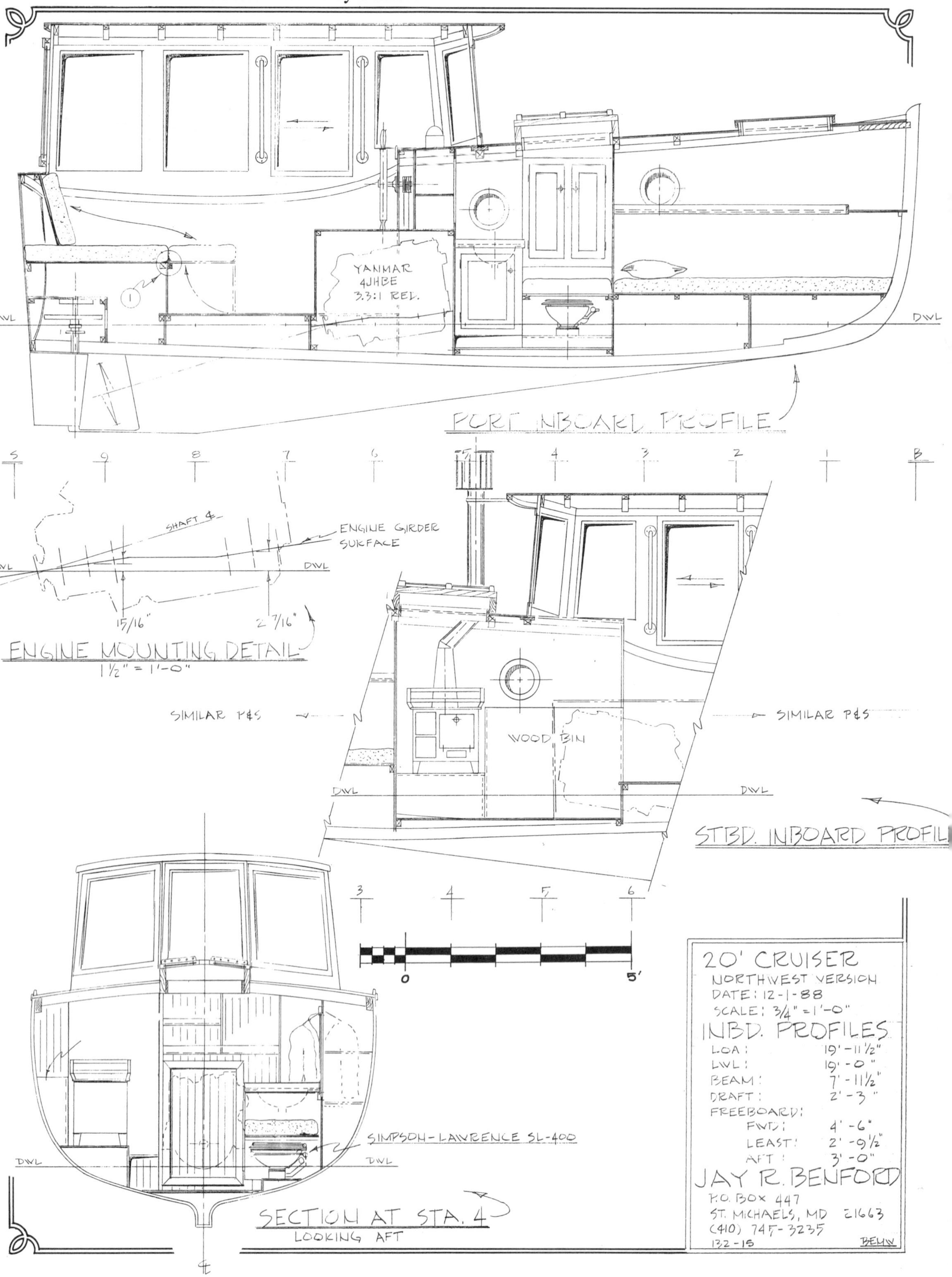

YANMAR
4JHBE
3.3:1 RED.

DWL

DWL

PORT INBOARD PROFILE

S 9 8 7 6 5 4 3 2 1 B

SHAFT ℄

ENGINE GIRDER SURFACE

DWL

DWL

15/16"

2 7/16"

ENGINE MOUNTING DETAIL
1½" = 1'-0"

SIMILAR P&S

SIMILAR P&S

WOOD BIN

DWL

DWL

STBD. INBOARD PROFIL

3 4 5 6

0

5'

SIMPSON-LAWRENCE SL-400

DWL

DWL

SECTION AT STA. 4
LOOKING AFT

℄

20' CRUISER
NORTHWEST VERSION
DATE: 12-1-88
SCALE: 3/4" = 1'-0"

INBD. PROFILES

LOA:	19'-11½"
LWL:	19'-0"
BEAM:	7'-11½"
DRAFT:	2'-3"
FREEBOARD:	
FWD:	4'-6"
LEAST:	2'-9½"
AFT:	3'-0"

JAY R. BENFORD
P.O. BOX 447
ST. MICHAELS, MD 21663
(410) 745-3235

132-15

BEHW

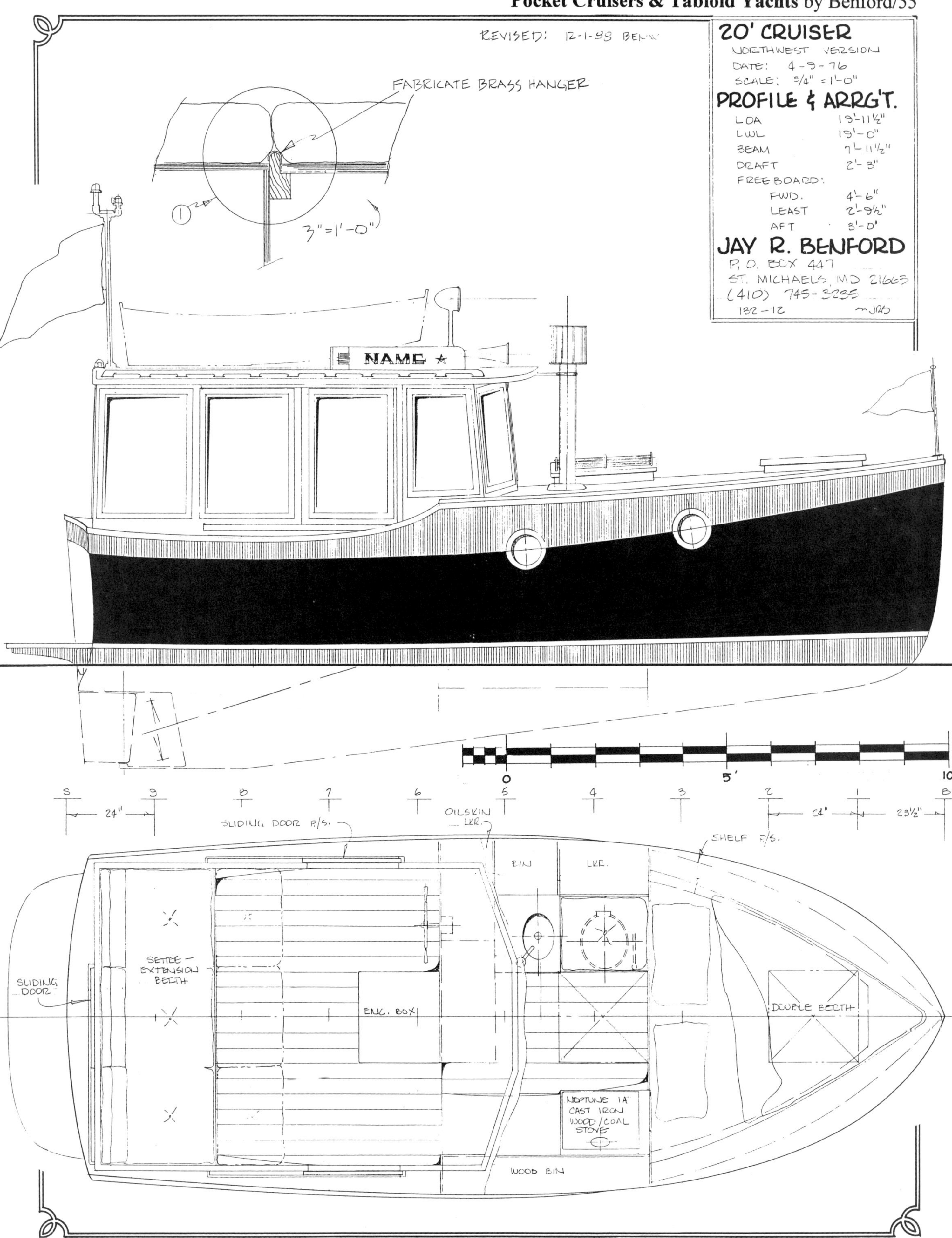
REVISED: 12-1-98 BENW
20' CRUISER
NORTHWEST VERSION
DATE: 4-9-76
SCALE: 3/4" = 1'-0"
PROFILE & ARRG'T.
LOA 19'-11½"
LWL 19'-0"
BEAM 7'-11½"
DRAFT 2'-3"
FREEBOARD:
FWD. 4'-6"
LEAST 2'-9½"
AFT 3'-0"
JAY R. BENFORD
P. O. BOX 447
ST. MICHAELS, MD 21663
(410) 745-3235
132-12
FABRICATE BRASS HANGER
3" = 1'-0"
NAME ★
0
5'
10'
24"
24"
23½"
SLIDING DOOR P/S.
OILSKIN LKR.
SHELF P/S.
BIN
LKR.
SETTEE - EXTENSION BERTH
SLIDING DOOR
ENG. BOX
DOUBLE BERTH
NEPTUNE 1A CAST IRON WOOD/COAL STOVE
WOOD BIN

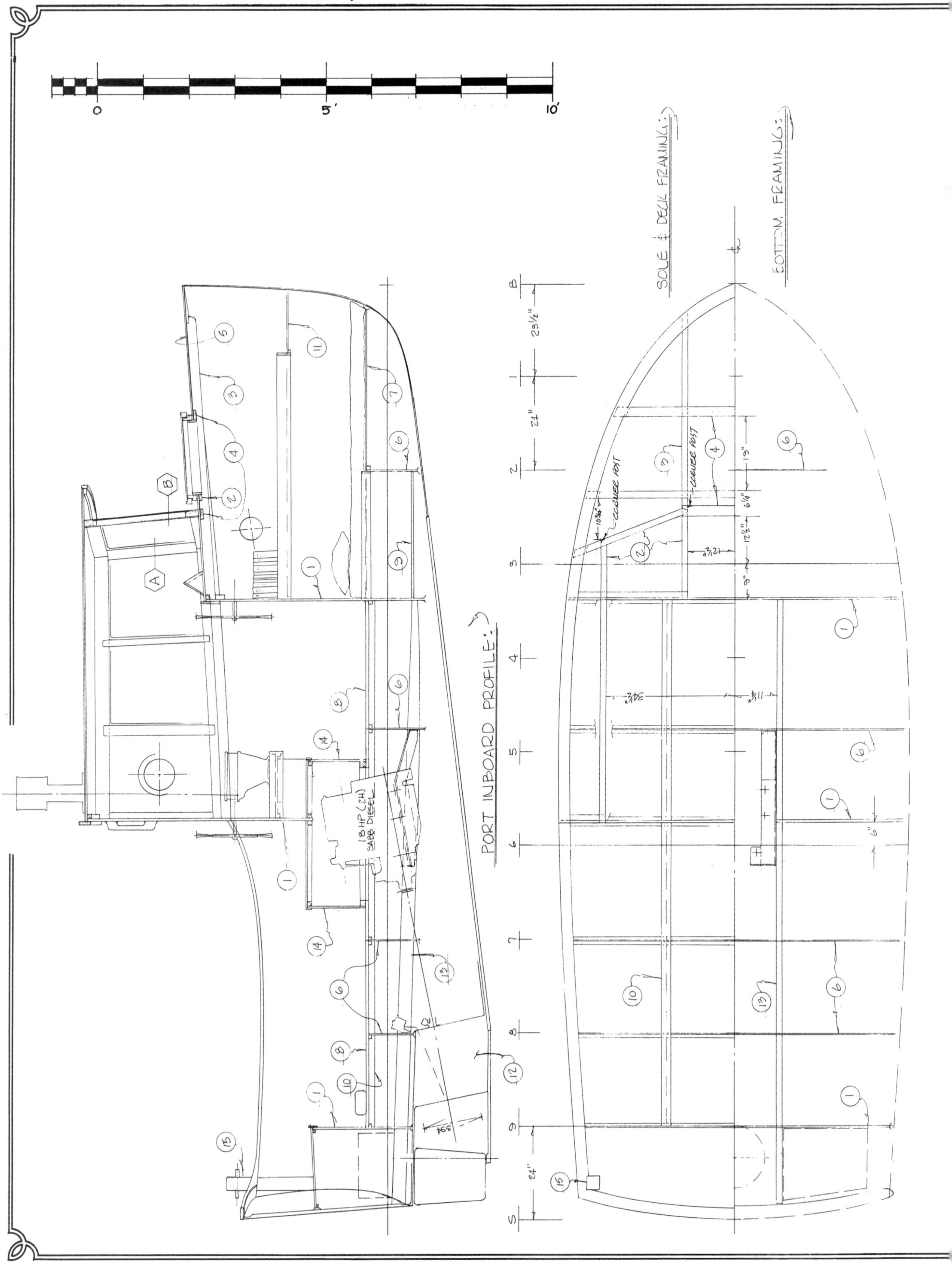
0
5'
10'
PORT INBOARD PROFILE:
SOLE & DECK FRAMING:
BOTTOM FRAMING:
18 HP (2H) SABB DIESEL
CORNER POST
24"
23½"
19"

NOTES:

1. BULKHEADS: 12 MM BRUYNZEEL
2. CARLINS: 3/4" x 1½" OAK—NOTCH THRU BEAMS & BH'DS. AS SHOWN — MAY BE LAPPED UNDER SHEER FLANGE OR CUT OFF JUST CLEAR OF IT.
3. LONG'L BEAMS: 1½" x 2½" OAK — LAP ONTO SHEER FLANGE W/TOPS FLUSH & BOLT TO FLANGE — NOTCH FOR CARLINS & LAP & BOLT TO FRAME ON BH'D.
4. WIDE CARLIN: 3/4" x 2½" OAK — TO PROVIDE BACKING FOR JOINT IN PLY. DECK & HATCH
5. DECK: 12MM BRUYNZEEL
6. FLOORS: 6MM BRUYNZEEL WITH 3/4" x 3/4" OAK FRAMES FOR SOLE AS SHOWN
7. BERTH FLAT: 10 MM BRUYNZEEL — PROVIDE LIFT TRAP ACCESS HATCHES TO SUIT
8. COCKPIT & CABIN SOLE: 18 MM BRUYNZEEL — SIDE PANELS 'GLASSED TO HULL & 36" WIDE CENTER PANEL (W/ENG. BOXES) LOOSE TO LIFT OFF
9. FOC'SLE SOLE: 12 MM BRUYNZEEL — LOOSE TO LIFT OUT
10. SOLE BEAMS: 2½" WIDE x 1½" OAK — BH'D. TO BH'D.
11. SHELF: 6 MM BRUYNZEEL W/ 3/4" x 3/4" OAK FRAME FOR ½" x 3½" FACIA
12. "DEADROCK": FILL THIS AREA AROUND STERN TUBE WITH CEMENT & 'GLASS OVER
13. ENGINE STRINGER: 1½" x 3½" FIR — RUNS FROM TRANSOM TO FOC'SLE BH'D. —TOP EDGE STRAIGHT
14. ENGINE BOX: 10 MM BRUYNZEEL OVER 1⅛" x 1⅛" OAK FRAME — 1½" x 1½" OAK FRAME AT SOLE (BOLTED TOGETHER)
15. BITTS: 3½" x 3½" HOND. MAHOG. — RUN DOWN & FIT & 'GLASS TO HULL — 3/4"⌀ x 8" BRZ. PIN
16. FOR ADDITIONAL DETAILS, SEE SHEET 132-4

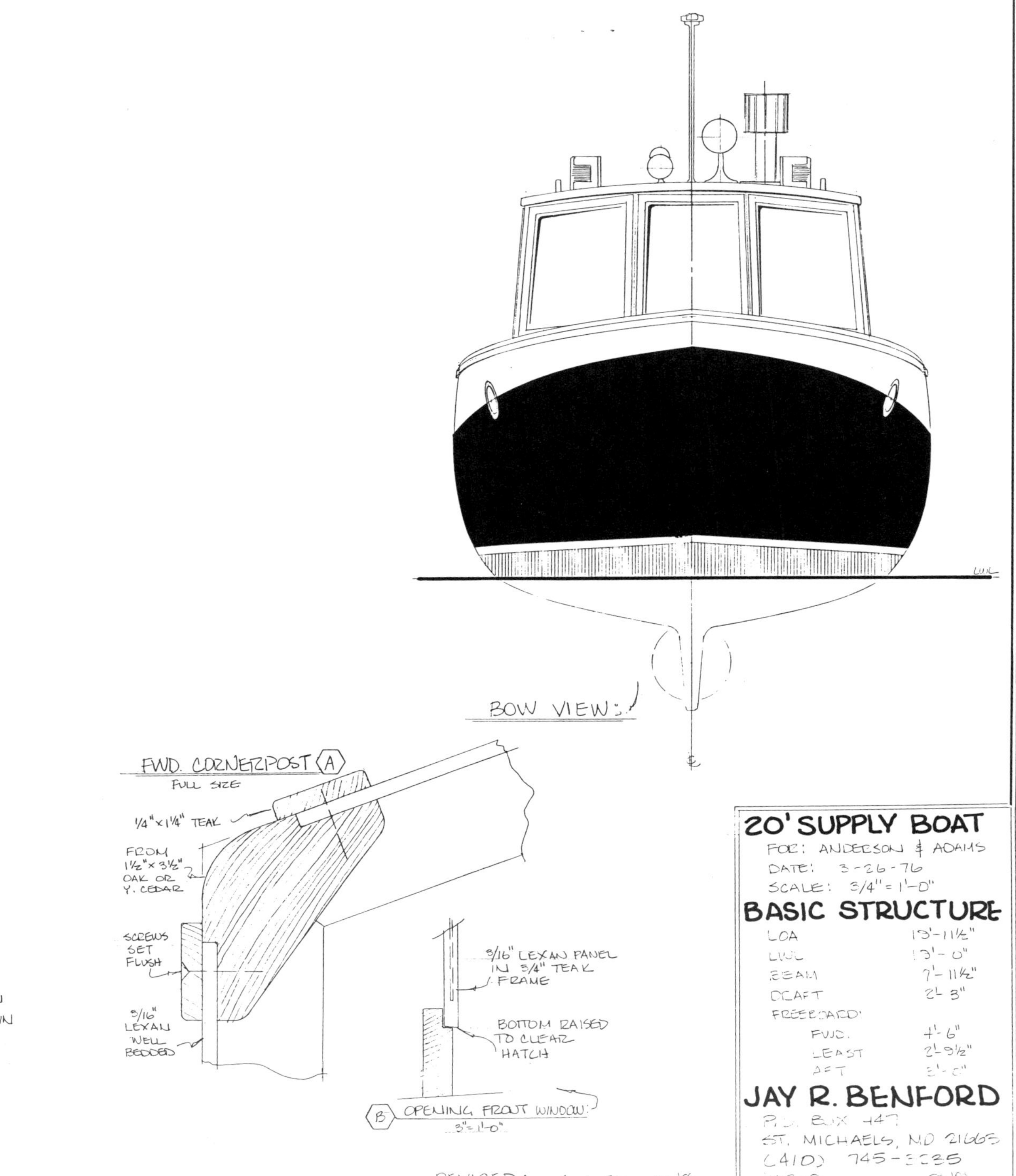

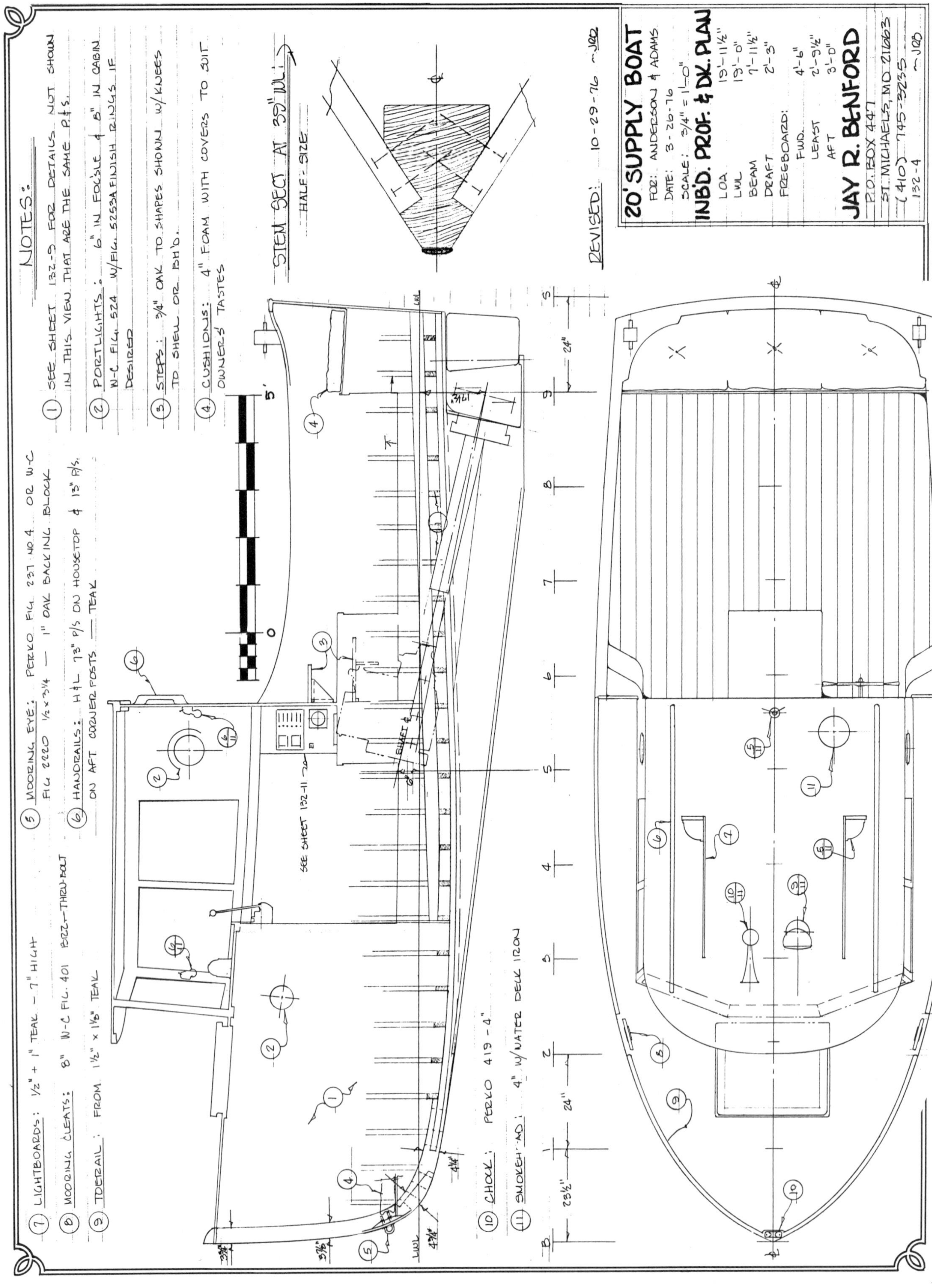

NOTES:

1. SEE SHEET 132-9 FOR DETAILS NOT SHOWN IN THIS VIEW THAT ARE THE SAME P & S.
2. PORTLIGHTS: 6" IN FOC'S'LE & 8" IN CABIN W-C FIG. 524 W/FIG. 5253A FINISH RINGS IF DESIRED
3. STEPS: 3/4" OAK TO SHAPES SHOWN W/KNEES TO SHELL OR BH'D.
4. CUSHIONS: 4" FOAM WITH COVERS TO SUIT OWNERS' TASTES
5. MOORING EYE: PERKO FIG 237 NO.4 OR W-C FIG 2220 1/2 x 3 1/4 — 1" OAK BACKING BLOCK
6. HANDRAILS: H & L 73" P/S ON HOUSETOP & 13" P/S. ON AFT CORNER POSTS — TEAK
7. LIGHTBOARDS: 1/2" + 1" TEAK – 7" HIGH
8. MOORING CLEATS: 8" W-C FIG. 401 BRZ—THRU-BOLT
9. TOERAIL: FROM 1 1/2" x 1 1/8" TEAK
10. CHOCK: PERKO 419 – 4"
11. SMOKEHEAD: 4" W/WATER DECK IRON

SEE SHEET 132-11

SHAFT ℄

LWL

0 5'

STEM SECT AT 39" WL

HALF - SIZE

B 1 2 3 4 5 6 7 8 9 S

23 1/2" 24" 24"

REVISED: 10-29-76 ~JRB

20' SUPPLY BOAT

FOR: ANDERSON & ADAMS

DATE: 3-26-76

SCALE: 3/4" = 1'-0"

INB'D. PROF. & DK. PLAN

LOA	19'-11 1/2"
LWL	19'-0"
BEAM	7'-11 1/2"
DRAFT	2'-3"
FREEBOARD:	
FWD.	4'-6"
LEAST	2'-9 1/2"
AFT	3'-0"

JAY R. BENFORD
P.O. BOX 447
ST. MICHAELS, MD 21663
(410) 745-3235

132-4 ~JRB

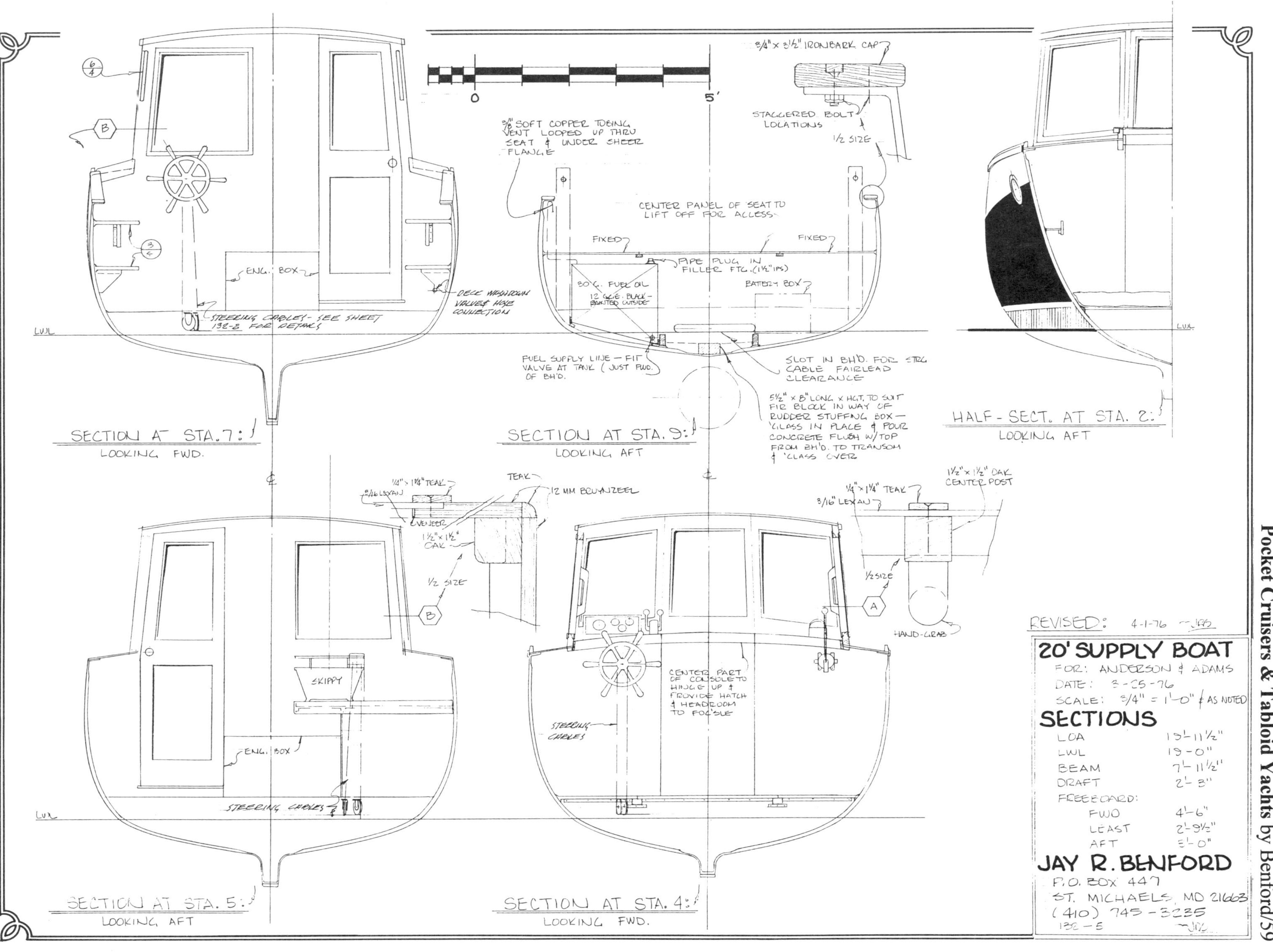

SECTION AT STA. 7:
LOOKING FWD.
STEERING CABLES - SEE SHEET 132-8 FOR DETAILS
ENG. BOX
DECK WASHDOWN VALVE & HOSE CONNECTION
0
5'
3/8" SOFT COPPER TUBING VENT LOOPED UP THRU SEAT & UNDER SHEER FLANGE
CENTER PANEL OF SEAT TO LIFT OFF FOR ACCESS
FIXED
PIPE PLUG IN FILLER FTG. (1½" IPS)
30 G. FUEL OIL
12 GAGE. BLACK-PAINTED OUTSIDE
BATTERY BOX
FUEL SUPPLY LINE — FIT VALVE AT TANK (JUST FWD. OF BH'D.
SLOT IN BH'D. FOR STRG CABLE FAIRLEAD CLEARANCE
5½" x 8" LONG x HGT. TO SUIT FIR BLOCK IN WAY OF RUDDER STUFFING BOX — 'GLASS IN PLACE & POUR CONCRETE FLUSH W/TOP FROM BH'D. TO TRANSOM & 'GLASS OVER
SECTION AT STA. 9:
LOOKING AFT
3/4" x 3½" IRONBARK CAP
STAGGERED BOLT LOCATIONS
1/2 SIZE
HALF-SECT. AT STA. 2:
LOOKING AFT
1/4" x 1¾" TEAK
3/16 LEXAN
VENEER
TEAK
12 MM BRUYNZEEL
1½" x 1½" OAK
1/2 SIZE
SKIPPY
ENG. BOX
STEERING CABLES
SECTION AT STA. 5:
LOOKING AFT
1/4" x 1¾" TEAK
3/16" LEXAN
1½" x 1½" OAK CENTER POST
1/2 SIZE
HAND-GRAB
CENTER PART OF CONSOLE TO HINGE UP & PROVIDE HATCH & HEADROOM TO FOC'SLE
STEERING CABLES
SECTION AT STA. 4:
LOOKING FWD.
REVISED: 4-1-76
20' SUPPLY BOAT
FOR: ANDERSON & ADAMS
DATE: 3-25-76
SCALE: 3/4" = 1'-0" & AS NOTED
SECTIONS
LOA 19'-11½"
LWL 19'-0"
BEAM 7'-11½"
DRAFT 2'-3"
FREEBOARD:
FWD 4'-6"
LEAST 2'-9½"
AFT 3'-0"
JAY R. BENFORD
P.O. BOX 447
ST. MICHAELS, MD 21663
(410) 745-3235
132-5

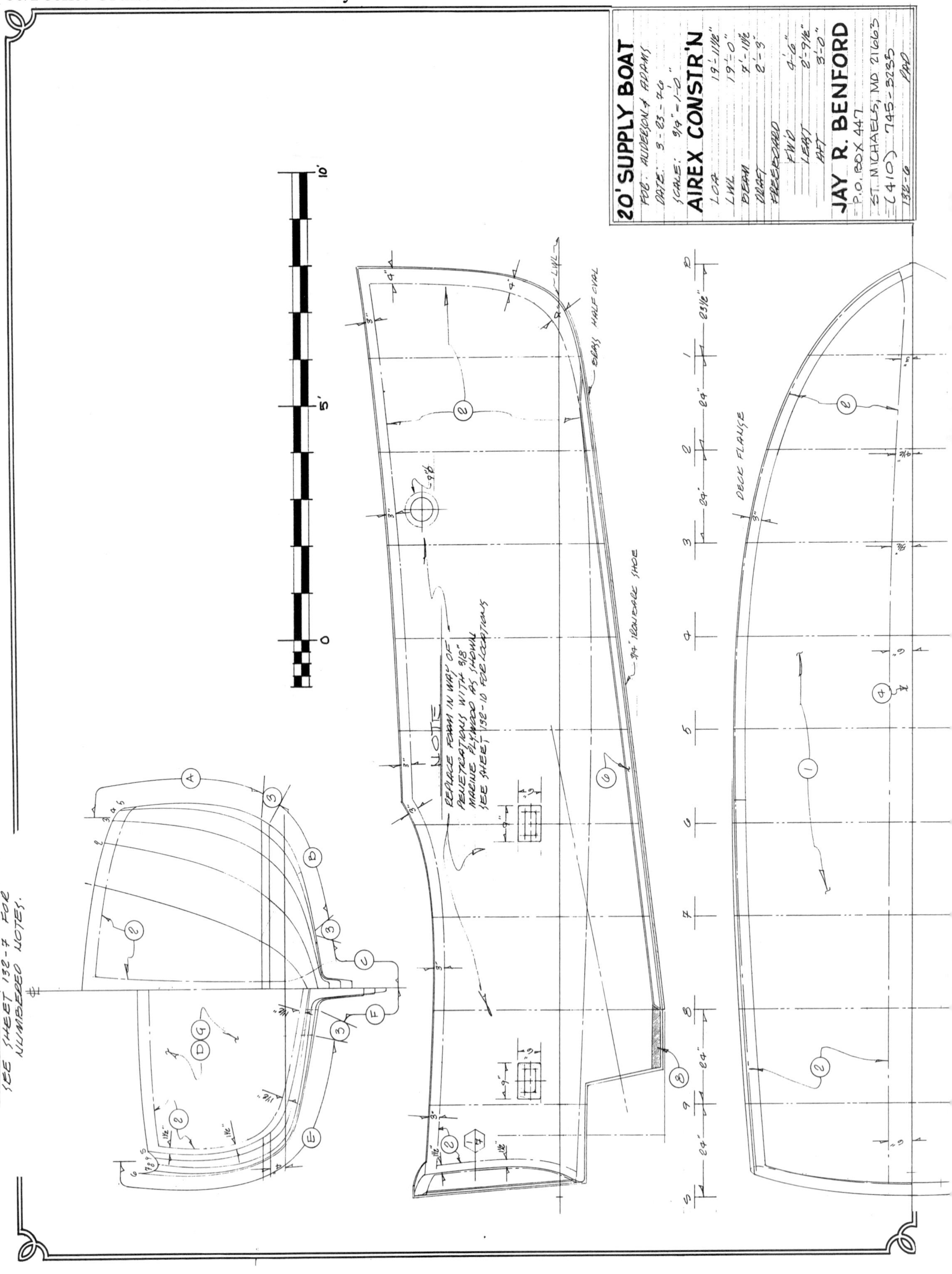

20' SUPPLY BOAT
FOR: ANDERSON & ADAMS
DATE: 3-23-76
SCALE: 3/4" = 1'-0"
AIREX CONSTR'N

LOA	19'-11½"
LWL	19'-0"
BEAM	7'-1½"
DRAFT	2'-3"
FREEBOARD	
FWD	4'-6"
LEAST	2'-9½"
AFT	3'-0"

JAY R. BENFORD
P.O. BOX 447
ST. MICHAELS, MD 21663
(410) 745-3235
132-6 PAD

NOTE
REPLACE FOAM IN WAY OF PENETRATIONS WITH 3/8" MARINE PLYWOOD AS SHOWN SEE SHEET 132-10 FOR LOCATIONS

NOTE
SEE SHEET 132-7 FOR NUMBERED NOTES.

BRASS HALF OVAL
3/4" IRONBARK SHOE
DECK FLANGE
LWL

NOTES

1. CORE - CORE MATERIAL TO BE 3/8" AIREX 01-18 PVC FOAM - 5LB. DENSITY.
2. LIMIT OF FOAM - CUT BACK FOAM 3" BELOW SHEER & AS SHOWN - CORE MATERIAL IS TO BE REDUCED IN THICKNESS WITH A TAPER OF NOT LESS THAN 1 IN 3.
3. TRANSITION ZONES - CHANGES IN LAMINATE WEIGHT (DRY WEIGHT OF GLASS) ARE TO OCCUR AT THE RATE OF 2 OZ. IN 2".
4. KEEL REINFORCEMENT - LAMINATE "F" IS TO RUN THE FULL LENGTH OF THE HULL FROM STEM HEAD TO BOTTOM OF TRANSOM.
5. LINES ARE TO BE LOFTED FULL SIZE & DEDUCTIONS MADE FOR OUTER SKIN, CORE, & BATTEN THICKNESSES TO OBTAIN MOLD SIZES.
6. MOLD KEELSON - TO BE 1½" W. OAK - LEAVE IN KEEL - GLASS OVER WITH INSIDE SKIN.
7. BULKHEAD ATTACHMENT - MOUNT BULKH'DS ON ½" THICK AIREX PADS & GLASS TO SHELL WITH 3-8" WIDE 1½ oz MAT STRIPS EACH SIDE - STAGGER LAYERS - SEE DETAIL
8. FILL SOLID WITH CASTING RESIN MIXED WITH PHENOLIC MICROSPHERES IN WAY OF GUDGEON.

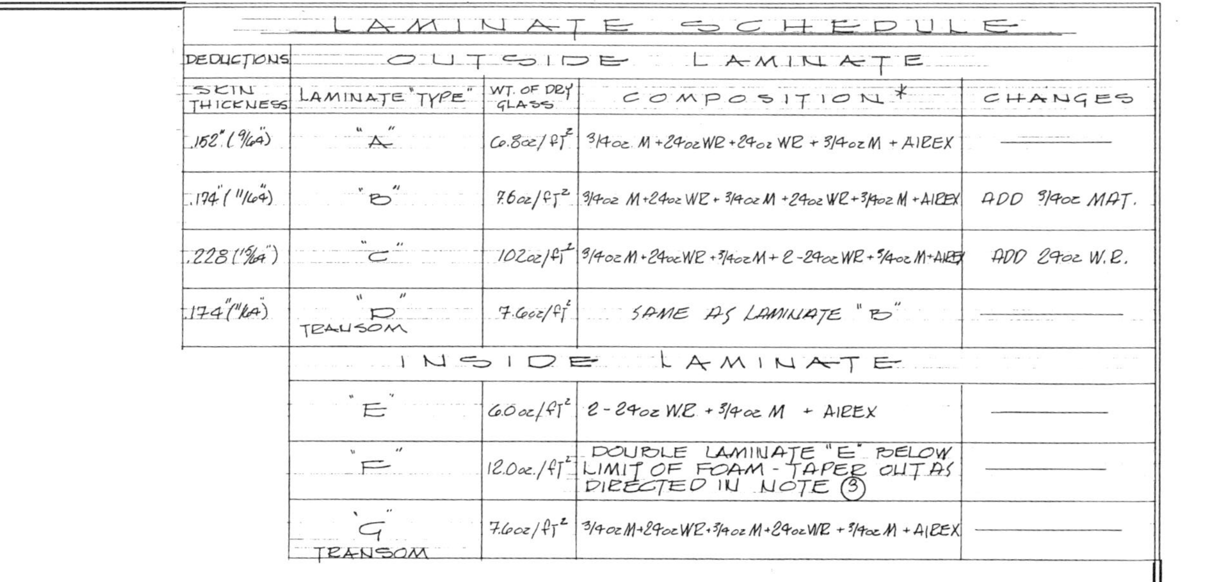

LAMINATE SCHEDULE

DEDUCTIONS	OUTSIDE LAMINATE			
SKIN THICKNESS	LAMINATE "TYPE"	WT. OF DRY GLASS	COMPOSITION *	CHANGES
.152" (9/64")	"A"	6.8oz/ft²	3/4oz M + 24oz WR + 24oz WR + 3/4oz M + AIREX	———
.174" (11/64")	"B"	7.6oz/ft²	3/4oz M + 24oz WR + 3/4oz M + 24oz WR + 3/4oz M + AIREX	ADD 3/4oz MAT.
.228 (15/64")	"C"	10.2oz/ft²	3/4oz M + 24oz WR + 3/4oz M + 2-24oz WR + 3/4oz M + AIREX	ADD 24oz W.R.
.174" (11/64")	"D" TRANSOM	7.6oz/ft²	SAME AS LAMINATE "B"	———
	INSIDE LAMINATE			
	"E"	6.0oz/ft²	2-24oz WR + 3/4oz M + AIREX	———
	"F"	12.0oz/ft²	DOUBLE LAMINATE "E" BELOW LIMIT OF FOAM - TAPER OUT AS DIRECTED IN NOTE (3)	———
	"G" TRANSOM	7.6oz/ft²	3/4oz M + 24oz WR + 3/4oz M + 24oz WR + 3/4oz M + AIREX	———

LAMINATE "A"
3/8" AIREX
1½"±
1½"±
LAMINATE "E"
LAMINATE "D"
LAMINATE "G"
1 IN 3 TAPER - SEE NOTE (2)

(1) SECTION THRU HULL-TRANSOM JOINT
APPROX. FULL SIZE

12 MM BRUYNZEEL PLYWOOD
3 PLIES 1½ oz MAT
½" AIREX PAD
HULL LAYUP

(2) TYPICAL BULKH'D CONNECTION
APPROX. FULL SIZE

20' SUPPLY BOAT
FOR: ANDERSON & ADAMS
DATE: 3-23-76
SCALE: AS NOTED

LAYUP & NOTES

LOA	19'-11½"
LWL	19'-0"
BEAM	7'-11½"
DRAFT	2'-3"
FREEBOARD	
FWD	4'-6"
LEAST	2'-9½"
AFT	3'-0"

JAY R. BENFORD
P.O. BOX 447
ST. MICHAELS, MD 21663
(410) 745-3235
132-7 PAD

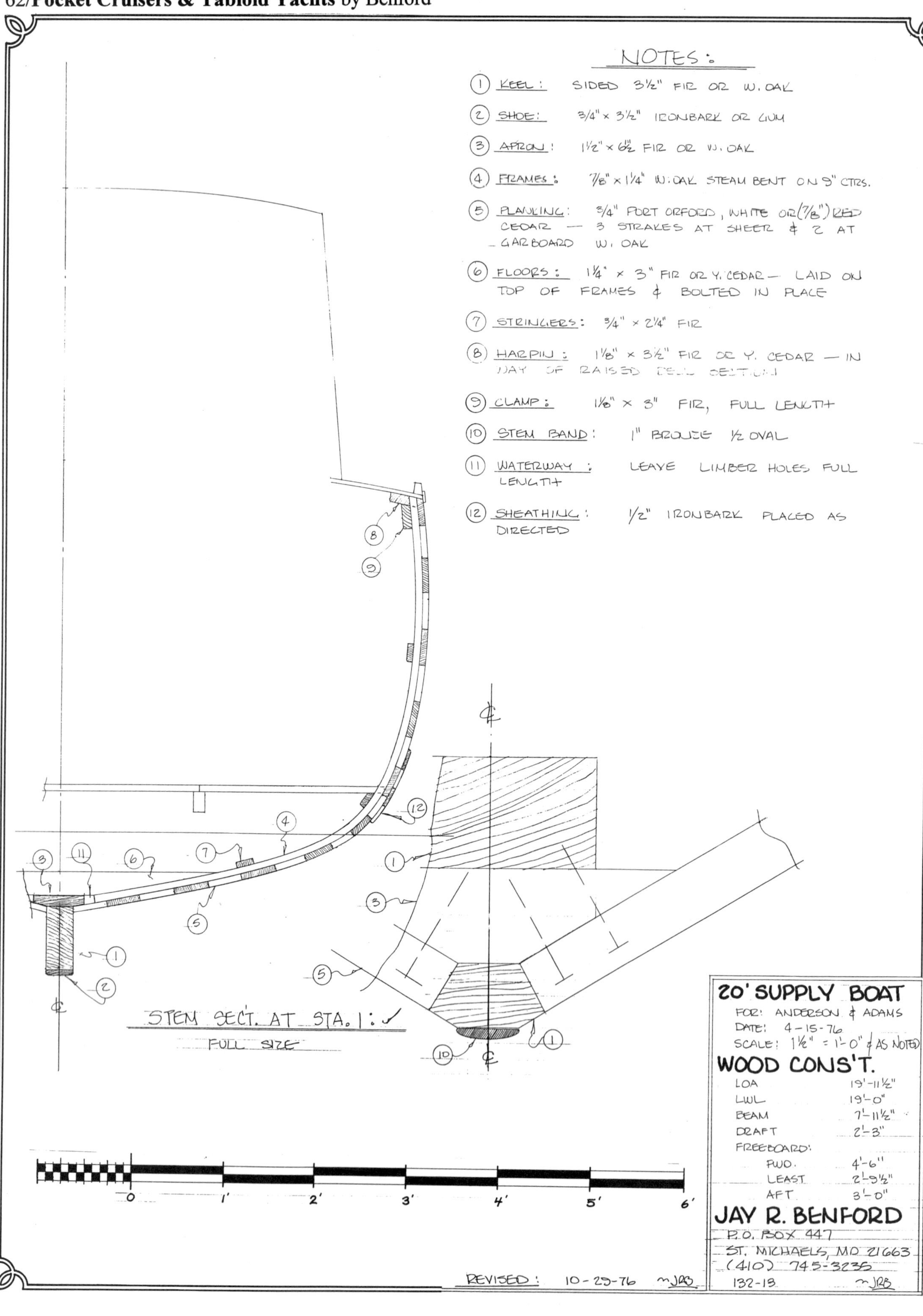
NOTES:
1 KEEL: SIDED 3½" FIR OR W. OAK
2 SHOE: 3/4" x 3½" IRONBARK OR GUM
3 APRON: 1½" x 6½" FIR OR W. OAK
4 FRAMES: 7/8" x 1¼" W. OAK STEAM BENT ON 9" CTRS.
5 PLANKING: 3/4" PORT ORFORD, WHITE OR (7/8") RED CEDAR — 3 STRAKES AT SHEER & 2 AT GARBOARD W. OAK
6 FLOORS: 1¼" x 3" FIR OR Y. CEDAR — LAID ON TOP OF FRAMES & BOLTED IN PLACE
7 STRINGERS: 3/4" x 2¼" FIR
8 HARPIN: 1⅛" x 3½" FIR OR Y. CEDAR — IN WAY OF RAISED DECK SECTION
9 CLAMP: 1⅛" x 3" FIR, FULL LENGTH
10 STEM BAND: 1" BRONZE ½ OVAL
11 WATERWAY: LEAVE LIMBER HOLES FULL LENGTH
12 SHEATHING: 1/2" IRONBARK PLACED AS DIRECTED
STEM SECT. AT STA. 1
FULL SIZE
0
1'
2'
3'
4'
5'
6'
20' SUPPLY BOAT
FOR: ANDERSON & ADAMS
DATE: 4-15-76
SCALE: 1½" = 1'-0" & AS NOTED
WOOD CONS'T.
LOA 19'-11½"
LWL 19'-0"
BEAM 7'-11½"
DRAFT 2'-3"
FREEBOARD:
FWD. 4'-6"
LEAST 2'-9½"
AFT 3'-0"
JAY R. BENFORD
P.O. BOX 447
ST. MICHAELS, MD 21663
(410) 745-3235
132-13
JRB
REVISED: 10-29-76 JRB

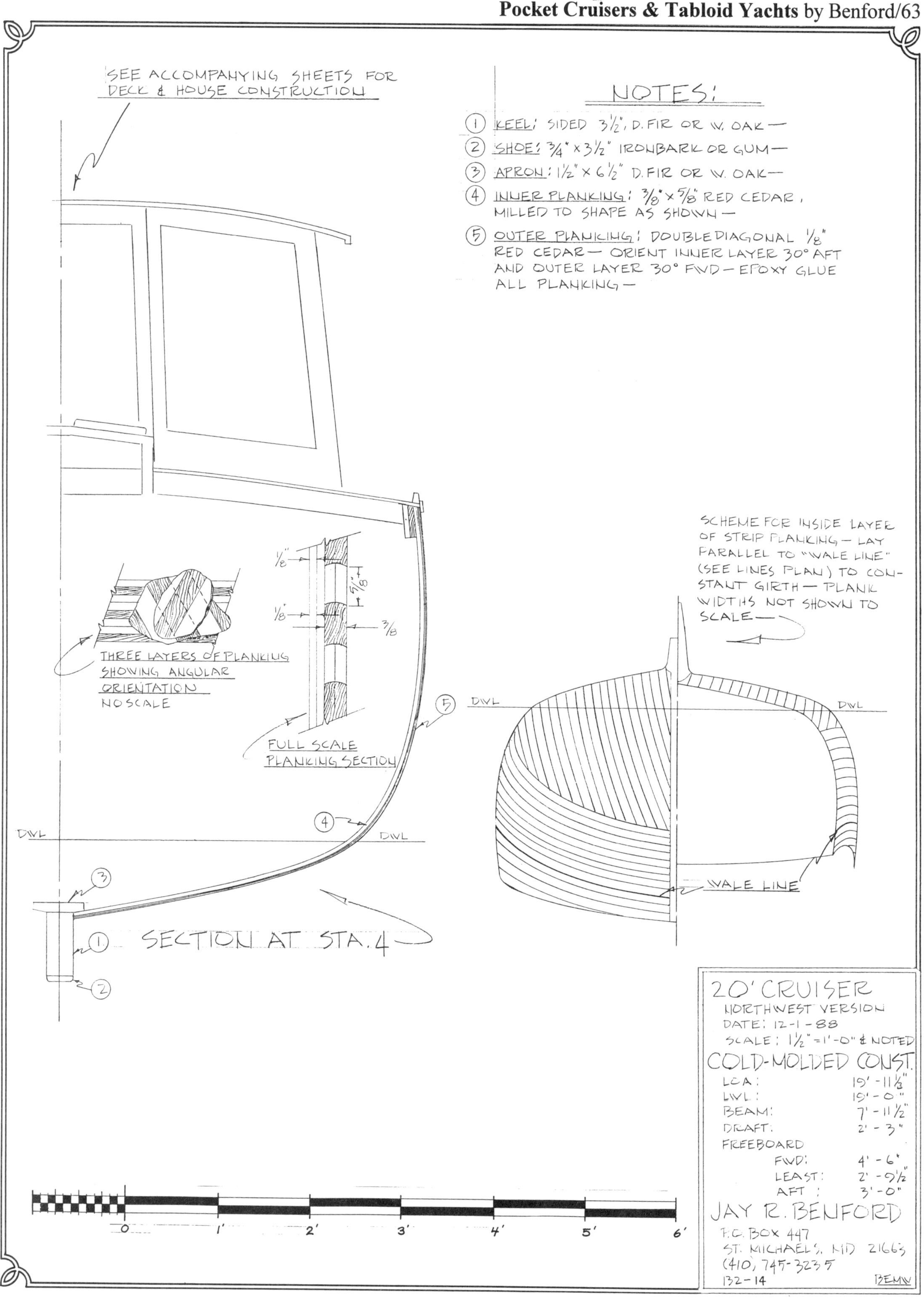
SEE ACCOMPANYING SHEETS FOR DECK & HOUSE CONSTRUCTION
NOTES:
1 KEEL: SIDED 3½", D. FIR OR W. OAK—
2 SHOE: ¾" x 3½" IRONBARK OR GUM—
3 APRON: 1½" x 6½" D. FIR OR W. OAK—
4 INNER PLANKING: ⅜" x ⅝" RED CEDAR, MILLED TO SHAPE AS SHOWN—
5 OUTER PLANKING: DOUBLE DIAGONAL ⅛" RED CEDAR— ORIENT INNER LAYER 30° AFT AND OUTER LAYER 30° FWD— EPOXY GLUE ALL PLANKING—
⅛"
⅝"
⅛"
⅜
THREE LAYERS OF PLANKING SHOWING ANGULAR ORIENTATION NO SCALE
FULL SCALE PLANKING SECTION
SCHEME FOR INSIDE LAYER OF STRIP PLANKING— LAY PARALLEL TO "WALE LINE" (SEE LINES PLAN) TO CONSTANT GIRTH— PLANK WIDTHS NOT SHOWN TO SCALE—
DWL
DWL
WALE LINE
DWL
DWL
SECTION AT STA. 4
0 1' 2' 3' 4' 5' 6'
20' CRUISER
NORTHWEST VERSION
DATE: 12-1-88
SCALE: 1½" = 1'-0" & NOTED
COLD-MOLDED CONST.
LOA: 19'-11½"
LWL: 19'-0"
BEAM: 7'-11½"
DRAFT: 2'-3"
FREEBOARD
FWD: 4'-6"
LEAST: 2'-9½"
AFT: 3'-0"
JAY R. BENFORD
P.O. BOX 447
ST. MICHAELS, MD 21663
(410) 745-3235
132-14
BEMW

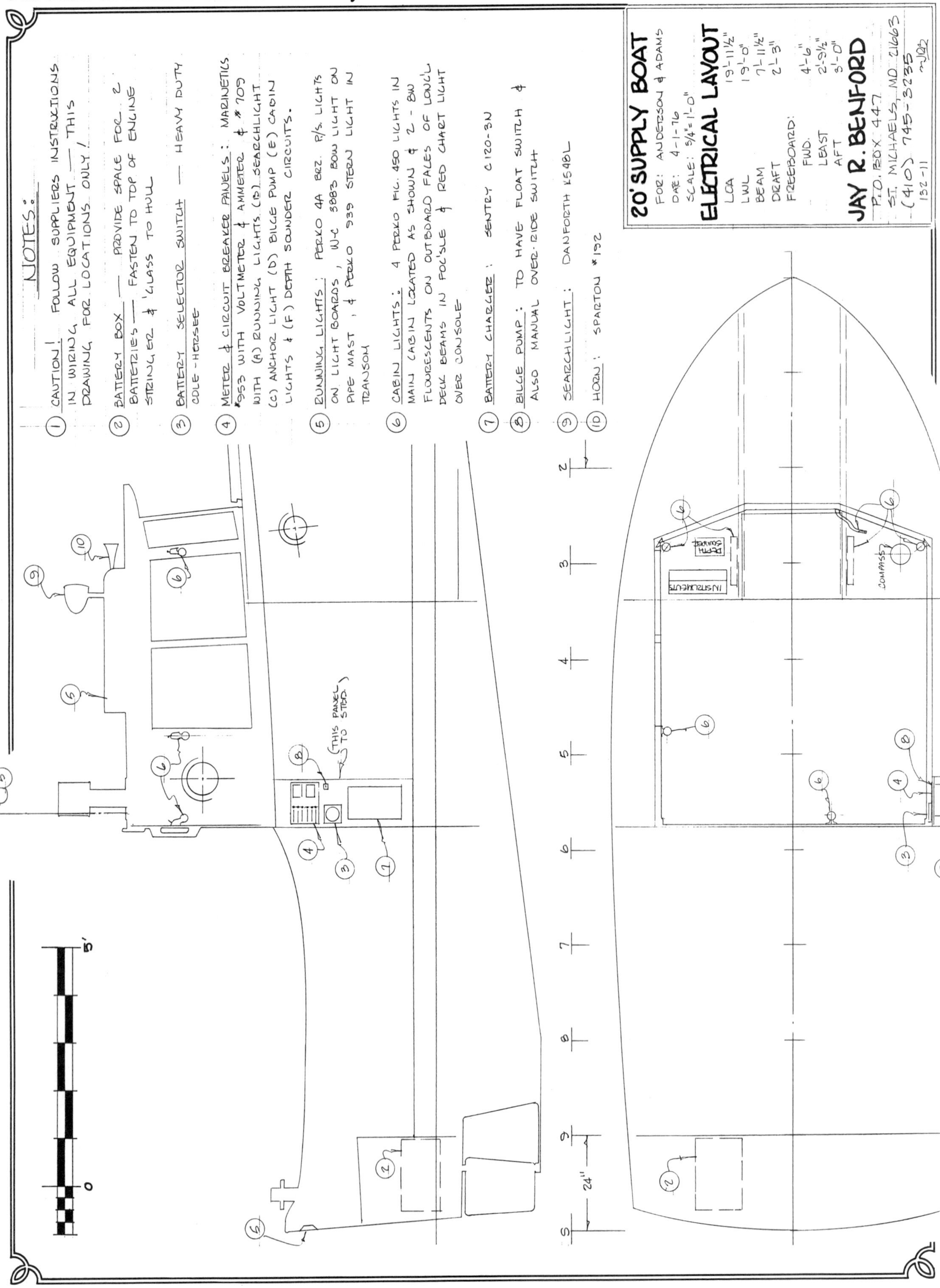

NOTES:

1. CAUTION! FOLLOW SUPPLIERS INSTRUCTIONS IN WIRING ALL EQUIPMENT — THIS DRAWING FOR LOCATIONS ONLY!
2. BATTERY BOX — PROVIDE SPACE FOR 2 BATTERIES — FASTEN TO TOP OF ENGINE STRINGER & 'GLASS TO HULL
3. BATTERY SELECTOR SWITCH — HEAVY DUTY COLE-HERSEE
4. METER & CIRCUIT BREAKER PANELS: MARINETICS #953 WITH VOLTMETER & AMMETER & #709 WITH (A) RUNNING LIGHTS (B) SEARCHLIGHT (C) ANCHOR LIGHT (D) BILGE PUMP (E) CABIN LIGHTS & (F) DEPTH SOUNDER CIRCUITS.
5. RUNNING LIGHTS: PERKO 4A BRZ. P/S. LIGHTS ON LIGHT BOARDS, W-C 3883 BOW LIGHT ON PIPE MAST, & PERKO 939 STERN LIGHT IN TRANSOM
6. CABIN LIGHTS: 4 PERKO FIG. 450 LIGHTS IN MAIN CABIN LOCATED AS SHOWN & 2 - 8W FLOURESCENTS ON OUTBOARD FACES OF LONG'L DECK BEAMS IN FOC'SLE & RED CHART LIGHT OVER CONSOLE
7. BATTERY CHARGER: SENTRY C120-3N
8. BILGE PUMP: TO HAVE FLOAT SWITCH & ALSO MANUAL OVER-RIDE SWITCH
9. SEARCHLIGHT: DANFORTH K548L
10. HORN: SPARTON #192

(THIS PANEL TO STBD.)

INSTRUMENTS

DEPTH SOUNDER

COMPASS

0 5'

S 9 8 7 6 5 4 3 2

24"

20' SUPPLY BOAT

FOR: ANDERSON & ADAMS

DATE: 4-1-76

SCALE: 3/4"=1'-0"

ELECTRICAL LAYOUT

LOA	19'-11½"
LWL	19'-0"
BEAM	7'-11½"
DRAFT	2'-3"
FREEBOARD:	
FWD.	4'-6"
LEAST	2'-9½"
AFT	3'-0"

JAY R. BENFORD

P.O. BOX 447

ST. MICHAELS, MD 21663

(410) 745-3235

132-11

JRB

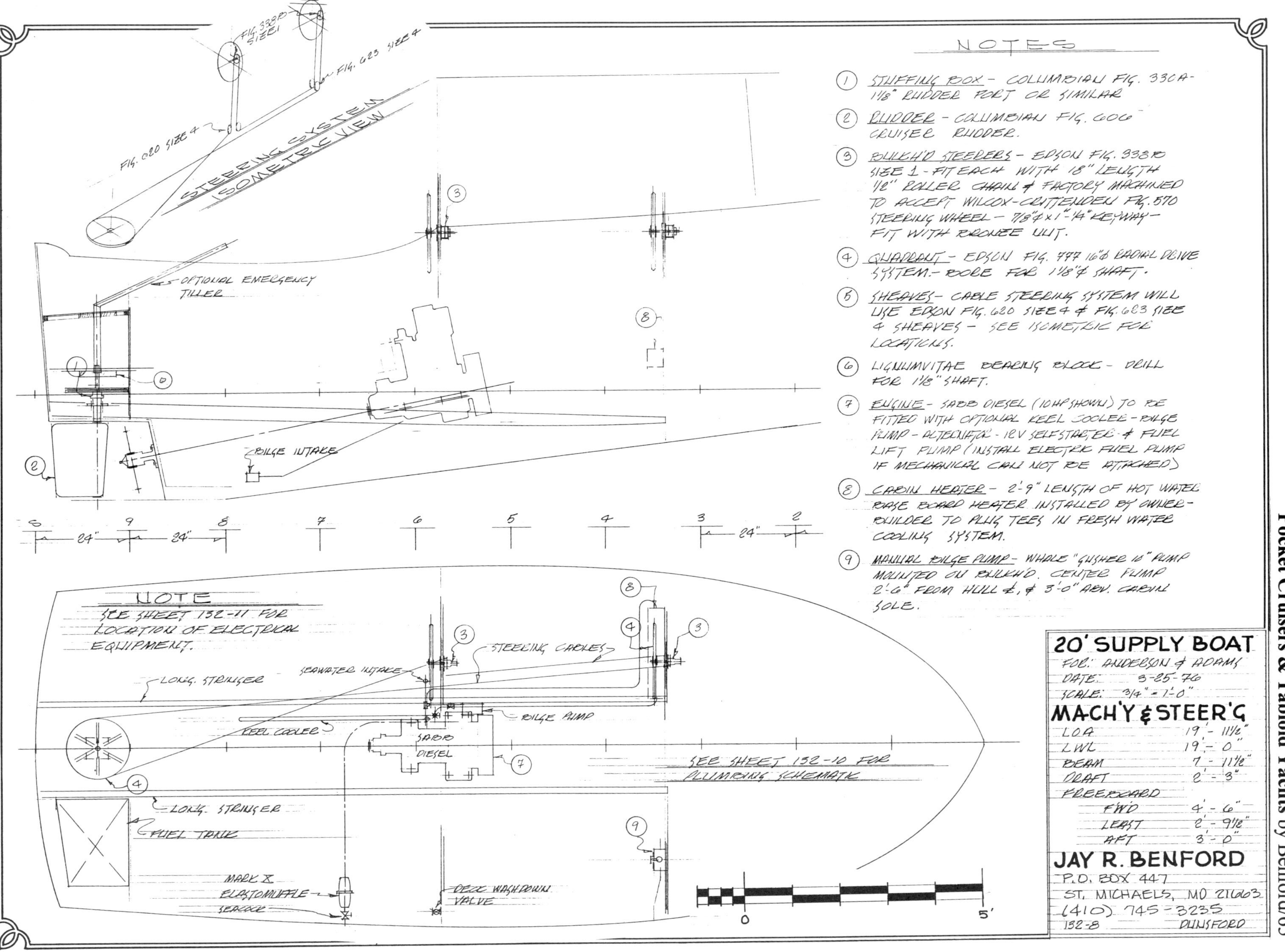
NOTES
1 STUFFING BOX - COLUMBIAN FIG. 330A - 1 1/8" RUDDER PORT OR SIMILAR
2 RUDDER - COLUMBIAN FIG. 606 CRUISER RUDDER.
3 BULKH'D STEERERS - EDSON FIG. 338B SIZE 1 - FIT EACH WITH 18" LENGTH 1/2" ROLLER CHAIN & FACTORY MACHINED TO ACCEPT WILCOX-CRITTENDEN FIG. 570 STEERING WHEEL - 7/8"⌀ x 1" - 1/4" KEYWAY - FIT WITH BRONZE NUT.
4 QUADRANT - EDSON FIG. 777 16"⌀ RADIAL DRIVE SYSTEM. - BORE FOR 1 1/8"⌀ SHAFT.
5 SHEAVES - CABLE STEERING SYSTEM WILL USE EDSON FIG. 620 SIZE 4 & FIG. 623 SIZE 4 SHEAVES - SEE ISOMETRIC FOR LOCATIONS.
6 LIGNUMVITAE BEARING BLOCK - DRILL FOR 1 1/8" SHAFT.
7 ENGINE - SABB DIESEL (10HP SHOWN) TO BE FITTED WITH OPTIONAL KEEL COOLER - BILGE PUMP - ALTERNATOR - 12V SELFSTARTER & FUEL LIFT PUMP (INSTALL ELECTRIC FUEL PUMP IF MECHANICAL CAN NOT BE ATTACHED)
8 CABIN HEATER - 2'-9" LENGTH OF HOT WATER BASE BOARD HEATER INSTALLED BY OWNER-BUILDER TO PLUG TEES IN FRESH WATER COOLING SYSTEM.
9 MANUAL BILGE PUMP - WHALE "GUSHER 10" PUMP MOUNTED ON BULKH'D. CENTER PUMP 2'-6" FROM HULL ℄, & 3'-0" ABV. CABIN SOLE.
STEERING SYSTEM ISOMETRIC VIEW
FIG. 338B SIZE 1
FIG. 623 SIZE 4
FIG. 620 SIZE 4
OPTIONAL EMERGENCY TILLER
BILGE INTAKE
NOTE
SEE SHEET 132-11 FOR LOCATION OF ELECTRICAL EQUIPMENT.
LONG. STRINGER
SEAWATER INTAKE
STEERING CABLES
BILGE PUMP
KEEL COOLER
SABB DIESEL
SEE SHEET 132-10 FOR PLUMBING SCHEMATIC
FUEL TANK
MARK X ELASTOMUFFLE
SEACOCK
DECK WASHDOWN VALVE
20' SUPPLY BOAT
FOR: ANDERSON & ADAMS
DATE: 3-25-76
SCALE: 3/4" = 1'-0"
MACH'Y & STEER'G
LOA 19'-11 1/2"
LWL 19'-0"
BEAM 7'-11 1/2"
DRAFT 2'-3"
FREEBOARD
FWD 4'-6"
LEAST 2'-9 1/2"
AFT 3'-0"
JAY R. BENFORD
P.O. BOX 447
ST. MICHAELS, MD 21663
(410) 745-3235
132-8
DUNSFORD

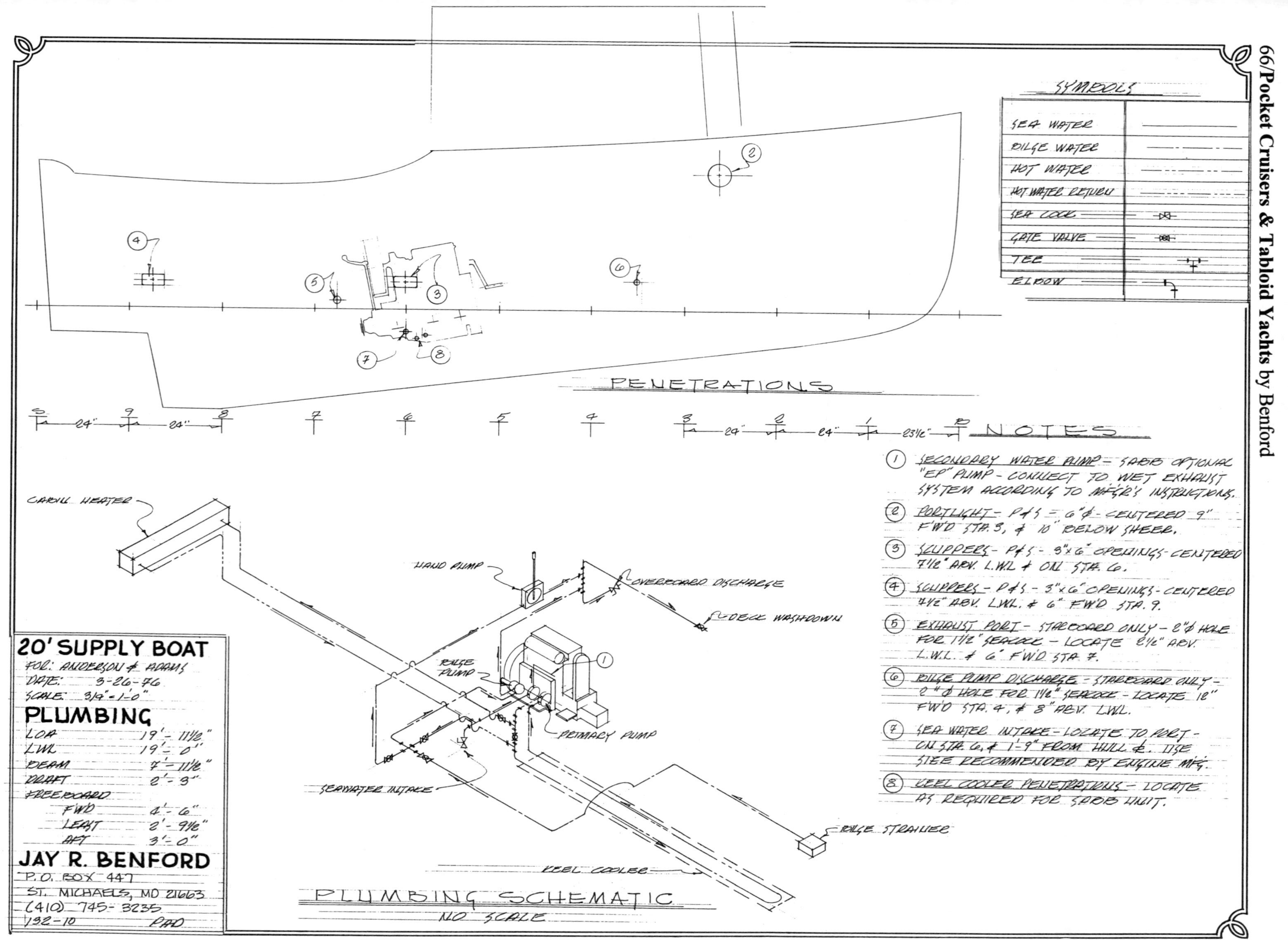
SYMBOLS
SEA WATER
BILGE WATER
HOT WATER
HOT WATER RETURN
SEA COCK
GATE VALVE
TEE
ELBOW
PENETRATIONS
NOTES
1 SECONDARY WATER PUMP - SABB OPTIONAL "EP" PUMP - CONNECT TO WET EXHAUST SYSTEM ACCORDING TO MFGR'S INSTRUCTIONS.
2 PORTLIGHT - PΦS = 6"Ø - CENTERED 9" FWD STA. 3, & 10" BELOW SHEER.
3 SCUPPERS - PΦS - 3"x6" OPENINGS - CENTERED 7½" ABV. L.W.L. & ON STA. 6.
4 SCUPPERS - PΦS - 3"x6" OPENINGS - CENTERED 4½" ABV. L.W.L. & 6" FWD STA. 9.
5 EXHAUST PORT - STARBOARD ONLY - 2"Ø HOLE FOR 1½" SEACOCK - LOCATE 8½" ABV. L.W.L. & 6" FWD STA. 7.
6 BILGE PUMP DISCHARGE - STARBOARD ONLY - 2"Ø HOLE FOR 1½" SEACOCK - LOCATE 12" FWD STA. 4, & 8" ABV. LWL.
7 SEA WATER INTAKE - LOCATE TO PORT - ON STA. 6, & 1'-9" FROM HULL ¢. USE SIZE RECOMMENDED BY ENGINE MFG.
8 KEEL COOLER PENETRATIONS - LOCATE AS REQUIRED FOR SABB UNIT.
CABIN HEATER
HAND PUMP
OVERBOARD DISCHARGE
DECK WASHDOWN
BILGE PUMP
PRIMARY PUMP
SEAWATER INTAKE
BILGE STRAINER
KEEL COOLER
PLUMBING SCHEMATIC
NO SCALE
20' SUPPLY BOAT
FOR: ANDERSON & ADAMS
DATE: 3-26-76
SCALE: 3/4" = 1'-0"
PLUMBING
LOA 19'-11½"
LWL 19'-0"
BEAM 7'-11½"
DRAFT 2'-3"
FREEBOARD
FWD 4'-6"
LEAST 2'-9½"
AFT 3'-0"
JAY R. BENFORD
P.O. BOX 447
ST. MICHAELS, MD 21663
(410) 745-3235
132-10 RAD

Chapter Five

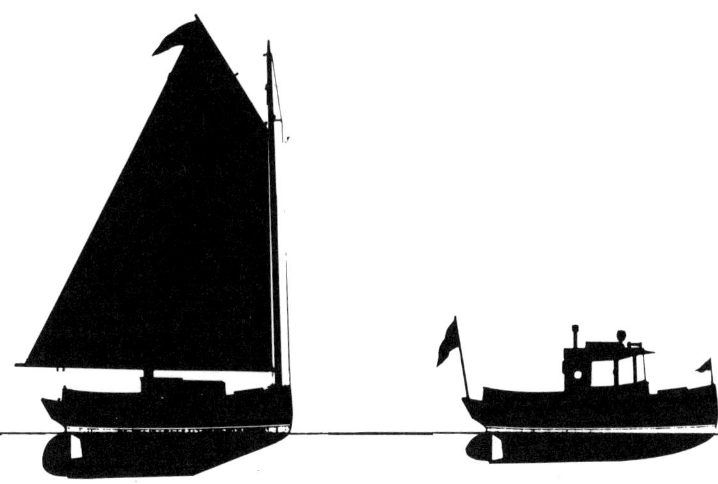

20' Catboat Joy & Tug Yacht

Design Number 137
1976

Some designs seem to spring to life, inspired by just the right spark, either in the form of a suggestion from a client or an inspiration from another source. This 20' catboat is one of them.

In the spring of 1976 we received a very interesting letter from Al Lewis. In it he said, *"I wonder if you would design a catboat for me.... I have been studying the books and journals for several years and have come across photographs of boats Mr. Benford has designed and they have given me great pleasure just to look at them. His* **Puffin** *has particularly delighted me....*

"...Reflecting further, I believe that if I had a design for a neat little....keel cat I might.... proceed with a....boat.... I had planned to sail her in the Columbia River and perhaps in the San Juan's....

"What I think I would like in a....cat is a beefy, beamy keelboat big enough to sleep two in the cabin and two or three (athwartship?) in the cockpit under a boom tent; a small galley and head; an inboard diesel engine powering a nice big prop. Perhaps twin bilge keels might be considered to avoid an overly deep draft but not if it will make her too slow in stays. I read that keelcats are already bad in this regard. I am uncertain as to whether I would be trailering the boat or mooring it in Puget Sound somewhere; most likely the latter. I still like lots of sheer and tumblehome and like the looks of a round counter-stern, cruiser stern or even a fantail. Bow would be tumblehome, plumb & sharp, or canoe. A classical gaff rigged "up and down "mainsail looks beautiful, loose footed or laced, whichever....

"I would think an LOA of 20' or so would be enough to incorporate the features I have mentioned, but smaller would be just fine and a little larger possibly OK too. The beam would be about half the LWL.

"The enclosed check....should be applied to the cost of a preliminary design if you agree to undertake the job."

This one struck just the right note with me. A couple days later I sent back the following letter:

"Thank you for your letter of April 15th, and your expression of interest in our designs. The project you outlined took my fancy with its

potential, and the enclosed print is the result. I think it ought to make a very handsome little cruiser, and we'd be delighted to have the opportunity to do up the plans!..."

The drawings that follow are the result of the design commission that resulted. The final boat is very close to the preliminary design I had laid out, having been so well inspired by the original request.

Quite a number of sisterships have been built and we have a mold for the hull that was taken from the original hull built for Al Lewis, from which several 'glass hulls have been pulled.

Some time after we'd done the design for the original catboat version, and a mold had been made from the hull, we started thinking about what sort of pocket cruiser could be created on that hull.

The 20' Cruiser or Tug Yacht is the result of that sketching. Several have been built from the molded hulls and at least one in wood. They have proven to be capable cruisers and the reports we get back from the owners indicate that they're having a lot of fun with them.

The drawings indicate a Yanmar diesel that's no longer a current model. I'd suggest their 1GM10 with a 3.2:1 gear as the current choice for a substitution. Of course, as further years come along, the choice of current models will change. The main point is that an engine in the six to ten horsepower range is what's needed and to get the most reduction you can so that the prop size is large enough to have good thrust. The engine compartment is roomy enough to let a variety of different engines fit in it, and the beds will just have to be modified to take into account differences in width and height of the mounts.

What about a centerboard version? We've done some sketching on a centerboard alternative version, but the drawings are not fully completed or detailed. The small drawing that follows shows the direction of our thinking. We've kept the board narrower than in traditional cats, to keep the trunk unobtrusive in the cabin and not push up the engine too much into the cockpit. The board would be a thick (10-15% of chord length) NACA foil shape to provide good lift.

Particulars:		**English**	**Metric**
Length overall		20'-0"	6.10 m
Length designed waterline		18'-0"	5.49 m
Beam		8'-0"	2.44 m
Draft		3'-6"	1.07 m
Tug		2'-3"	0.69 m
Freeboard:	Forward	3'-7½"	1.10 m
	Least	2'-0"	0.61 m
	Aft	2'-6"	0.76 m
Displacement, cruising trim		5,260 lbs.	2,385 kg
Tug		4,800 lbs.	2,177 kg
Displacement-length ratio		403	
Tug		367	
Ballast		1,600 lbs.	726 kg
Tug		750 lbs.	340 kg
Ballast ratio		30%	
Tug		16%	
Sail area		310 sq. ft.	28.8 sq.m
Sail area-displacement ratio		16.4	
Prismatic coefficient		.557	
Pounds per inch immersion		466	83 kg/cm
Entrance half-angle		26°	
Water tankage		14 Gals.	53 litres
Tug		20 Gals.	76 litres
Fuel tankage		15 Gals.	57 litres
Tug		30 Gals.	114 litres
Headroom		5'-0"	1.52 m
Tug		6'-3"	1.91 m

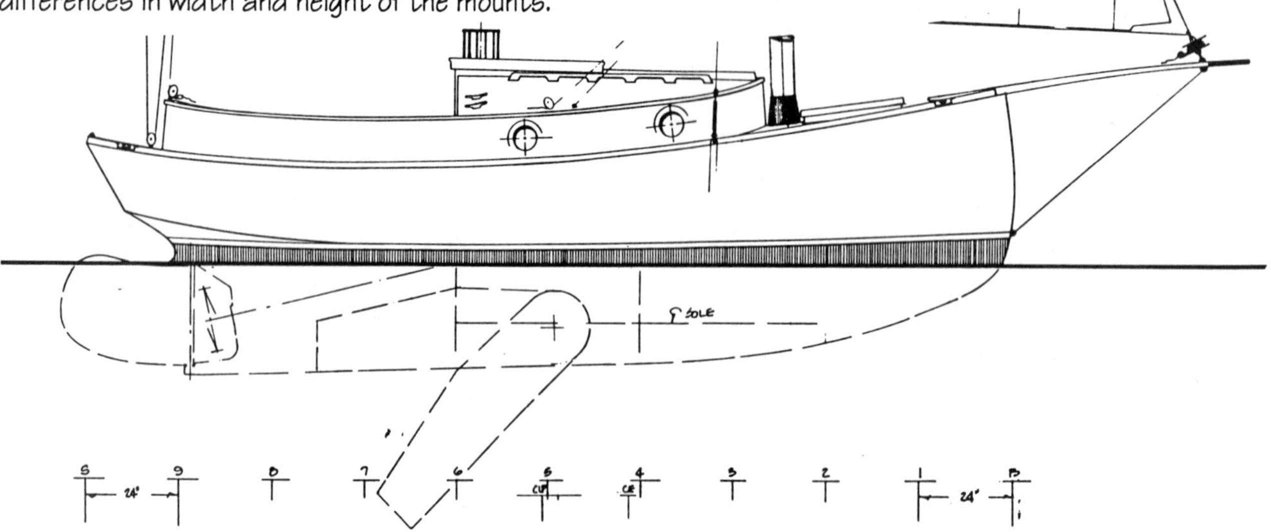

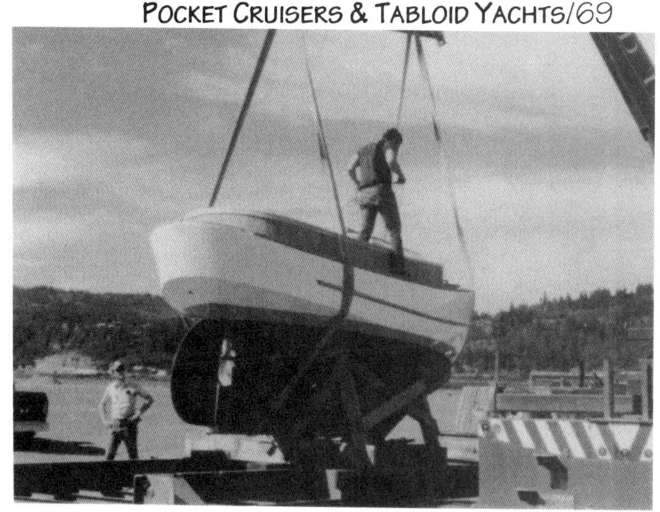

The original 20' Cat **Joy** *being launched by Heritage Boat Company. Photos courtesy of the builder.*

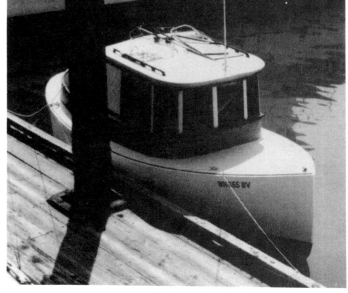

The 20-footer above is one of the first of the fiberglass hulled versions of this design. We met up with her on a cruise to Bellingham, Washington.

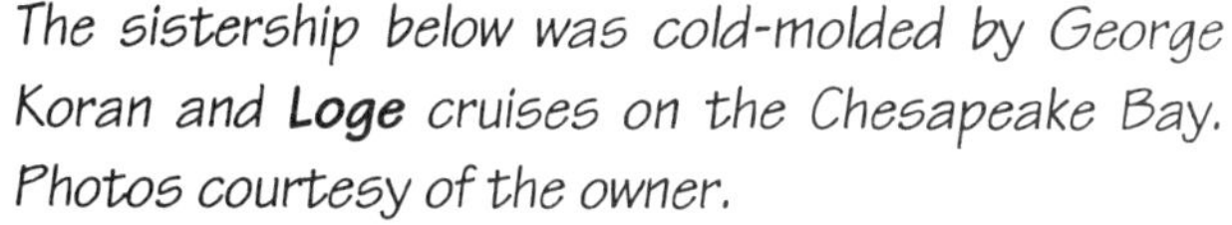

The sistership below was cold-molded by George Koran and **Loge** *cruises on the Chesapeake Bay. Photos courtesy of the owner.*

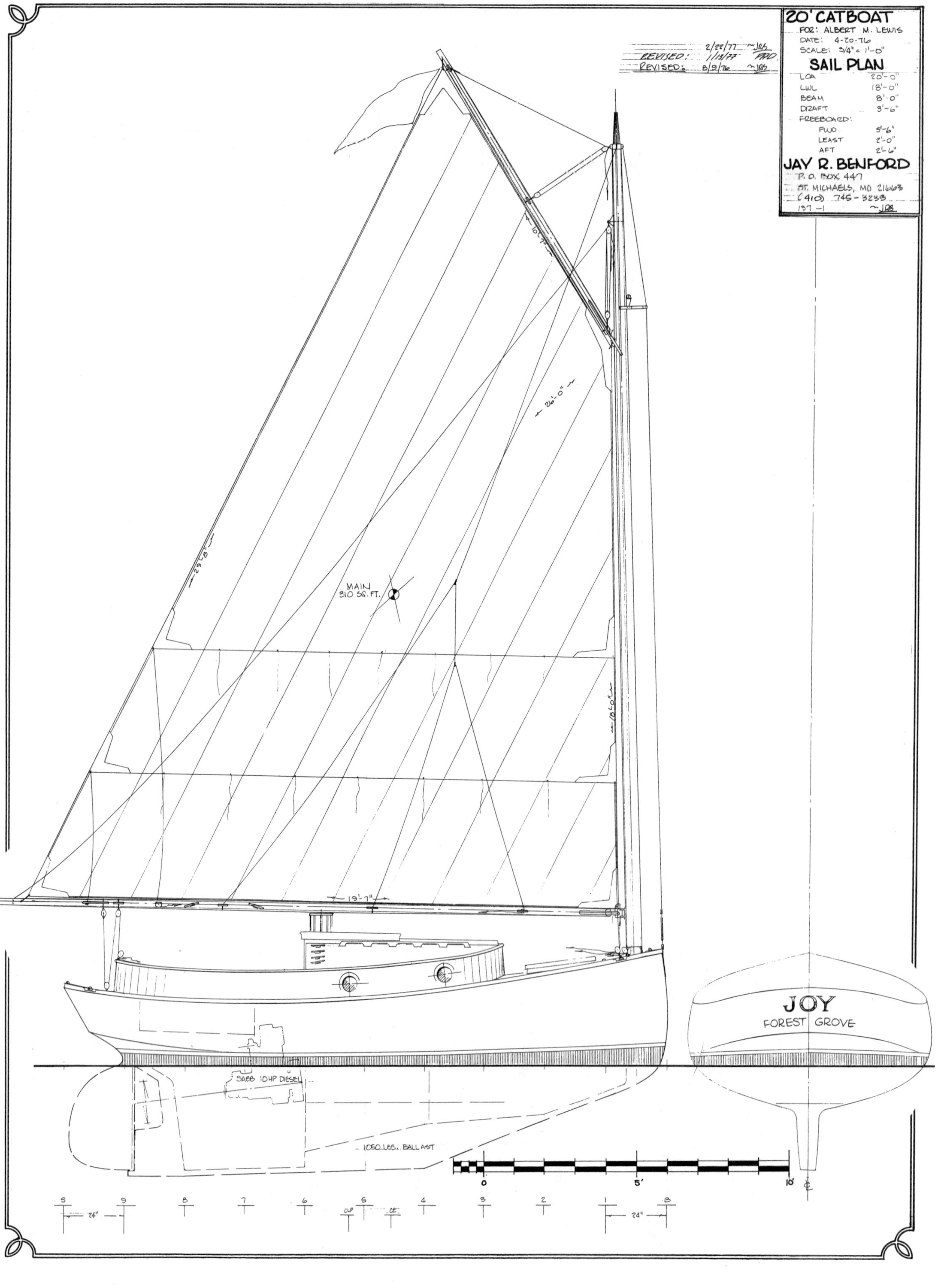

20' CATBOAT
FOR: ALBERT M. LEWIS
DATE: 4-20-76
SCALE: 3/4" = 1'-0"
SAIL PLAN

LOA	20'-0"
LWL	18'-0"
BEAM	8'-0"
DRAFT	3'-6"
FREEBOARD:	
FWD.	3'-6"
LEAST	2'-0"
AFT	2'-6"

JAY R. BENFORD
P. O. BOX 447
ST. MICHAELS, MD 21663
(410) 745-3235
137-1

REVISED: 8/9/76
REVISED: 1/13/77
2/22/77

MAIN
310 SQ. FT.

JOY
FOREST GROVE

SAAB 10HP DIESEL
1050 LBS. BALLAST

STA.	HEIGHTS (℄ TO:)								HALF-BREADTHS (℄ TO:)										DIAGONALS		
	KEEL	FAIRBODY	B1	B2	B3	BOOTTOP	KNUCKLE	SHEER	KEEL BOTTOM	KEEL TRACE	36" WL	42" WL	48" WL	57" WL	66" WL	KNUCKLE	SHEER	21" WL	A	B	C
1	3-0-0	3-0-5	4-2-5	—	—	4-7-6	—	7-3-0	0-0-4	0-0-4	—	0-5-6	0-10-5	1-3-0	1-5-3	—	1-7-3	—	0-8-1	1-1-7	1-5-2
2	2-3-0	2-8-6	3-3-6	4-2-6	—	4-7-0	—	6-10-6	0-0-4	0-2-0	0-6-1	1-3-1	1-9-7	2-3-5	2-6-5	—	2-8-4	—	1-1-5	1-9-5	2-4-6
3	1-6-0	2-6-7	2-11-0	3-5-3	4-6-2	4-6-2	—	6-7-0	0-0-4	0-3-3	1-2-3	2-1-2	2-7-7	3-1-4	3-3-7	—	3-4-5	0-1-2	1-5-6	2-3-2	3-1-0
4	0-9-0	2-6-1	2-9-1	3-1-3	3-7-4	4-5-6	—	6-3-6	0-0-4	0-4-1	1-8-5	2-9-7	3-3-7	3-8-4	3-9-2	—	3-8-7	0-3-1	1-7-6	2-6-5	3-7-4
5	0-8-2	2-6-0	2-8-7	3-0-2	3-4-7	4-5-3	—	6-1-4	0-3-0	0-4-4	1-11-4	3-2-3	3-8-6	3-11-6	3-11-4	—	3-10-2	0-4-1	1-8-4	2-7-6	3-11-0
6	0-7-4	2-6-4	2-9-7	3-1-2	3-5-2	4-5-1+	—	6-0-3	0-4-0	0-4-2	1-8-5	3-2-1	3-9-0	4-0-0	3-11-4	—	3-10-0	0-4-2	1-7-6	2-6-7	3-11-1
7	0-6-6	2-10-0	3-1-2	3-4-4	3-8-7	4-5-2	4-4-4	6-0-0	0-3-6	0-3-6	0-7-6	2-5-2	3-4-5	3-9-7	3-9-6	3-9-0	3-8-3	0-3-6	1-3-6	2-3-1	3-7-3
8	0-6-0	3-4-6	3-7-6	3-10-6	4-4-2	4-5-4	4-6-6	6-0-4	0-2-3	0-2-3	—	0-5-2	2-3-2	3-4-0	3-4-4	3-3-6	3-4-2	0-2-3	0-8-2	1-7-4	2-11-5
9	0-6-0	4-4-7	4-6-2	4-9-2	—	4-6-3	4-10-1	6-2-2	0-0-3	0-0-3	—	—	0-0-6	1-10-6	2-5-5	2-2-4	2-7-6	0-0-3	—	0-5-6	1-10-3
S	—	5-6-6					5-3-3	6-6-0	—	—	—	—	—	—	—	—	-0-	—	—	—	

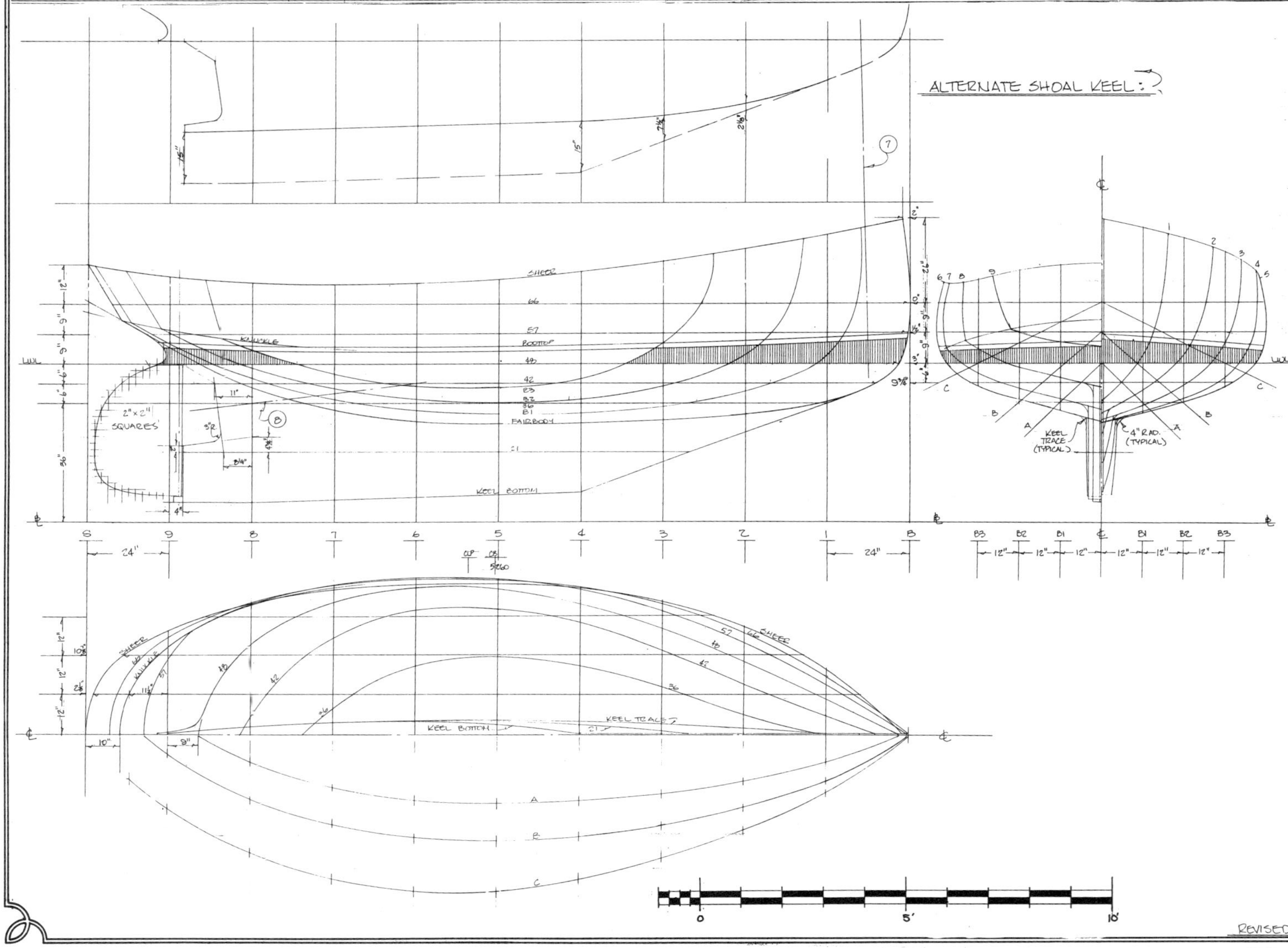

ALTERNATE SHOAL KEEL:

NOTES:

1. LINES & OFFSETS TO OUTSIDE OF HULL IN FEET—INCHES—EIGHTHS. DEDUCT FOR HULL THICKNESS PER CONSTRUCTION PLAN. DO NOT SCALE PRINTS!
2. ANY ALTERATION FROM THESE PLANS RELIEVES THE DESIGNERS FROM ANY FURTHER RESPONSIBILITY
3. THESE PLANS & PRINTS ARE THE PROPERTY OF THE DESIGNERS & MAY BE USED ONLY AS AUTHORIZED IN WRITING.
4. IT IS UNDERSTOOD THAT NO MORE THAN ONE BOAT WILL BE BUILT FROM THESE PLANS WITHOUT WRITTEN PERMISSION FROM THE DESIGNERS.
5. BOOTTOP STRIPE IS 1½" HIGH IN PROFILE. OFFSETS TO TOP EDGE OF STRIPE.
6. LINES MUST BE LOFTED & FAIRED FULL SIZE.
7. MAST ℄ CROSSES LWL 12" AFT OF STA. B & RAKES AFT 1" IN 36" OF HEIGHT
8. SHAFT ℄ CROSSES 42" WL AT STA 6 & IS 13¼" BELOW LWL AT CROSSING APERTURE OUTLINE
9.

REVISED: 3/13/77 ~JRB 8/5/76 ~JRB

20' CATBOAT
FOR: ALBERT M. LEWIS
DATE: 5-6-76
SCALE: 3/4" = 1'-0"

LINES & OFFSETS

LOA	20'-0"
LWL	18'-0"
BEAM	8'-0"
DRAFT	3'-6"
FREEBOARD:	
FWD.	3'-7½"
LEAST	2'-0"
AFT	2'-6"

JAY R. BENFORD
P.O. BOX 447
ST. MICHAELS, MD 21663
(410) 745-3235
137-2 ~JRB

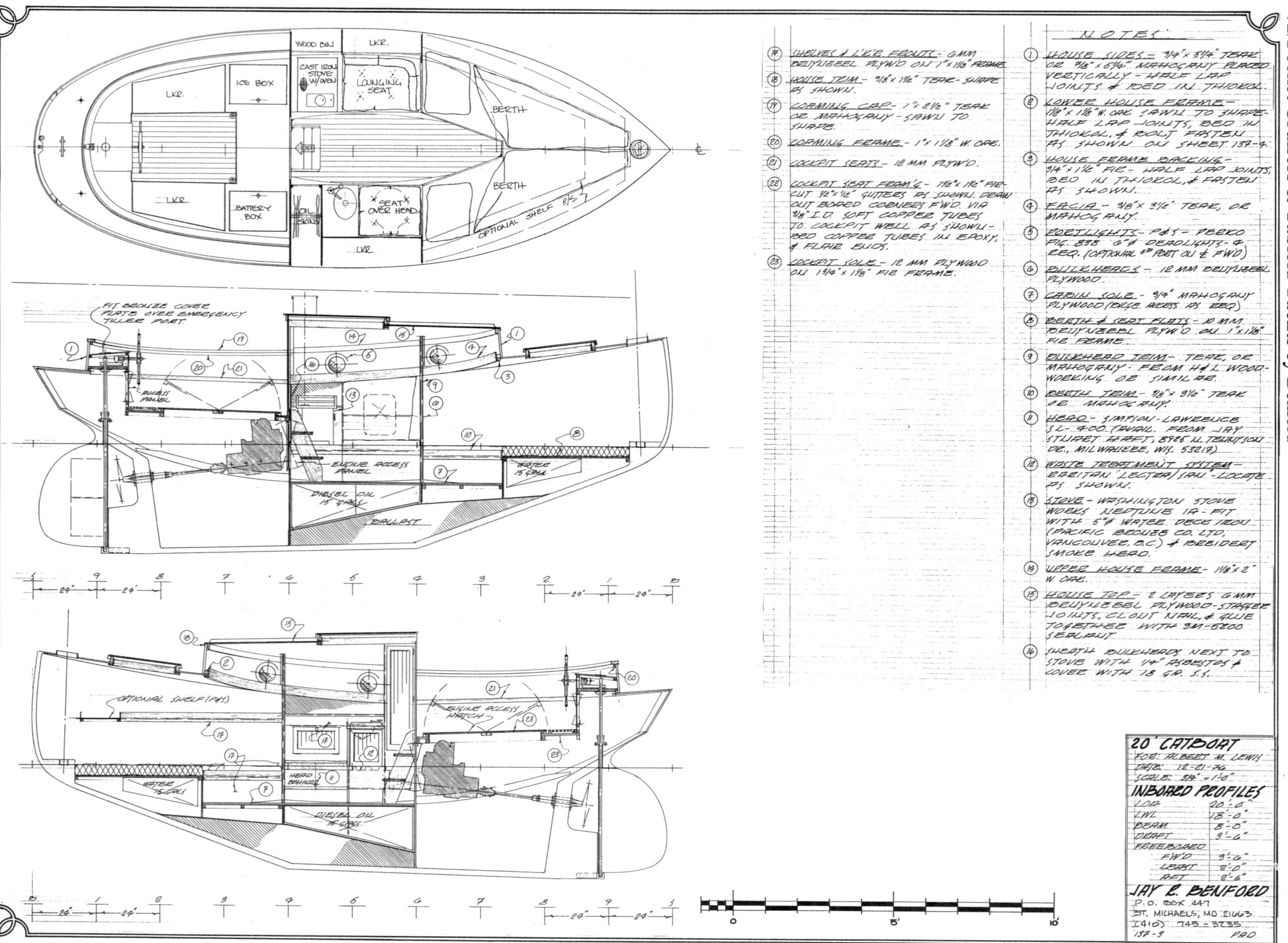
WOOD BIN
LKR.
CAST IRON STOVE W/OVEN
LOUNGING SEAT
ICE BOX
LKR.
BERTH
BERTH
LKR.
BATTERY BOX
OIL SKINS
SEAT OVER HEAD
LKR.
OPTIONAL SHELF P/S
FIT BRONZE COVER PLATE OVER EMERGENCY TILLER PORT.
ACCESS PANEL
ENGINE ACCESS PANEL
WATER 15 GALS.
DIESEL OIL 15 GALS.
BALLAST
OPTIONAL SHELF (P&S)
ENGINE ACCESS HATCH
HEAD BEHIND
WATER 15 GALS.
DIESEL OIL 15 GALS.
NOTES
1 HOUSE SIDES - 3/4" x 5 1/4" TEAK OR 7/8" x 5 1/4" MAHOGANY PLACED VERTICALLY - HALF LAP JOINTS & BED IN THIOKOL.
2 LOWER HOUSE FRAME - 1 1/8" x 1 1/8" W. OAK SAWN TO SHAPE. HALF LAP JOINTS, BED IN THIOKOL, & BOLT FASTEN AS SHOWN ON SHEET 137-4.
3 HOUSE FRAME BACKING - 3/4" x 1 1/2" FIR - HALF LAP JOINTS, BED IN THIOKOL, & FASTEN AS SHOWN.
4 FACIA - 3/8" x 3 1/2" TEAK, OR MAHOGANY.
5 PORTLIGHTS - P&S - PERKO FIG. 838 6"⌀ DEADLIGHTS - 4 REQ. (OPTIONAL 6" PORT ON ℄ FWD)
6 BULKHEADS - 12 MM BRUYNZEEL PLYWOOD.
7 CABIN SOLE - 3/4" MAHOGANY PLYWOOD (TAKE ACCESS AS REQ)
8 BERTH & SEAT FLATS - 12 MM BRUYNZEEL PLYW'D ON 1" x 1 1/8" FIR FRAME.
9 BULKHEAD TRIM - TEAK, OR MAHOGANY - FROM H & L WOODWORKING OR SIMILAR.
10 BERTH TRIM - 3/8" x 3 1/2" TEAK OR MAHOGANY.
11 HEAD - SIMPSON-LAWRENCE SL-400. (AVAIL. FROM JAY STUART HAFT, 8925 N. TENNYSON DR., MILWAUKEE, WIS. 53217)
12 WASTE TREATMENT SYSTEM - RARITAN "LECTRA/SAN" - LOCATE AS SHOWN.
13 STOVE - WASHINGTON STOVE WORKS NEPTUNE IA - FIT WITH 5"⌀ WATER DECK IRON (PACIFIC BRONZE CO. LTD, VANCOUVER, B.C.) & BREIDERT SMOKE HEAD.
14 UPPER HOUSE FRAME - 1 1/8" x 2" W. OAK.
15 HOUSE TOP - 2 LAYERS 6 MM BRUYNZEEL PLYWOOD - STAGGER JOINTS, CLOUT NAIL, & GLUE TOGETHER WITH 3M-5200 SEALANT.
16 SHEATH BULKHEADS NEXT TO STOVE WITH 1/4" ASBESTOS & COVER WITH 18 GA. S.S.
17 SHELVES & LKR FRONTS - 6 MM BRUYNZEEL PLYW'D. ON 1" x 1 1/8" FRAME.
18 HOUSE TRIM - 3/8" x 1 1/2" TEAK - SHAPE AS SHOWN.
19 COAMING CAP - 1" x 2 1/2" TEAK OR MAHOGANY - SAWN TO SHAPE.
20 COAMING FRAME - 1" x 1 1/8" W. OAK.
21 COCKPIT SEATS - 12 MM PLYW'D.
22 COCKPIT SEAT FRAM'G - 1 1/8" x 1 1/2" FIR - CUT 1/2" x 1/2" GUTTERS AS SHOWN. DRAIN OUTBOARD CORNERS FWD VIA 3/8" I.D. SOFT COPPER TUBES TO COCKPIT WELL AS SHOWN - BED COPPER TUBES IN EPOXY, & FLAIR ENDS.
23 COCKPIT SOLE - 12 MM PLYWOOD ON 1 3/4" x 1 1/8" FIR FRAME.
20' CATBOAT
FOR: ALBERT M. LEWIS
DATE: 12-21-76
SCALE: 3/4" = 1'-0"
INBOARD PROFILES
LOA 20'-0"
LWL 18'-0"
BEAM 8'-0"
DRAFT 3'-6"
FREEBOARD
FWD 3'-6"
LEAST 2'-0"
AFT 2'-6"
JAY R. BENFORD
P.O. BOX 447
ST. MICHAELS, MD 21663
(410) 745-3235
137-3
P.A.O.
0
5'
10'

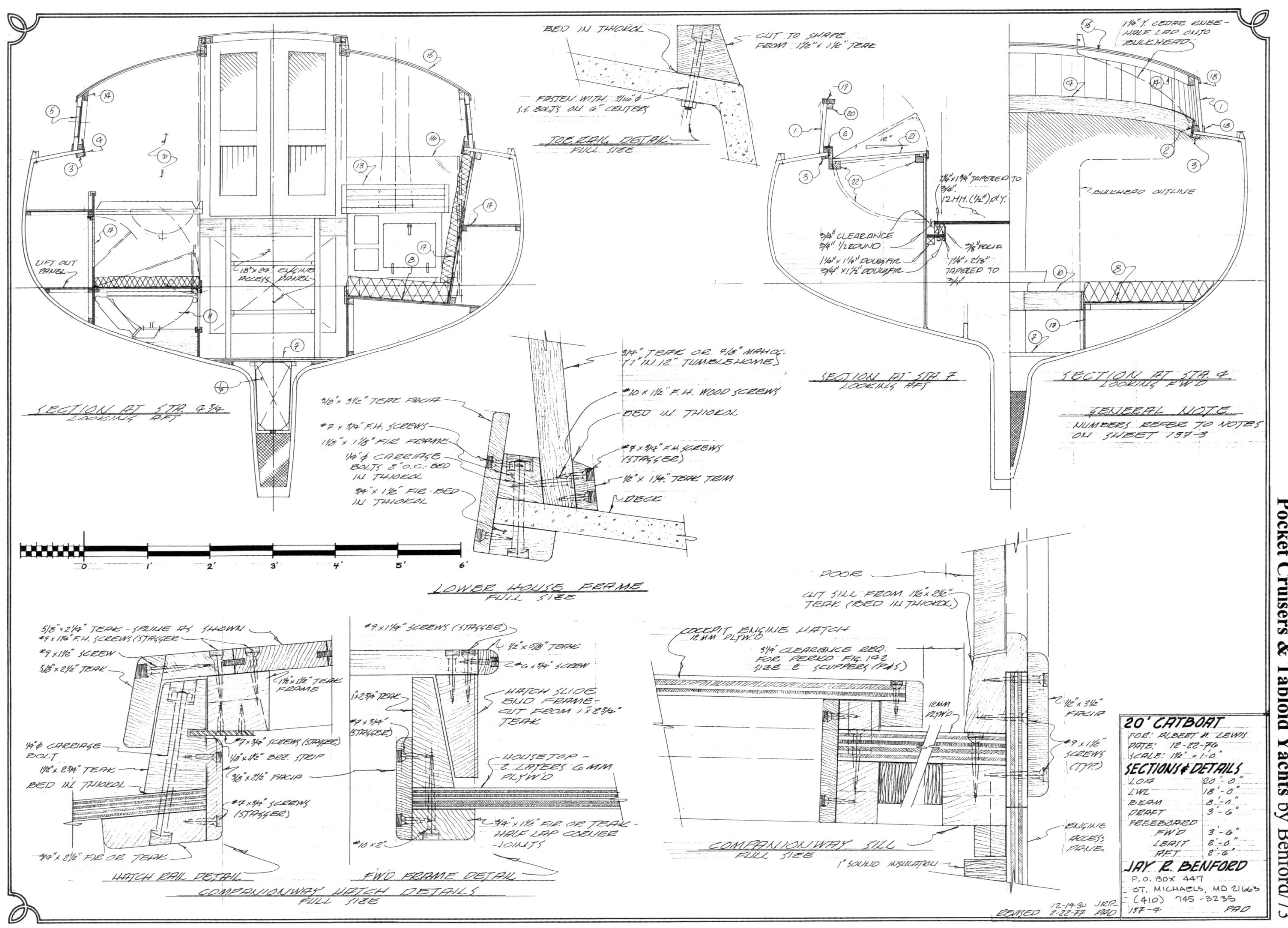

SECTION AT STA. 4 3/4 LOOKING AFT
LIFT OUT PANEL
18" x 24" ENGINE ACCESS PANEL
BED IN THIOKOL
CUT TO SHAPE FROM 1 1/2" x 1 1/2" TEAK
FASTEN WITH 3/16" Ø S.S. BOLTS ON 6" CENTERS
TOERAIL DETAIL FULL SIZE
1 1/4" x 1 3/4" TAPERED TO 3/4"
12MM. (1/2") PLY.
3/4" CLEARANCE
3/4" 1/2 ROUND
1 1/4" x 1 1/4" DOUG FIR
3/4" x 1 1/2" DOUG FIR
7/8" FACIA
1 1/4" x 2 1/8" TAPERED TO 3/4"
SECTION AT STA. 7 LOOKING AFT
1 1/4" Y. CEDAR KNEE - HALF LAP ONTO BULKHEAD
BULKHEAD OUTLINE
SECTION AT STA. 4 LOOKING FWD
GENERAL NOTE
NUMBERS REFER TO NOTES ON SHEET 137-3
3/4" TEAK OR 7/8" MAHOG. (1" IN 12" TUMBLEHOME)
#10 x 1 1/2" F.H. WOOD SCREWS
BED IN THIOKOL
3/8" x 3 1/2" TEAK FACIA
#7 x 3/4" F.H. SCREWS
1 1/8" x 1 1/8" FIR FRAME
1/4" Ø CARRIAGE BOLTS 8" O.C. - BED IN THIOKOL
3/4" x 1 1/2" FIR - BED IN THIOKOL
#7 x 3/4" F.H. SCREWS (STAGGER)
1/2" x 1 1/4" TEAK TRIM
DECK
0 1' 2' 3' 4' 5' 6'
LOWER HOUSE FRAME FULL SIZE
DOOR
CUT SILL FROM 1 1/2" x 8 1/2" TEAK (BED IN THIOKOL)
COCKPIT ENGINE HATCH 12MM PLYWD
3/4" CLEARANCE REQ. FOR PERKO FIG. 142 SIZE 2 SCUPPERS (PAS)
12MM PLYWD
1/2" x 3 1/2" FACIA
#9 x 1 1/2" SCREWS (TYP.)
ENGINE ACCESS PANEL
COMPANIONWAY SILL FULL SIZE
1" SOUND INSULATION
5/8" x 2 1/4" TEAK - SPLINE AS SHOWN
#9 x 1 3/4" F.H. SCREWS (STAGGER)
#9 x 1 1/2" SCREW
5/8" x 2 1/2" TEAK
1 1/2" x 1 1/2" TEAK FRAME
1/4" Ø CARRIAGE BOLT
1 1/2" x 2 3/4" TEAK
BED IN THIOKOL
#7 x 3/4" SCREWS (STAGGER)
1/8" x 1/2" BRZ. STRIP
3/8" x 2 1/2" FACIA
#7 x 3/4" SCREWS (STAGGER)
3/4" x 2 1/2" FIR OR TEAK
HATCH RAIL DETAIL
#9 x 1 1/4" SCREWS (STAGGER)
1/2" x 5/8" TEAK
#6 x 3/4" SCREW
HATCH SLIDE END FRAME - CUT FROM 1 x 8 3/4" TEAK
1 x 2 3/4" TEAK
#7 x 3/4" (STAGGER)
HOUSETOP - 2 LAYERS 6MM PLYWD
3/4" x 1 1/2" FIR OR TEAK - HALF LAP CORNER JOINTS
#10 x 2"
FWD FRAME DETAIL
COMPANIONWAY HATCH DETAILS FULL SIZE
20' CATBOAT
FOR: ALBERT A. LEWIS
DATE: 12-22-76
SCALE: 1 1/2" = 1'-0"
SECTIONS & DETAILS
LOA 20'-0"
LWL 18'-0"
BEAM 8'-0"
DRAFT 3'-6"
FREEBOARD FWD 3'-6"
LEAST 2'-0"
AFT 2'-6"
JAY R. BENFORD
P.O. BOX 447
ST. MICHAELS, MD 21663
(410) 745-3235
137-4 PAD
12-14-80 JRB
REVISED 2-22-77 PAD

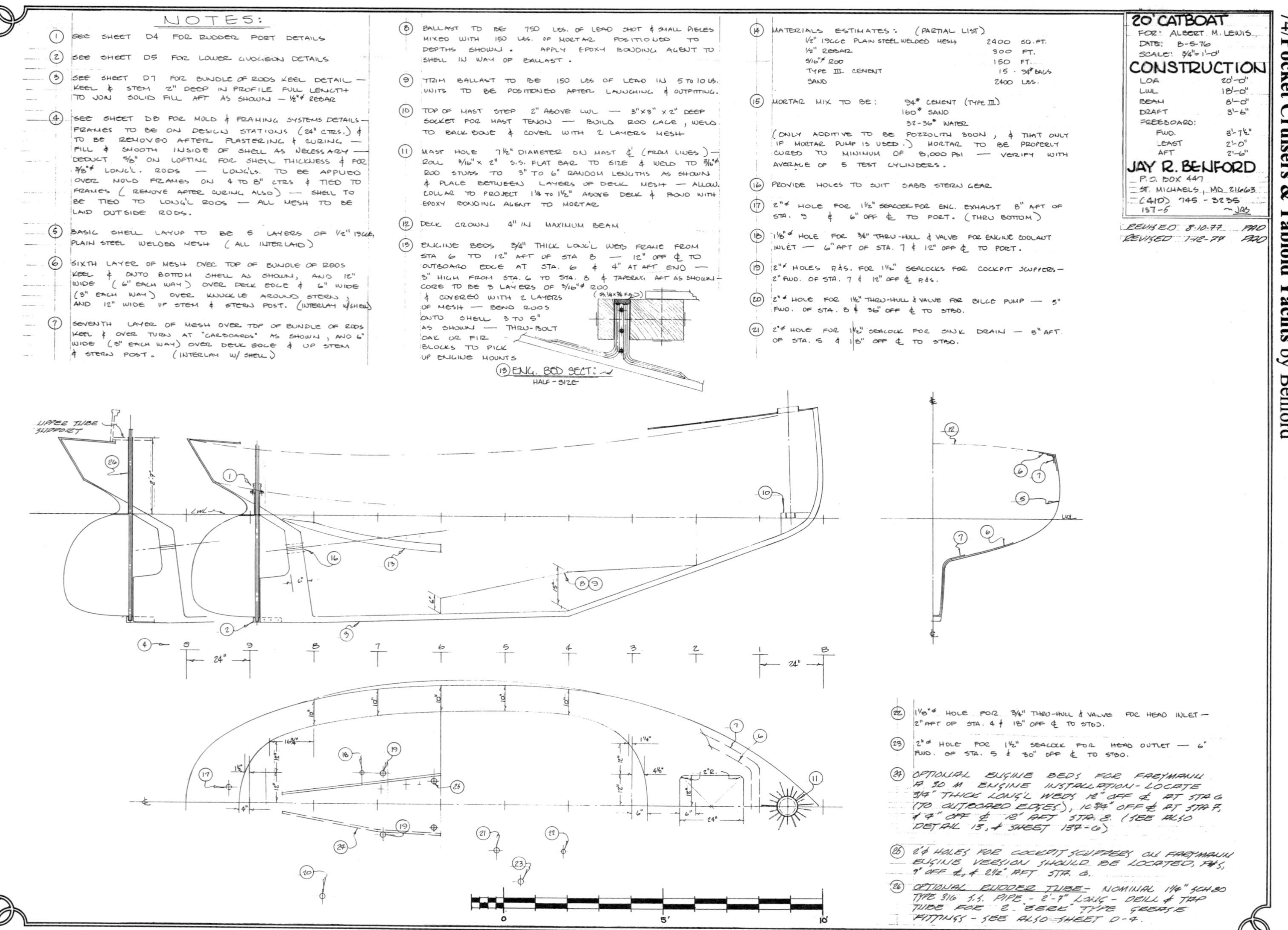
NOTES:
1 SEE SHEET D4 FOR RUDDER PORT DETAILS
2 SEE SHEET D5 FOR LOWER GUDGEON DETAILS
3 SEE SHEET D7 FOR BUNDLE OF RODS KEEL DETAIL — KEEL & STEM 2" DEEP IN PROFILE FULL LENGTH TO JOIN SOLID FILL AFT AS SHOWN — 1/2"⌀ REBAR
4 SEE SHEET D8 FOR MOLD & FRAMING SYSTEMS DETAILS — FRAMES TO BE ON DESIGN STATIONS (24" CTRS.) & TO BE REMOVED AFTER PLASTERING & CURING — FILL & SMOOTH INSIDE OF SHELL AS NECESSARY — DEDUCT 5/8" ON LOFTING FOR SHELL THICKNESS & FOR 3/8"⌀ LONG'L. RODS — LONG'LS. TO BE APPLIED OVER MOLD FRAMES ON 4 TO 8" CTRS & TIED TO FRAMES (REMOVE AFTER CURING ALSO) — SHELL TO BE TIED TO LONG'L RODS — ALL MESH TO BE LAID OUTSIDE RODS.
5 BASIC SHELL LAYUP TO BE 5 LAYERS OF 1/2" 19GGE. PLAIN STEEL WELDED MESH (ALL INTERLAID)
6 SIXTH LAYER OF MESH OVER TOP OF BUNDLE OF RODS KEEL & ONTO BOTTOM SHELL AS SHOWN, AND 12" WIDE (6" EACH WAY) OVER DECK EDGE & 6" WIDE (3" EACH WAY) OVER KNUCKLE AROUND STERN, AND 12" WIDE UP STEM & STERN POST. (INTERLAY W/SHELL)
7 SEVENTH LAYER OF MESH OVER TOP OF BUNDLE OF RODS KEEL & OVER TURN AT "CARDBOARDS" AS SHOWN, AND 6" WIDE (3" EACH WAY) OVER DECK EDGE & UP STEM & STERN POST. (INTERLAY W/ SHELL)
8 BALLAST TO BE 750 LBS. OF LEAD SHOT & SMALL PIECES MIXED WITH 150 LBS. OF MORTAR POSITIONED TO DEPTHS SHOWN. APPLY EPOXY BONDING AGENT TO SHELL IN WAY OF BALLAST.
9 TRIM BALLAST TO BE 150 LBS OF LEAD IN 5 TO 10 LBS. UNITS TO BE POSITIONED AFTER LAUNCHING & OUTFITTING.
10 TOP OF MAST STEP 2" ABOVE LWL — 3"X3" X 2" DEEP SOCKET FOR MAST TENON — BUILD ROD CAGE, WELD TO BACKBONE & COVER WITH 2 LAYERS MESH
11 MAST HOLE 7 1/2" DIAMETER ON MAST ℄ (FROM LINES) — ROLL 3/16"X 2" S.S. FLAT BAR TO SIZE & WELD TO 5/16"⌀ ROD STUBS TO 3" TO 6" RANDOM LENGTHS AS SHOWN & PLACE BETWEEN LAYERS OF DECK MESH — ALLOW COLLAR TO PROJECT 1 1/4 TO 1 1/2" ABOVE DECK & BOND WITH EPOXY BONDING AGENT TO MORTAR
12 DECK CROWN 4" IN MAXIMUM BEAM
13 ENGINE BEDS 3/4" THICK LONG'L WEB FRAME FROM STA 6 TO 12" AFT OF STA 8 — 12" OFF ℄ TO OUTBOARD EDGE AT STA. 6 & 4" AT AFT END — 3" HIGH FROM STA. 6 TO STA. 8 & TAPERING AFT AS SHOWN — CORE TO BE 3 LAYERS OF 5/16"⌀ ROD & COVERED WITH 2 LAYERS OF MESH — BEND RODS ONTO SHELL 3 TO 5" AS SHOWN — THRU-BOLT OAK OR FIR BLOCKS TO PICK UP ENGINE MOUNTS
(5/16 x 3/8 F.G.)
13 ENG. BED SECT.
HALF-SIZE
14 MATERIALS ESTIMATES: (PARTIAL LIST)
1/2" 19GGE PLAIN STEEL WELDED MESH 2400 SQ. FT.
1/2" REBAR 300 FT.
5/16"⌀ ROD 150 FT.
TYPE III CEMENT 15 - 94# BAGS
SAND 2400 LBS.
15 MORTAR MIX TO BE: 94# CEMENT (TYPE III)
160# SAND
32-36# WATER
(ONLY ADDITIVE TO BE POZZOLITH 300N, & THAT ONLY IF MORTAR PUMP IS USED.) MORTAR TO BE PROPERLY CURED TO MINIMUM OF 8,000 PSI — VERIFY WITH AVERAGE OF 5 TEST CYLINDERS.
16 PROVIDE HOLES TO SUIT SABB STERN GEAR
17 2"⌀ HOLE FOR 1 1/2" SEACOCK FOR ENG. EXHAUST 8" AFT OF STA. 9 & 6" OFF ℄ TO PORT. (THRU BOTTOM)
18 1 1/8"⌀ HOLE FOR 3/4" THRU-HULL & VALVE FOR ENGINE COOLANT INLET — 6" AFT OF STA. 7 & 12" OFF ℄ TO PORT.
19 2"⌀ HOLES P&S. FOR 1 1/2" SEACOCKS FOR COCKPIT SCUPPERS — 2" FWD. OF STA. 7 & 12" OFF ℄ P&S.
20 2"⌀ HOLE FOR 1 1/2" THRU-HULL & VALVE FOR BILGE PUMP — 3" FWD. OF STA. 8 & 36" OFF ℄ TO STBD.
21 2"⌀ HOLE FOR 1 1/2" SEACOCK FOR SINK DRAIN — 3" AFT OF STA. 5 & 18" OFF ℄ TO STBD.
22 1 1/8"⌀ HOLE FOR 3/4" THRU-HULL & VALVE FOR HEAD INLET — 2" AFT OF STA. 4 & 18" OFF ℄ TO STBD.
23 2"⌀ HOLE FOR 1 1/2" SEACOCK FOR HEAD OUTLET — 6" FWD. OF STA. 5 & 30" OFF ℄ TO STBD.
24 OPTIONAL ENGINE BEDS FOR FARYMANN A 30 M ENGINE INSTALLATION - LOCATE 3/4" THICK LONG'L WEBS 12" OFF ℄ AT STA 6 (TO OUTBOARD EDGES), 10 3/4" OFF ℄ AT STA 7, & 7" OFF ℄ 12" AFT STA 8. (SEE ALSO DETAIL 13, & SHEET 137-6)
25 2"⌀ HOLES FOR COCKPIT SCUPPERS ON FARYMANN ENGINE VERSION SHOULD BE LOCATED, P&S, 9" OFF ℄, & 2 1/2" AFT STA. 6.
26 OPTIONAL RUDDER TUBE - NOMINAL 1 1/4" SCH 80 TYPE 316 S.S. PIPE - 2'-7" LONG - DRILL & TAP TUBE FOR 2 "ZERK" TYPE GREASE FITTINGS - SEE ALSO SHEET D-4.
20' CATBOAT
FOR: ALBERT M. LEWIS
DATE: 8-5-76
SCALE: 3/4" = 1'-0"
CONSTRUCTION
LOA 20'-0"
LWL 18'-0"
BEAM 8'-0"
DRAFT 3'-6"
FREEBOARD:
FWD. 3'-7 1/2"
LEAST 2'-0"
AFT 2'-6"
JAY R. BENFORD
P.O. BOX 447
ST. MICHAELS, MD 21663
(410) 745-3235
137-5 ~JRB
REVISED 8-10-77 PAD
REVISED 1-12-77 PAD
UPPER TUBE SUPPORT
LWL
9 8 7 6 5 4 3 2 1 B
24"
0 5' 10'

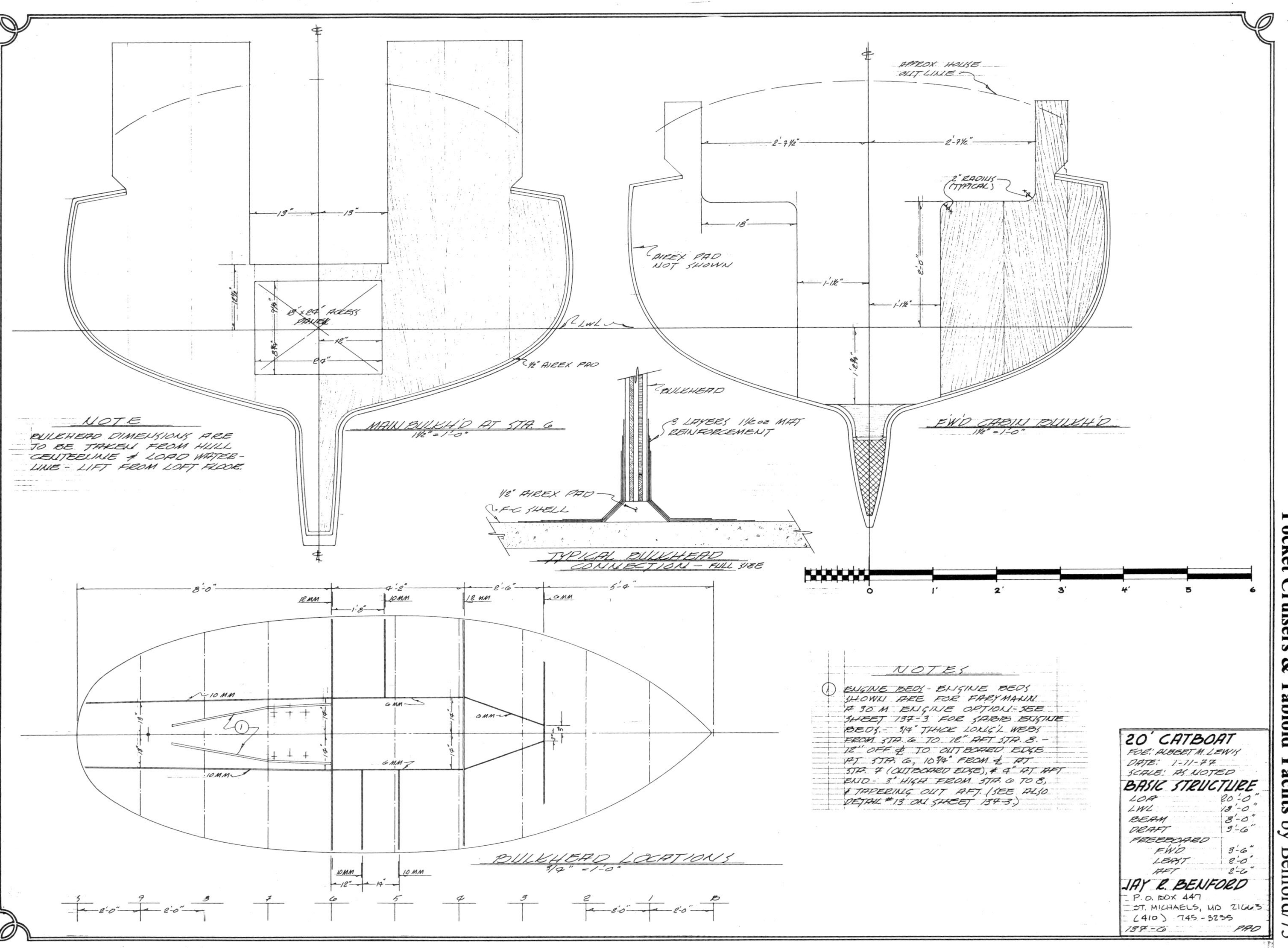
APPROX. HOUSE OUTLINE
2" RADIUS (TYPICAL)
AIREX PAD NOT SHOWN
LWL
1/2" AIREX PAD
18" x 24" ACCESS PANEL
NOTE
BULKHEAD DIMENSIONS ARE TO BE TAKEN FROM HULL CENTERLINE & LOAD WATERLINE - LIFT FROM LOFT FLOOR.
MAIN BULKH'D AT STA. 6
1 1/2" = 1'-0"
BULKHEAD
3 LAYERS 1 1/2 oz MAT REINFORCEMENT
1/2" AIREX PAD
F-C SHELL
TYPICAL BULKHEAD CONNECTION - FULL SIZE
FWD CABIN BULKH'D
1 1/2" = 1'-0"
NOTES
1 ENGINE BEDS - ENGINE BEDS SHOWN ARE FOR FARYMANN A 30 M ENGINE OPTION - SEE SHEET 137-3 FOR SABB ENGINE BEDS. - 3/4" THICK LONG'L WEBS FROM STA. 6 TO 12" AFT STA. 8. - 12" OFF ℄ TO OUTBOARD EDGE AT STA. 6, 10 3/4" FROM ℄ AT STA. 7 (OUTBOARD EDGE), & 9" AT AFT END - 3" HIGH FROM STA. 6 TO 8, & TAPERING OUT AFT. (SEE ALSO DETAIL #13 ON SHEET 137-3.)
BULKHEAD LOCATIONS
3/4" = 1'-0"
20' CATBOAT
FOR: ALBERT M. LEWIS
DATE: 1-11-77
SCALE: AS NOTED
BASIC STRUCTURE
LOA 20'-0"
LWL 18'-0"
BEAM 8'-0"
DRAFT 3'-6"
FREEBOARD
FWD 3'-6"
LEAST 2'-0"
AFT 2'-6"
JAY R. BENFORD
P.O. BOX 447
ST. MICHAELS, MD 21663
(410) 745-3235
137-6

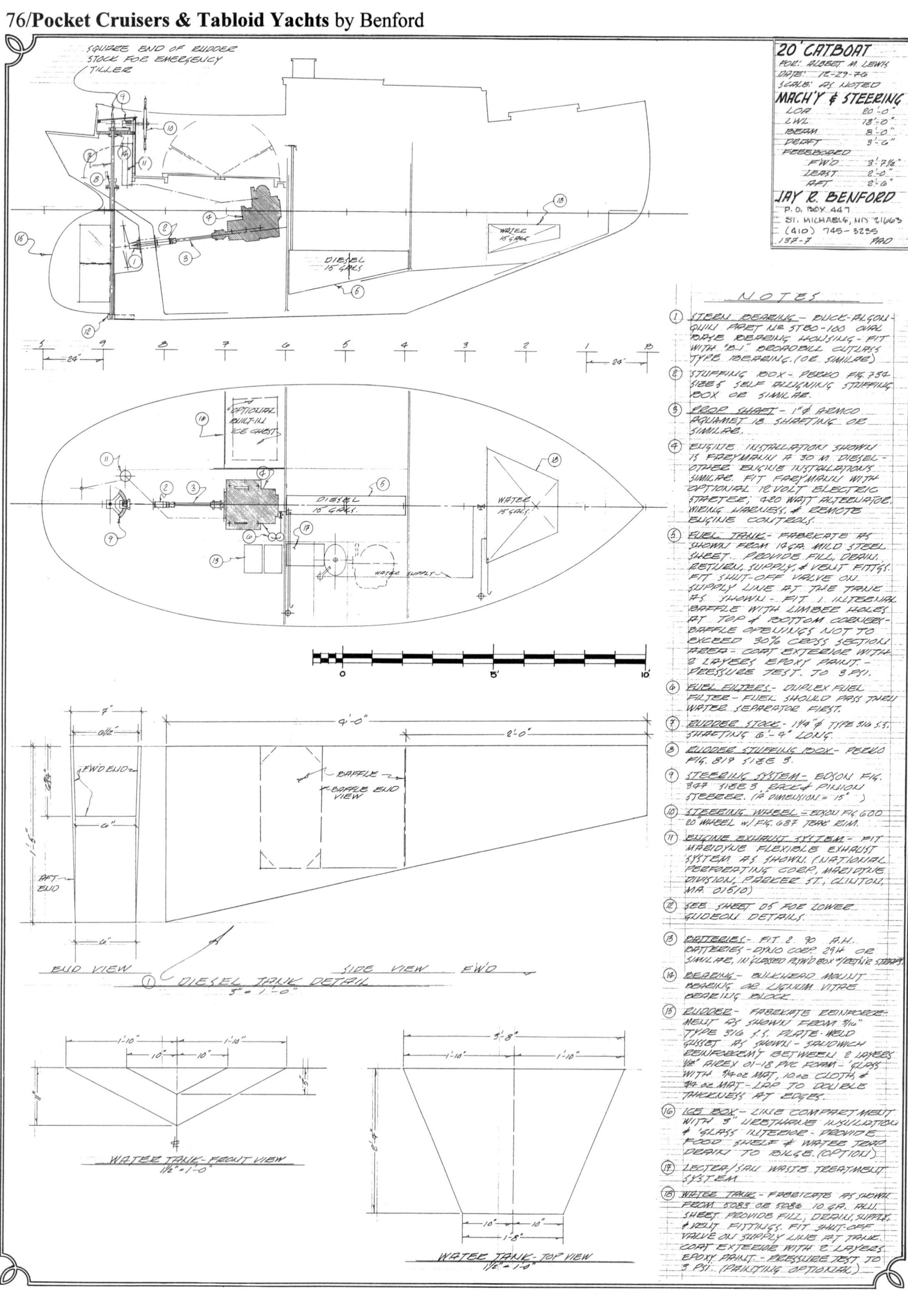
20' CATBOAT
FOR: ALBERT M. LEWIS
DATE: 12-29-76
SCALE: AS NOTED
MACH'Y & STEERING
LOA 20'-0"
LWL 18'-0"
BEAM 8'-0"
DRAFT 3'-6"
FREEBOARD
FWD 3'-7½"
LEAST 2'-0"
AFT 2'-6"
JAY R. BENFORD
P.O. BOX 447
ST. MICHAELS, MD 21663
(410) 745-3235
137-7 PAO
SQUARE END OF RUDDER STOCK FOR EMERGENCY TILLER
DIESEL 15 GALS
WATER 15 GALS
OPTIONAL BUILT-IN ICE CHEST
WATER SUPPLY
24"
0
5'
10'
NOTES
1 STERN BEARING - BUCK-ALGONQUIN PART Nº ST80-100 OVAL BASE BEARING HOUSING - FIT WITH "B-J" BROADBILL CUTLASS TYPE BEARING. (OR SIMILAR)
2 STUFFING BOX - PERKO FIG. 754 SIZE 5 SELF ALIGNING STUFFING BOX OR SIMILAR.
3 PROP SHAFT - 1"⌀ ARMCO AQUAMET 18 SHAFTING OR SIMILAR.
4 ENGINE INSTALLATION SHOWN IS FARYMANN A 30 M DIESEL - OTHER ENGINE INSTALLATIONS SIMILAR. FIT FARYMANN WITH OPTIONAL 12 VOLT ELECTRIC STARTER, 420 WATT ALTERNATOR, WIRING HARNESS, & REMOTE ENGINE CONTROLS.
5 FUEL TANK - FABRICATE AS SHOWN FROM 14 GA. MILD STEEL SHEET. PROVIDE FILL, DRAIN, RETURN, SUPPLY, & VENT FITT'GS. FIT SHUT-OFF VALVE ON SUPPLY LINE AT THE TANK AS SHOWN - FIT 1 INTERNAL BAFFLE WITH LIMBER HOLES AT TOP & BOTTOM CORNERS - BAFFLE OPENINGS NOT TO EXCEED 30% CROSS SECTION AREA - COAT EXTERIOR WITH 2 LAYERS EPOXY PAINT. - PRESSURE TEST TO 3 PSI.
6 FUEL FILTERS - DUPLEX FUEL FILTER - FUEL SHOULD PASS THRU WATER SEPARATOR FIRST.
7 RUDDER STOCK - 1¼"⌀ TYPE 316 S.S. SHAFTING 6'-4" LONG.
8 RUDDER STUFFING BOX - PERKO FIG. 817 SIZE 3.
9 STEERING SYSTEM - EDSON FIG. 347 SIZE 3 RACK & PINION STEERER. (A DIMENSION = 15")
10 STEERING WHEEL - EDSON FIG. 600 20" WHEEL W/ FIG. 687 TEAK RIM.
11 ENGINE EXHAUST SYSTEM - FIT MARIDYNE FLEXIBLE EXHAUST SYSTEM AS SHOWN. (NATIONAL PERFORATING CORP. MARIDYNE DIVISION, PARKER ST., CLINTON, MA. 01510)
12 SEE SHEET 05 FOR LOWER GUDGEON DETAILS.
13 BATTERIES - FIT 2 90 A.H. BATTERIES - DYNO CORP. 29H OR SIMILAR, IN GLASSED PLYWD BOX W/ LEATHER STRAPS.
14 BEARING - BULKHEAD MOUNT BEARING OR LIGNUM VITAE BEARING BLOCK.
15 RUDDER - FABRICATE REINFORCEMENT AS SHOWN FROM 3/16" TYPE 316 S.S. PLATE. WELD GUSSET AS SHOWN - SANDWICH REINFORCEMENT BETWEEN 2 LAYERS 1/2" AIREX 01-18 PVC FOAM - 'GLASS WITH 3/4 OZ MAT, 10 OZ CLOTH & 3/4 OZ MAT - LAP TO DOUBLE THICKNESS AT EDGES.
16 ICE BOX - LINE COMPARTMENT WITH 3" URETHANE INSULATION & 'GLASS INTERIOR - PROVIDE FOOD SHELF & WATER TRAP DRAIN TO BILGE. (OPTION)
17 LECTRA/SAN WASTE TREATMENT SYSTEM
18 WATER TANK - FABRICATE AS SHOWN FROM 5083 OR 5086 10 GA. ALU. SHEET. PROVIDE FILL, DRAIN, SUPPLY, & VENT FITTINGS. FIT SHUT-OFF VALVE ON SUPPLY LINE AT TANK. COAT EXTERIOR WITH 2 LAYERS EPOXY PAINT. - PRESSURE TEST TO 3 PSI. (PAINTING OPTIONAL)
7"
6½"
FWD END
1'-5"
6"
AFT END
4'-0"
2'-0"
BAFFLE
BAFFLE END VIEW
END VIEW
SIDE VIEW FWD
DIESEL TANK DETAIL
3" = 1'-0"
1'-10"
10"
11"
5"
WATER TANK - FRONT VIEW
1½" = 1'-0"
3'-8"
2'-4"
1'-8"
WATER TANK - TOP VIEW
1½" = 1'-0"

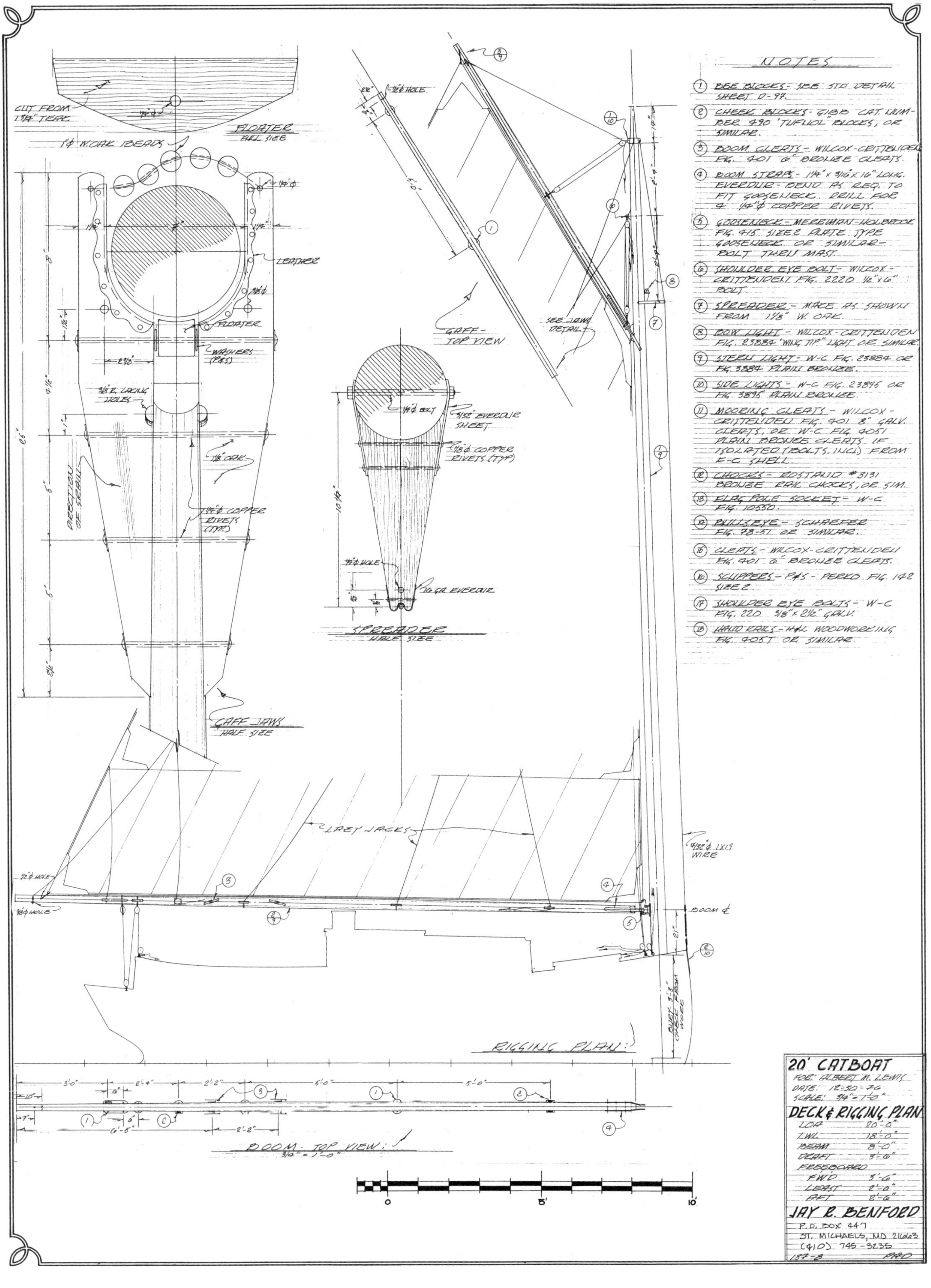

CUT FROM 1¾" TEAK

FLOATER
FULL SIZE

1" ϕ W. OAK BEADS

LEATHER

FLOATER

WASHERS (P&S)

3/16" ϕ LACING HOLES

1/2" OAK

1/4" ϕ COPPER RIVETS (TYP)

DIRECTION OF GRAIN

GAFF JAWS
HALF SIZE

GAFF – TOP VIEW

SEE JAWS DETAIL

1/4" ϕ BOLT

3/32" EVERDUR SHEET

1/8" ϕ COPPER RIVETS (TYP)

1/2" ϕ HOLE

16 GA. EVERDUR

SPREADER
HALF SIZE

LAZY JACKS

9/32" ϕ 1X19 WIRE

BOOM ℄

RIGGING PLAN

BOOM: TOP VIEW
3/4" = 1'-0"

NOTES

1. BEE BLOCKS – SEE STD DETAIL SHEET D-97.
2. CHEEK BLOCKS – GIBB CAT. NUMBER 490 "TUFNOL" BLOCKS, OR SIMILAR.
3. BOOM CLEATS – WILCOX-CRITTENDEN FIG. 401 6" BRONZE CLEATS.
4. BOOM STRAPS – 1¼" × 3/16" × 16" LONG. EVERDUR – BEND AS REQ. TO FIT GOOSENECK. DRILL FOR 4 1/4" ϕ COPPER RIVETS.
5. GOOSENECK – MERRIMAN-HOLBROOK FIG. 415 SIZE 2 PLATE TYPE GOOSENECK OR SIMILAR – BOLT THRU MAST.
6. SHOULDER EYE BOLT – WILCOX-CRITTENDEN FIG. 2220 1/2" × 6" BOLT.
7. SPREADER – MAKE AS SHOWN FROM 1⅛" W. OAK.
8. BOW LIGHT – WILCOX-CRITTENDEN FIG. 23884 "WING TIP" LIGHT OR SIMILAR.
9. STERN LIGHT – W-C FIG. 23884 OR FIG. 3884 PLAIN BRONZE.
10. SIDE LIGHTS – W-C FIG. 23895 OR FIG. 3895 PLAIN BRONZE.
11. MOORING CLEATS – WILCOX-CRITTENDEN FIG. 401 8" GALV. CLEATS, OR W-C FIG 4051 PLAIN BRONZE CLEATS IF ISOLATED (BOLTS, INCL.) FROM F-G SHELL.
12. CHOCKS – ROSTAND #3131 BRONZE RAIL CHOCKS, OR SIM.
13. FLAG POLE SOCKET – W-C FIG. 10550.
14. BULLSEYE – SCHAEFER FIG. 78-51 OR SIMILAR.
15. CLEATS – WILCOX-CRITTENDEN FIG. 401 6" BRONZE CLEATS.
16. SCUPPERS – P&S – PERKO FIG. 142 SIZE 2.
17. SHOULDER EYE BOLTS – W-C FIG. 220 3/8" × 2½" GALV.
18. HAND RAILS – H&L WOODWORKING FIG. 4057 OR SIMILAR.

0 5' 10'

20' CATBOAT

FOR: ALBERT M. LEWIS
DATE: 12-30-76
SCALE: 3/4" = 1'-0"

DECK & RIGGING PLAN

LOA	20'-0"
LWL	18'-0"
BEAM	8'-0"
DRAFT	3'-6"
FREEBOARD	
FWD	3'-6"
LEAST	2'-0"
AFT	2'-6"

JAY R. BENFORD
P.O. BOX 447
ST. MICHAELS, MD 21663
(410) 745-3235

157-8 PRD

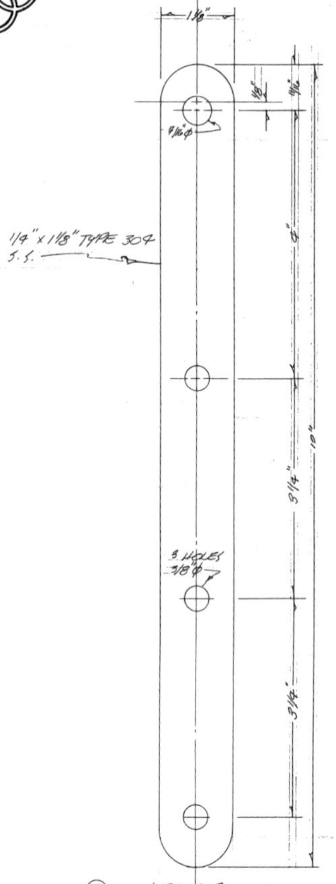

RIGGING SCHEDULE

NAME	NUMBER REQ'D	CONFIGURATION	LINE DIA. & CONST'N	LENGTH	FITTINGS
PEAK HALYARD	1	SPLICED EYE; SINGLE; STROP; DOUBLE; DOUBLE; EYE BOLT	3/8" φ DAC. 3-STRAND	120'	1-SINGLE BL'K 2-DOUBLE BL'KS 2-1/4" SHACKLES
THROAT HALYARD	1	TRIPLE BLOCK; STROP; SINGLE W/BECKET; EMPTY SHEAVE PEAK HALY'D DECK BLOCK	3/8"φ DAC. 3-STRAND	80'	1-SINGLE BL'K 1-TRIPLE BL'K 1-3/8" THIMBLE
TOPPING LIFT	1	EMPTY SHEAVE THROAT HALY'D TRIPLE; MATTHEW WALKER KNOT; DOUBLE; EYE BOLT	3/8"φ DAC. 3-STRAND	70'	1-DOUBLE
1ST REEF LUFF LINE	1	SAIL CRINGLE; EYE BOLT; EMPTY SHEAVE TOP'G LIFT DECK BLOCK	3/8"φ DAC. BRAID	24'	1-3/8" THIMBLE 1-SHACKLE
1ST REEF LEACH LINE	1	SAIL CRINGLE; MATTHEW WALKER KNOT; BEE BLOCK W/SHEAVE	3/8"φ DAC. BRAID	14'	1-BEE BLOCK W/ SHEAVE.
2ND REEF LEACH LINE	1	SAIL CRINGLE; CHEEK BLOCK; MATTHEW WALKER KNOT	3/8"φ DAC. BRAID	19'	1-CHEEK BL'K
MAIN SHEET	1	STROPS	3/8"φ DAC. 3-STRAND	115'	1-SINGLE W/ BECKET 3-SINGLE BL'KS 1-SINGLE W/CAM CLEAT 1-3/8" THIMBLE
LAZY-JACKS		SEE SAIL PLAN FOR ARRANGEMENT.	1/4"φ NYLON BRAID	180'	6-1/4" THIMBLES
HEAD STAY	1	LENGTH LISTED INCLUDES T'BUCKLE 1/2 OPEN	7/32"φ 1X19 S.S.	APPX 26'	1-3/8" TURNBUCKLE.
DOCK LINES	4		3/8"φ NYLON 3-STRAND	40'	
LIGHT GROUND TACKLE	1	6' CHAIN; 12-H DANFORTH	1/2" NYLON 3-STRAND	100'	1-1/2" THIMBLE 2- SHACKLES

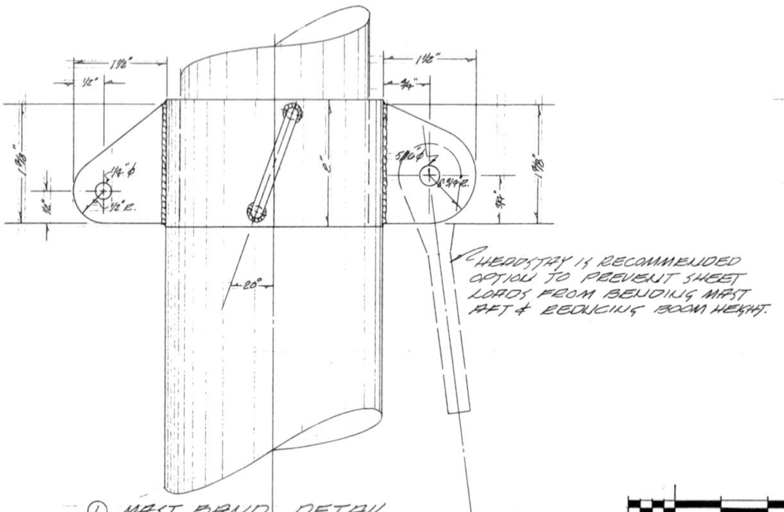

1 1/8"

1/2"

1 1/16"

9/16"φ

1/4" x 1 1/8" TYPE 304 S.S.

6"

3 1/4"

10"

3 HOLES 3/8"φ

3 1/4"

② CHAINPLATE
FULL SIZE

1 1/16"

1/2"

1 1/16"

3/4"

1 3/8"

1/4"φ

1/2"R.

5/16"φ

3/4"R.

6"

1 3/8"

20°

HEADSTAY IS RECOMMENDED OPTION TO PREVENT SHEET LOADS FROM BENDING MAST AFT & REDUCING BOOM HEIGHT.

① MAST BAND DETAIL
FULL SIZE

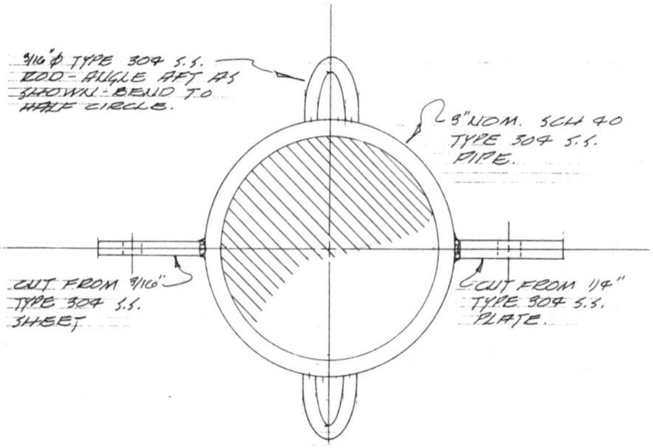

3/16"φ TYPE 304 S.S. ROD-ANGLE AFT AS SHOWN-BEND TO HALF CIRCLE.

3" NOM. SCH 40 TYPE 304 S.S. PIPE.

CUT FROM 3/16" TYPE 304 S.S. SHEET

CUT FROM 1/4" TYPE 304 S.S. PLATE.

0 5' 10'

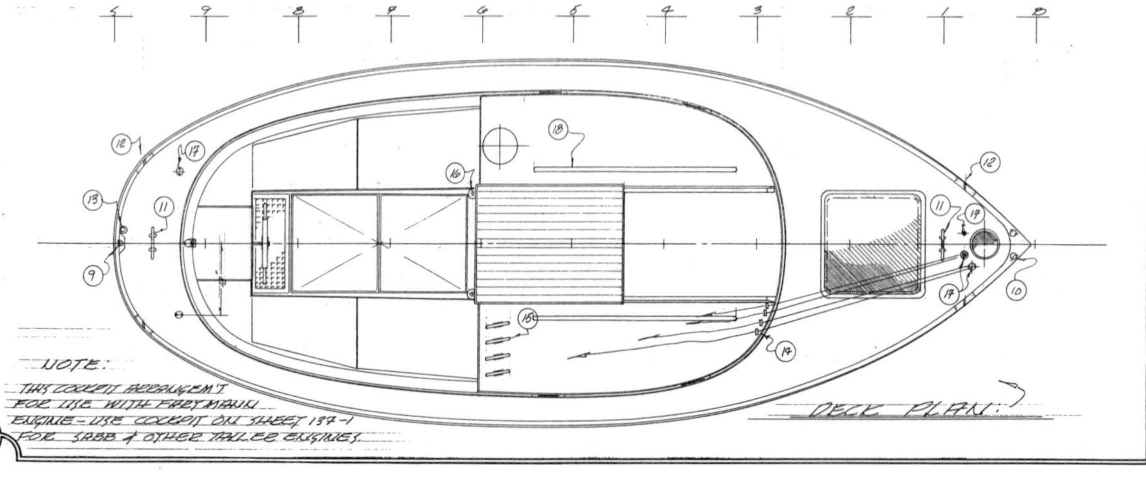

10 9 8 7 6 5 4 3 2 1 0

12 17 18 16 13 11 9 11 19 12 10 17 15 14

NOTE:
THIS COCKPIT ARRANGEM'T FOR USE WITH FARYMANN ENGINE-USE COCKPIT ON SHEET 137-1 FOR SABB & OTHER TALLER ENGINES.

DECK PLAN.

20' CATBOAT
FOR: ALBERT M. LEWIS
DATE: 1-6-77
SCALE: AS NOTED

RIG DETAILS

LOA	20'-0"
LWL	18'-0"
BEAM	8'-0"
DRAFT	3'-6"
FREEBOARD	
FWD	3'-6"
LEAST	2'-0"
AFT	2'-6"

JAY R. BENFORD
P. O. BOX 447
ST. MICHAELS, MD 21663
(410) 745-3235
137-10 PAD

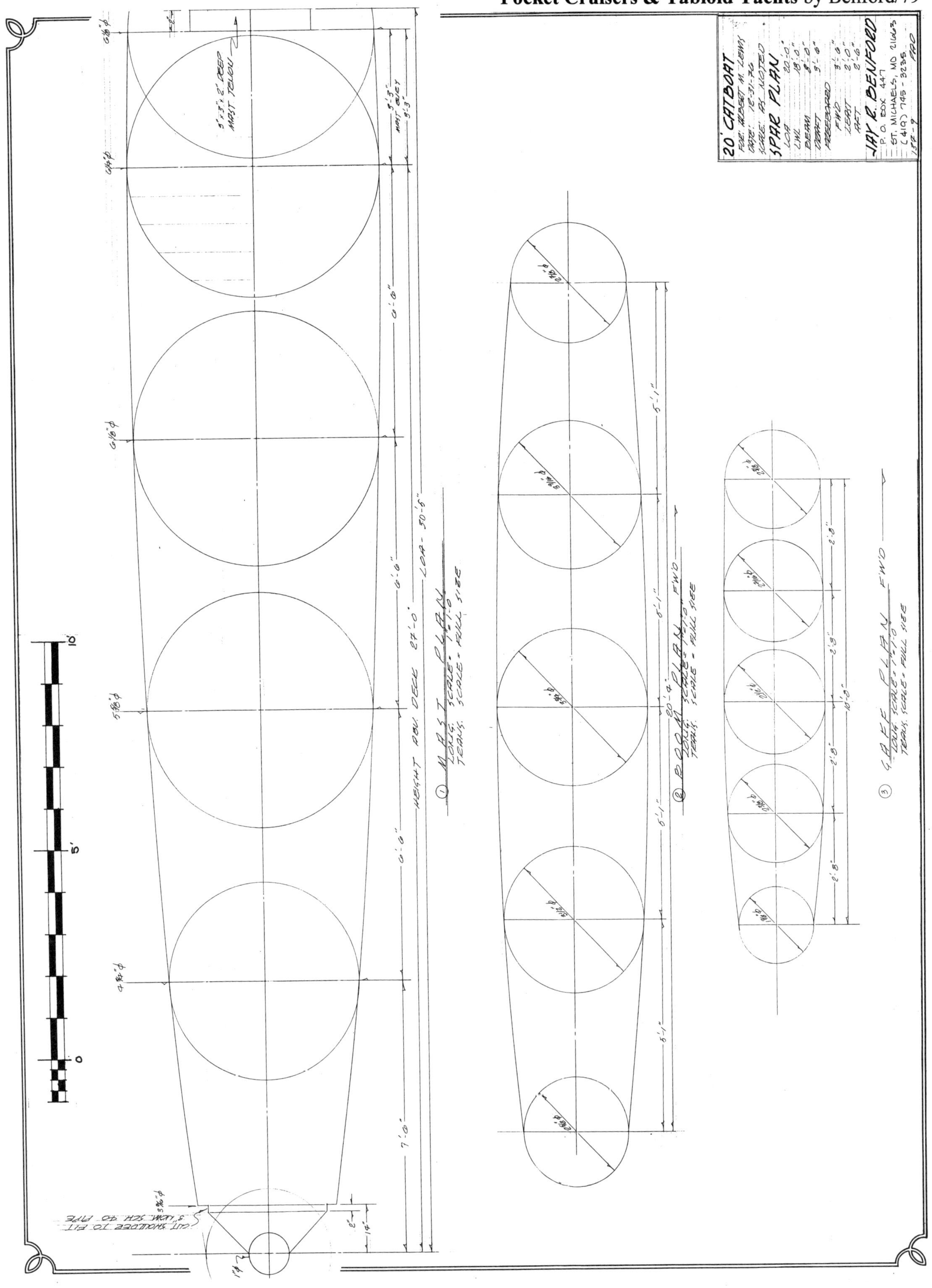

0 5' 10'

CUT SHOULDER TO FIT 3" NOM. SCH. 40 PIPE

3 9/16"ϕ 4 3/4"ϕ 5 5/8"ϕ 6 1/8"ϕ 6 1/4"ϕ 6 1/8"ϕ

1"ϕ

5" x 3" x 2" DEEP MAST TENON

2" 14"

7'-0" 6'-6" 6'-6" 6'-6" 3'-3" MAST BURY 3'-3"

HEIGHT ABV. DECK 27'-0"

LOA - 30'-5"

① MAST PLAN
LONG. SCALE = 1" = 1'-0"
TRANS. SCALE = FULL SIZE

5'-1" 5'-1" 5'-1" 5'-1"

20'-4"

② BOOM PLAN FWD
LONG. SCALE = 1" = 1'-0"
TRANS. SCALE = FULL SIZE

2'-8" 2'-8" 2'-8" 2'-8"

10'-8"

③ GAFF PLAN FWD
LONG. SCALE = 1" = 1'-0"
TRANS. SCALE = FULL SIZE

20' CATBOAT
FOR: ALBERT M. LEWIS
DATE: 12-31-76
SCALE: AS NOTED

SPAR PLAN

LOA	20'-0"
LWL	18'-0"
BEAM	8'-0"
DRAFT	3'-6"
FREEBOARD	
FWD	3'-6"
LEAST	2'-0"
AFT	2'-6"

JAY R. BENFORD
P. O. BOX 447
ST. MICHAELS, MD 21663
(410) 745-3235

137-9 PRO

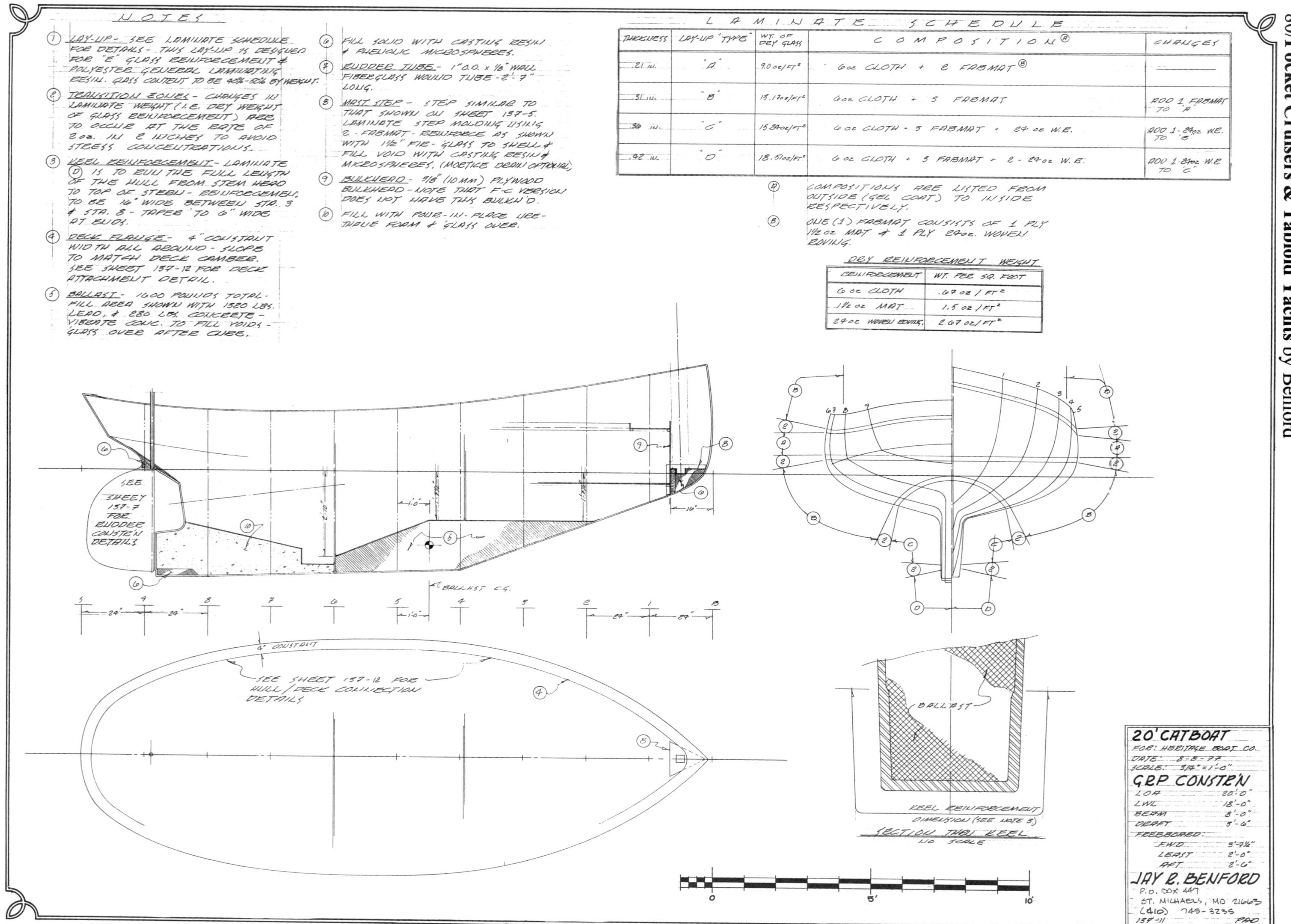
NOTES
1 LAY-UP- SEE LAMINATE SCHEDULE FOR DETAILS - THIS LAY-UP IS DESIGNED FOR "E" GLASS REINFORCEMENT & POLYESTER GENERAL LAMINATING RESIN. GLASS CONTENT TO BE 40%-50% BY WEIGHT.
2 TRANSITION ZONES - CHANGES IN LAMINATE WEIGHT (I.E. DRY WEIGHT OF GLASS REINFORCEMENT) ARE TO OCCUR AT THE RATE OF 2oz. IN 2 INCHES TO AVOID STRESS CONCENTRATIONS.
3 KEEL REINFORCEMENT - LAMINATE D IS TO RUN THE FULL LENGTH OF THE HULL FROM STEM HEAD TO TOP OF STERN - REINFORCEMENT TO BE 16" WIDE BETWEEN STA. 3 & STA. 8 - TAPER TO 6" WIDE AT ENDS.
4 DECK FLANGE - 4" CONSTANT WIDTH ALL AROUND - SLOPE TO MATCH DECK CAMBER. SEE SHEET 137-12 FOR DECK ATTACHMENT DETAIL.
5 BALLAST - 1600 POUNDS TOTAL - FILL AREA SHOWN WITH 1320 LBS. LEAD, & 280 LBS. CONCRETE - VIBRATE CONC. TO FILL VOIDS - GLASS OVER AFTER CURE.
6 FILL SOLID WITH CASTING RESIN & PHENOLIC MICROSPHERES.
7 RUDDER TUBE - 1" O.D. x 1/8" WALL FIBERGLASS WOUND TUBE - 2'-7" LONG.
8 MAST STEP - STEP SIMILAR TO THAT SHOWN ON SHEET 137-5. LAMINATE STEP MOLDING USING 2 - FABMAT - REINFORCE AS SHOWN WITH 1 1/2" FIR - GLASS TO SHELL & FILL VOID WITH CASTING RESIN & MICROSPHERES, (MORTICE DRAIN OPTIONAL)
9 BULKHEAD - 3/8" (10 MM) PLYWOOD BULKHEAD - NOTE THAT F-C VERSION DOES NOT HAVE THIS BULKH'D.
10 FILL WITH POUR-IN-PLACE URETHANE FOAM & GLASS OVER.
LAMINATE SCHEDULE
THICKNESS	LAY-UP "TYPE"	WT. OF DRY GLASS	COMPOSITION (A)	CHANGES
.21 in.	"A"	9.0 oz/FT²	6oz CLOTH + 2 FABMAT (B)	——
.31 in.	"B"	13.17oz/FT²	6oz CLOTH + 3 FABMAT	ADD 1 FABMAT TO "A"
.36 in.	"C"	15.84oz/FT²	6oz CLOTH + 3 FABMAT + 24 oz W.R.	ADD 1-24oz W.R. TO "B"
.42 in.	"D"	18.51oz/FT²	6oz CLOTH + 3 FABMAT + 2 - 24oz W.R.	ADD 1-24oz W.R. TO "C"
(A) COMPOSITIONS ARE LISTED FROM OUTSIDE (GEL COAT) TO INSIDE RESPECTIVELY.
(B) ONE (1) FABMAT CONSISTS OF 1 PLY 1 1/2oz MAT & 1 PLY 24oz. WOVEN ROVING.
DRY REINFORCEMENT WEIGHT
REINFORCEMENT	WT. PER SQ. FOOT
6 oz CLOTH	.67 oz / FT²
1 1/2 oz MAT	1.5 oz / FT²
24 oz WOVEN ROVING	2.67 oz / FT²
SEE SHEET 137-7 FOR RUDDER CONSTR'N DETAILS
BALLAST C.G.
4" CONSTANT
SEE SHEET 137-12 FOR HULL/DECK CONNECTION DETAILS
BALLAST
KEEL REINFORCEMENT DIMENSION (SEE NOTE 3)
SECTION THRU KEEL
NO SCALE
20' CATBOAT
FOR: HERITAGE BOAT CO.
DATE: 8-8-77
SCALE: 3/4" = 1'-0"
GRP CONSTR'N
LOA 20'-0"
LWL 18'-0"
BEAM 8'-0"
DRAFT 5'-6"
FREEBOARD:
FWD. 3'-7 1/4"
LEAST 2'-0"
AFT 2'-6"
JAY R. BENFORD
P.O. BOX 447
ST. MICHAELS, MD 21663
(410) 745-3235
137-11
PAO

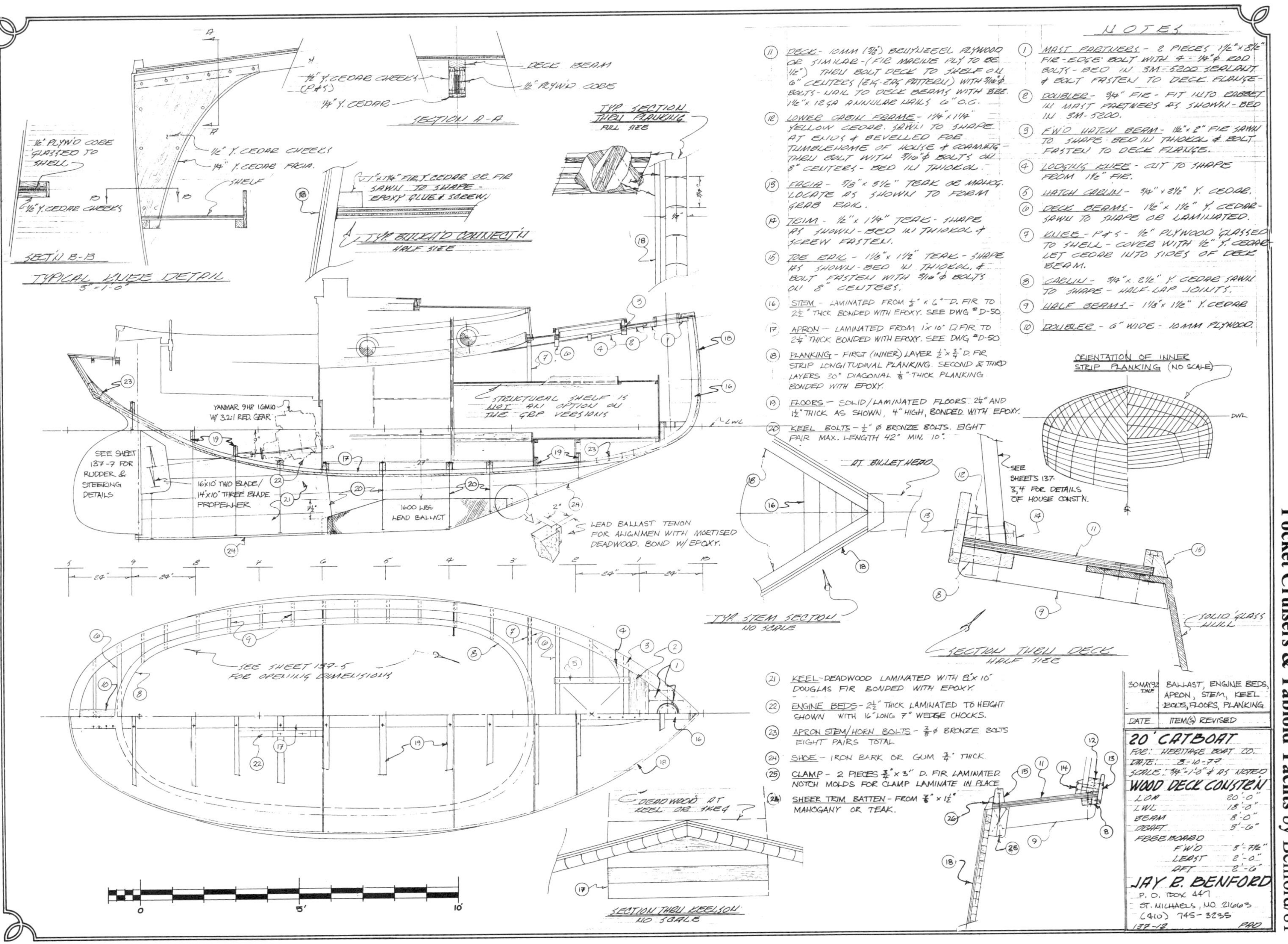
NOTES
(1) MAST PARTNERS - 2 PIECES 1½" x 8½" FIR-EDGE BOLT WITH 4 - ¼"ø ROD BOLTS - BED IN 3M-5200 SEALANT & BOLT FASTEN TO DECK FLANGE
(2) DOUBLER - ¾" FIR - FIT INTO RABBET IN MAST PARTNERS AS SHOWN - BED IN 3M-5200.
(3) FWD HATCH BEAM - 1½" x 2" FIR SAWN TO SHAPE - BED IN THIOKOL & BOLT FASTEN TO DECK FLANGE.
(4) LODGING KNEE - CUT TO SHAPE FROM 1½" FIR.
(5) HATCH CARLIN - ¾" x 2½" Y. CEDAR.
(6) DECK BEAMS - 1½" x 1½" Y. CEDAR - SAWN TO SHAPE OR LAMINATED.
(7) KNEE - P&S - ½" PLYWOOD GLASSED TO SHELL - COVER WITH ½" Y. CEDAR - LET CEDAR INTO SIDES OF DECK BEAM.
(8) CARLIN - ¾" x 2½" Y. CEDAR SAWN TO SHAPE - HALF-LAP JOINTS.
(9) HALF BEAMS - 1⅛" x 1½" Y. CEDAR
(10) DOUBLER - 6" WIDE - 10MM PLYWOOD.
(11) DECK - 10MM (⅜") BRUYNZEEL PLYWOOD OR SIMILAR - (FIR MARINE PLY TO BE ½") THRU BOLT DECK TO SHELF ON 6" CENTERS (ZIG-ZAG PATTERN) WITH 5/16"ø BOLTS - NAIL TO DECK BEAMS WITH BRZ. 1½" x 12GA ANNULAR NAILS 6" O.C.
(12) LOWER CABIN FRAME - 1¼" x 1¼" YELLOW CEDAR. SAWN TO SHAPE AT ENDS & BEVELLED FOR TUMBLEHOME OF HOUSE & COAMING - THRU BOLT WITH 5/16"ø BOLTS ON 8" CENTERS - BED IN THIOKOL.
(13) FACIA - 5/8" x 3½" TEAK OR MAHOG. LOCATE AS SHOWN TO FORM GRAB RAIL.
(14) TRIM - ½" x 1¼" TEAK - SHAPE AS SHOWN - BED IN THIOKOL & SCREW FASTEN.
(15) TOE RAIL - 1⅛" x 1½" TEAK - SHAPE AS SHOWN - BED IN THIOKOL & BOLT FASTEN WITH 5/16"ø BOLTS ON 8" CENTERS.
(16) STEM - LAMINATED FROM ½" x 6" D. FIR TO 2½" THICK BONDED WITH EPOXY. SEE DWG #D-50
(17) APRON - LAMINATED FROM 1x10" D. FIR TO 2¼" THICK BONDED WITH EPOXY. SEE DWG #D-50
(18) PLANKING - FIRST (INNER) LAYER ½" x ¾" D. FIR STRIP LONGITUDINAL PLANKING. SECOND & THIRD LAYERS 30° DIAGONAL ⅛" THICK PLANKING BONDED WITH EPOXY.
(19) FLOORS - SOLID/LAMINATED FLOORS 2¼" AND 1½" THICK AS SHOWN, 4" HIGH, BONDED WITH EPOXY.
(20) KEEL BOLTS - ½" ø BRONZE BOLTS. EIGHT PAIR MAX. LENGTH 42" MIN. 10".
(21) KEEL-DEADWOOD LAMINATED WITH 8" x 10" DOUGLAS FIR BONDED WITH EPOXY.
(22) ENGINE BEDS - 2½" THICK LAMINATED TO HEIGHT SHOWN WITH 16" LONG 7" WEDGE CHOCKS.
(23) APRON STEM/HORN BOLTS - ⅜"ø BRONZE BOLTS EIGHT PAIRS TOTAL
(24) SHOE - IRON BARK OR GUM ⅞" THICK.
(25) CLAMP - 2 PIECES ¾" x 3" D. FIR LAMINATED. NOTCH MOLDS FOR CLAMP LAMINATE IN PLACE
(26) SHEER TRIM BATTEN - FROM ⅞" x 1½" MAHOGANY OR TEAK.
ORIENTATION OF INNER STRIP PLANKING (NO SCALE)
DWL
DECK BEAM
½" PLYWD CORE
½" Y. CEDAR CHEEKS (P&S)
¼" Y. CEDAR
SECTION A-A
½" PLYWD CORE GLASSED TO SHELL
½" Y. CEDAR CHEEKS
½" Y. CEDAR CHEEKS
¼" Y. CEDAR FACIA.
SHELF
SECT'N B-B
TYPICAL KNEE DETAIL
3" = 1'-0"
1" x 1¼" FIR, Y. CEDAR OR FIR SAWN TO SHAPE - EPOXY GLUE & SCREW.
TYP. BULKHEAD CONNECT'N
HALF SIZE
TYP. SECTION THRU PLANKING
FULL SIZE
YANMAR 9HP 1GM10 W/ 3.2:1 RED. GEAR
STRUCTURAL SHELF IS NOT AN OPTION ON THE GRP VERSIONS
LWL
SEE SHEET 137-7 FOR RUDDER & STEERING DETAILS
16x10 TWO BLADE/ 14"x10" THREE BLADE PROPELLER
1600 LBS. LEAD BALLAST
LEAD BALLAST TENON FOR ALIGNMENT WITH MORTISED DEADWOOD. BOND W/ EPOXY.
AT BILLETHEAD
TYP. STEM SECTION
NO SCALE
SEE SHEETS 137-3, 4 FOR DETAILS OF HOUSE CONST'N.
SOLID GLASS HULL
SECTION THRU DECK
HALF SIZE
SEE SHEET 137-5 FOR OPENING DIMENSIONS
DEADWOOD AT KEEL OR KEG
SECTION THRU KEELSON
NO SCALE
0
5'
10'
30MAY92 T.W.F. BALLAST, ENGINE BEDS, APRON, STEM, KEEL BOLTS, FLOORS, PLANKING
DATE ITEM(S) REVISED
20' CATBOAT
FOR: HERITAGE BOAT CO.
DATE: 3-10-77
SCALE: ¾" = 1'-0" & AS NOTED
WOOD DECK CONSTR'N
LOA 20'-0"
LWL 18'-0"
BEAM 8'-0"
DRAFT 3'-6"
FREEBOARD
FWD 3'-7½"
LEAST 2'-0"
AFT 2'-6"
JAY R. BENFORD
P. O. BOX 447
ST. MICHAELS, MD 21663
(410) 745-3235
137-12 PRD

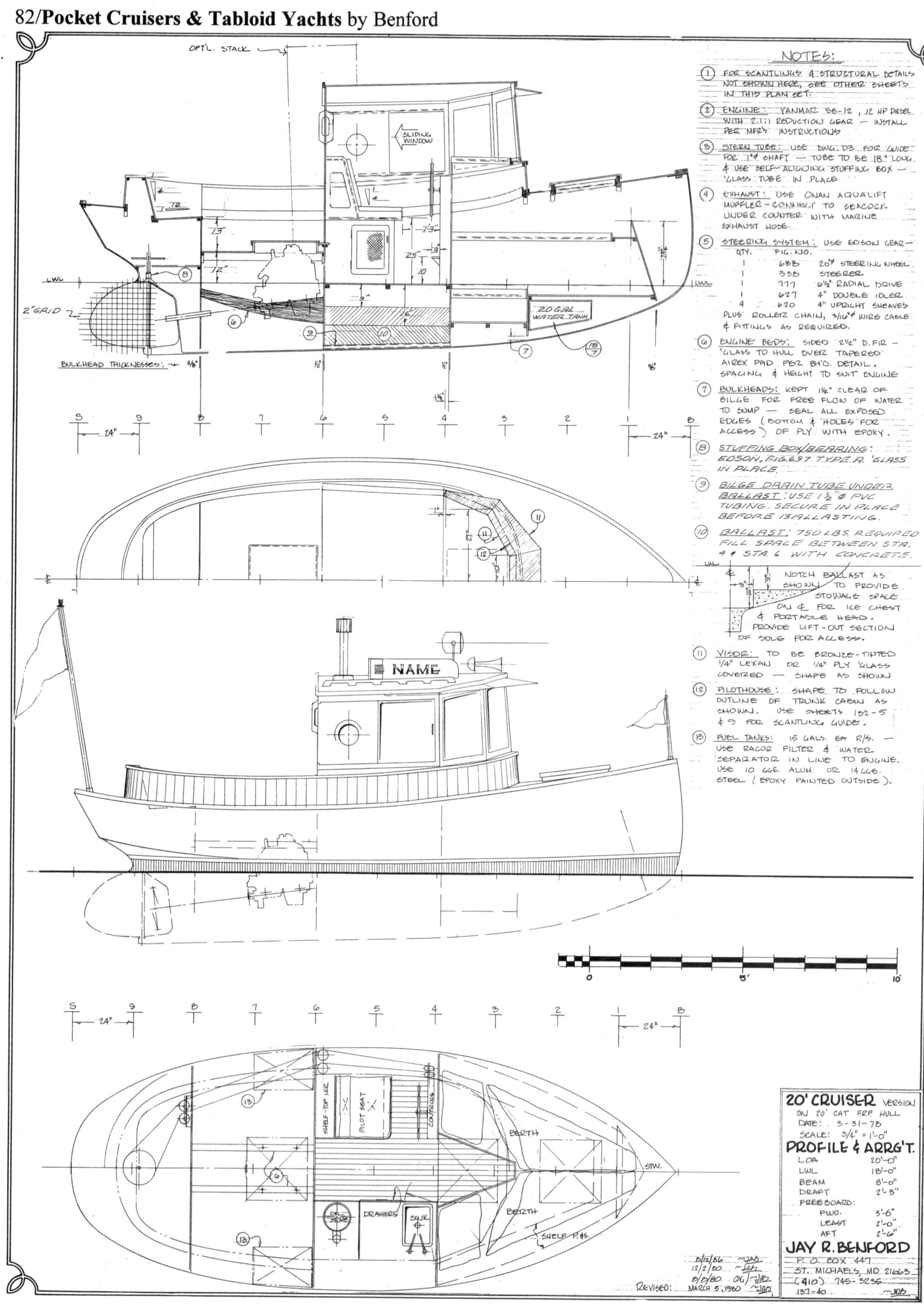

OPT'L. STACK
SLIDING WINDOW
LWL
2" GRID
20 GAL. WATER TANK
BULKHEAD THICKNESSES:
NOTES:
1 FOR SCANTLINGS & STRUCTURAL DETAILS NOT SHOWN HERE, SEE OTHER SHEETS IN THIS PLAN SET.
2 ENGINE: YANMAR SB-12, 12 HP DIESEL WITH 2.1:1 REDUCTION GEAR — INSTALL PER MFR'S. INSTRUCTIONS
3 STERN TUBE: USE DWG. D3 FOR GUIDE FOR 1"ø SHAFT — TUBE TO BE 18" LONG & USE SELF-ALIGNING STUFFING BOX — 'GLASS TUBE IN PLACE
4 EXHAUST: USE ONAN AQUALIFT MUFFLER — CONNECT TO SEACOCK UNDER COUNTER WITH MARINE EXHAUST HOSE.
5 STEERING SYSTEM: USE EDSON GEAR —
QTY. FIG. NO.
1 688 20"ø STEERING WHEEL
1 358 STEERER
1 777 6½" RADIAL DRIVE
1 627 4" DOUBLE IDLER
4 620 4" UPRIGHT SHEAVES
PLUS ROLLER CHAIN, 3/16"ø WIRE CABLE & FITTINGS AS REQUIRED.
6 ENGINE BEDS: SIDED 2½" D. FIR — 'GLASS TO HULL OVER TAPERED AIREX PAD PER BH'D. DETAIL. SPACING & HEIGHT TO SUIT ENGINE
7 BULKHEADS: KEPT 1½" CLEAR OF BILGE FOR FREE FLOW OF WATER TO SUMP — SEAL ALL EXPOSED EDGES (BOTTOM & HOLES FOR ACCESS) OF PLY WITH EPOXY.
8 STUFFING BOX/BEARING: EDSON, FIG. 697 TYPE A. 'GLASS IN PLACE.
9 BILGE DRAIN TUBE UNDER BALLAST: USE 1½"ø PVC TUBING. SECURE IN PLACE BEFORE BALLASTING.
10 BALLAST: 750 LBS. REQUIRED FILL SPACE BETWEEN STA. 4 & STA. 6 WITH CONCRETE.
NOTCH BALLAST AS SHOWN TO PROVIDE STOWAGE SPACE ON ℄ FOR ICE CHEST & PORTABLE HEAD. PROVIDE LIFT-OUT SECTION OF SOLE FOR ACCESS.
11 VISOR: TO BE BRONZE-TINTED 1/4" LEXAN OR 1/4" PLY 'GLASS COVERED — SHAPE AS SHOWN
12 PILOTHOUSE: SHAPE TO FOLLOW OUTLINE OF TRUNK CABIN AS SHOWN. USE SHEETS 132-5 & 9 FOR SCANTLING GUIDE.
13 FUEL TANKS: 15 GALS. EA. P/S. — USE RACOR FILTER & WATER SEPARATOR IN LINE TO ENGINE. USE 10 GGE. ALUM. OR 14 GGE. STEEL (EPOXY PAINTED OUTSIDE).
NAME
0 5' 10'
SHELF-TOP LKR.
PILOT SEAT
CONTROLS
BERTH
STW.
STOVE
DRAWERS
SINK
SHELF P. & S.
20' CRUISER VERSION ON 20' CAT FRP HULL
DATE: 3-31-78
SCALE: 3/4" = 1'-0"
PROFILE & ARRG'T.
LOA 20'-0"
LWL 18'-0"
BEAM 8'-0"
DRAFT 2'-3"
FREEBOARD:
FWD. 3'-6"
LEAST 2'-0"
AFT 2'-6"
JAY R. BENFORD
P. O. BOX 447
ST. MICHAELS, MD 21663
(410) 745-3235
137-40
REVISED: MARCH 5, 1980

Chapter Six

25' Fantail Steam Launch *Beverley*

Design Number 131
1975

This design was originally started for a couple of different clients before we had someone come along who actually went ahead and built her. She was so nice that I kept pulling out the drawings to show to prospective builders, and I was pleased to eventually see there were a number of plans sold for her.

She's a launch only slightly smaller than the one made famous as the **African Queen.** This one has some extra touches that lend an air of greater elegance. These range from the graceful fantail stern to the elliptical coaming and the fringed canopy overhead.

There is plenty of seating for day cruises, with storage under the end decks and under the seats.

A modified version has been built as a diesel launch with a 23' 6" waterline and 2' 0" draft. Her construction was cold-molded over strip-planking. Both versions are shown on the drawings in this chapter.

We'd originally thought of doing her as an Airex® cored fiberglass hull, and she would be suitable for this and other one-off 'glass techniques.

Shortly before this book was completed, we received the following kind letter with a number of lovely photos enclosed:

"Dear Mr. Benford,

"What do the **African Queen** *and the Benford Design 25' steam launch have in common? A double acting compound steam engine! Both engines were made by the same company, Langley Engineering in Sussex, England.*

"On launching day January 25, 1992, several reporters attended. One wrote up the launching in the **Newport Pilot** *newspaper, and the other, from what I hear, will have an article in the next issue of* **WoodenBoat**. *She is the only operating steam launch on Balboa Bay and Newport Harbor, and, as you can imagine, she attracts a lot of attention.*

"She was built of laminated wood construction by MacMillan Yachts in Suffolk, England. Her bottom is fiberglass. She has teak decks and

Honduran mahogany trim.

"The propeller is 22" in diameter and has a 36" pitch. The engine turns 400 to 500 RPMs. The engine is from 15 to 19 horsepower. The boiler is of a fire tube type, with 87 square feet of surface area.

"It took about three years to complete the boat and engine. Actually, the boat took only about six months, but construction of the steam engine took a long period of time because of interruptions and the financial conditions of the builder.

"The boat is fast, very comfortable, and is enjoyable to be aboard. Her graceful lines remind one of a beauty contestant and one's eyes are drawn to her.

"She uses either wood or coal for fuel and has a Windermere teakettle, which will boil in about seven seconds with steam heating. I believe she will do over 8 knots. I am very pleased with the boat. It will be an honor to have the steam launch, which is named **Beverley**, mentioned in your publication.

"Sincerely,
"Carl B. Ziesmer, M.D."

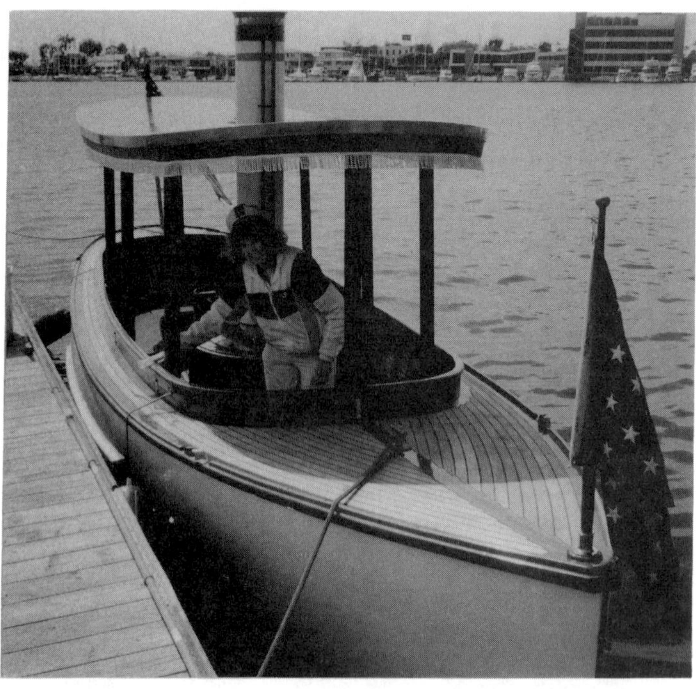

Some of his photos are on the cover of this book and some follow on this and the next page:

Particulars:		**English**	**Metric**
Length overall		25'-0"	7.62 m
Length waterline		22'-6"	6.86 m
Beam		7'-0"	2.13 m
Draft		3'-3"	0.99 m
Freeboard:	Forward	3'-0"	0.91 m
	Least	1'-6"	0.46 m
	Aft	2'-0"	0.61 m
Displacement, cruising trim		5,585 lbs.	2,533 kg
Displacement-length ratio		219	
Prismatic coefficient		.593	
Pounds per inch immersion		528	239 kg/cm
Entrance half-angle		21°	

***CAUTION:** The displacement quoted here is for the boat in cruising trim. That is, with the fuel and water tanks filled, the crew on board, as well as the crews' gear and stores in the lockers. This should not be confused with the "shipping weight" often quoted as "displacement" by some manufacturers. This should be taken into account when comparing figures and ratios between this and other designs.

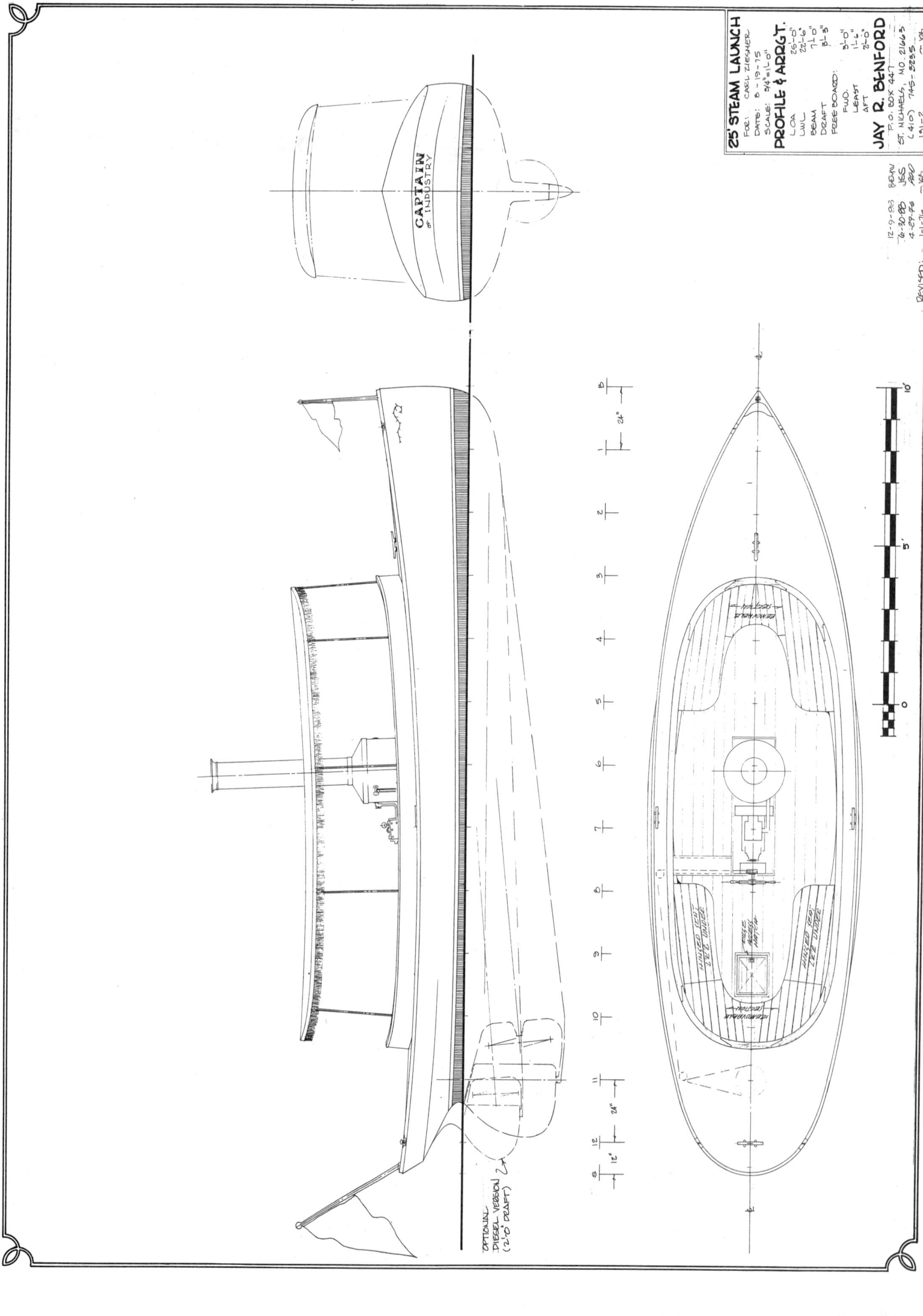

CAPTAIN OF INDUSTRY

OPTIONAL DIESEL VERSION (2'-0" DRAFT)

S 12 11 10 9 8 7 6 5 4 3 2 1 B

12" 24" 24"

HINGED SEAT, L'KR UNDER

REMOVABLE SECTION

BILGE ACCESS HATCH

REMOVABLE SECTION

HINGED SEAT, L'KR UNDER

0 5' 10'

25' STEAM LAUNCH

FOR: CARL ZIESMER

DATE: 8-19-75

SCALE: 3/4"=1'-0"

PROFILE & ARRG'T.

LOA	25'-0"
LWL	22'-6"
BEAM	7'-0"
DRAFT	3'-3"
FREEBOARD:	
FWD.	3'-0"
LEAST	1'-6"
AFT	2'-0"

JAY R. BENFORD

P.O. BOX 447

ST. MICHAELS, MD. 21663

(410) 745-3235

131-2

REVISED:	
12-9-93	BEMV
6-30-88	JSS
4-29-76	RDD
1-1-76	JRB

STATIONS	12	11	10	9	8	7	6	5	4	3	2	1
	HEIGHTS											
℄ TO KEEL	—	0-10-0	0-9-0	←		STRAIGHT				→	2-9-4	3-0-4
" " FAIRBODY	5-0-2	(4-0-0) 5-9-4	3-2-7	2-9-7	2-8-0	2-8-0	2-8-0	2-8-0	2-8-1	2-8-5	2-10-0	3-0-6
" " B1	5-2-3	4-4-0	3-7-1	3-1-5	2-11-3	2-10-5	2-10-6	2-11-3	3-0-3	3-2-4	3-8-0	6-5-2
" " B2	—	5-0-1	4-2-0	3-7-1	3-3-5	3-2-4	3-2-6	3-3-7	3-7-5	4-10-2	—	—
LWL TO BOOTTOP	(0-6-2)	0-5-5	0-5-1	0-4-5	0-4-3	0-4-2	0-4-2	0-4-3	0-4-6	0-5-2	0-5-7	0-6-6
" " KNUCKLE	1-5-1	1-0-6	0-11-2	0-10-3	—	—	—	—	—	—	—	—
" " SHEER	1-10-5	1-8-5	1-7-3	1-6-3	1-6-0	1-6-2	1-6-7	1-8-3	1-10-3	2-1-1	2-4-3	2-8-0
	HALF-BREADTHS											
℄ TO KEEL ½ SIDING	—	—	0-0-2	0-1-6	0-2-5	0-3-1	0-3-1	0-2-5	0-2-0	0-1-2	0-0-2	—
" " 40" WL	—	—	0-3-6	1-9-5	2-5-1	2-7-6	2-7-2	2-4-2	1-11-1	1-4-4	0-10-0	0-3-4
" " 48" WL	—	0-1-7	2-1-1	2-10-6	3-3-2	3-4-5	3-3-5	3-0-2	2-7-1	2-0-2	1-4-6	0-8-[illegible]
" " 56" WL	—	1-11-0	2-9-1	3-2-5	3-4-7	3-5-6	3-5-6	3-3-6	2-10-1	2-3-3	1-7-3	0-10-2
" " KNUCKLE	1-4-1	2-4-5	2-10-3	3-2-1	—	—	—	—	—	—	—	—
" " SHEER	1-9-2	2-6-2	2-11-2	3-2-1	3-3-6	3-4-2	3-4-1	3-2-6	3-0-2	2-7-5	2-0-2	1-2-5

NOTES:

1. OFFSETS TO OUTSIDE OF SHELL IN FEET-INCHES-EIGHTHS — DEDUCT FOR MOLDS AS DIRECTED.
2. LINES MUST BE LOFTED & FAIRED FULL SIZE — DO NOT SCALE PRINTS.
3. BOOTTOP OFFSETS ARE TO TOP EDGE OF STRIPE — STRIPE IS 1½" HIGH IN PROFILE.
4. ANY ALTERATION FROM THESE PLANS RELIEVES THE DESIGNER FROM RESPONSIBILITY.
5. IT IS UNDERSTOOD THAT NO MORE THAN ONE BOAT WILL BE BUILT FROM THESE PLANS WITHOUT WRITTEN PERMISSION FROM THE DESIGNER.
6. THESE PLANS ARE THE PROPERTY OF JAY R. BENFORD & ASSOC., INC., & MAY BE USED ONLY AS AUTHORIZED BY THEM.

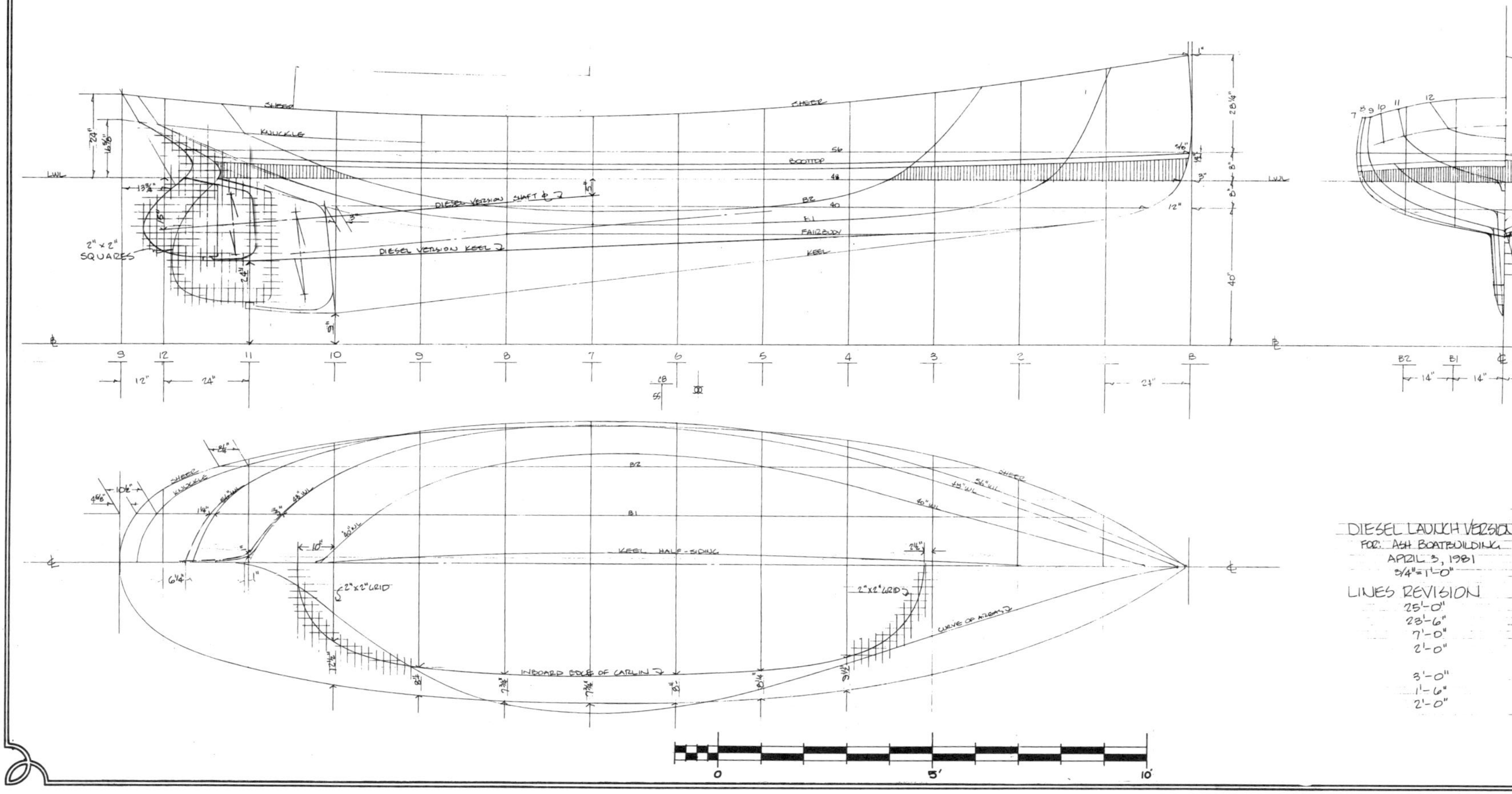

DIESEL LAUNCH VERSION
FOR: ASH BOATBUILDING
APRIL 3, 1981
3/4" = 1'-0"

LINES REVISION
25'-0"
23'-6"
7'-0"
2'-0"

3'-0"
1'-6"
2'-0"

REV.	DATE	ITEM(S) REVISED
C	4-29-91	ADD'L DIESEL VERS. DETAILS
B	4-3-81	DIESEL VERSION
A	12-30-75	MISC.

25' STEAM LAUNCH
FOR: CARL ZIESMER
DATE: 8-19-75
SCALE: 3/4" = 1'-0"

LINES & OFFSETS

LOA	25'-0"
LWL	22'-6"
BEAM	7'-0"
DRAFT	5'-3"
FREEBOARD:	
FWD. -	3'-0"
LEAST	1'-6"
AFT	2'-0"

JAY R. BENFORD
P.O. BOX 447
ST. MICHAELS, MD 21663
(410) 745-3235
131-1 ~JRB

NOTES:

1. INNER PLANKING: 1/2" x 3/4" RED CEDAR MILLED TO SHAPE SHOWN — GLUE AND EDGE NAIL —
2. OUTER PLANKING: DOUBLE DIAGONAL 1/8" VERTICAL GRAIN RED CEDAR — ORIENT INNER LAYER 30° AFT & OUTER LAYER 30° FWD — EPOXY GLUE ALL PLANKING SURFACES —
3. KEEL & DEADWOOD: 1 1/2" D. FIR SHAPED TO SUIT —
4. APRON: 1 1/2" x 7 1/2" D. FIR —
5. SOLE: 5/8" MARINE PLY OR 5/8" TEAK OR H. MAHOGANY —
6. CLAMP: TWO PIECES 3/4" x 2 1/2" D. FIR —
7. DECK BEAM: 1" x 1 1/2" D. FIR —
8. FACIA: 1/2" x 3" TEAK OR H. MAHOGANY
9. SILL: 1" x 1" D. FIR —
10. CLEAT: 3/4" x 3/4" D. FIR —
11. CAP RAIL: SHAPE TO SUIT FROM 1" x 2 1/2" TEAK OR H. MAHOGANY —
12. COAMING: TWO LAYERS 1/4" MARINE PLY, GLUED & FASTENED TOGETHER —
13. TOE RAIL: 1 1/4" x 1 1/2" TEAK OR H. MAHOGANY —
14. TRIM: 1/2" x 1 1/2" TEAK OR H. MAHOGANY —
15. FLOOR: 1/4" MARINE PLY W/ 3/4" x 3/4" D. FIR FRAME —
16. SEAT FLAT: 5/8" MARINE PLY OR 5/8" TEAK OR H. MAHOGANY —
17. CLEAT: 1" x 1" D. FIR —
18. FRAME: 1 1/2" x 2 1/2" D. FIR —
19. LEG: 1" x 1" OR 1" Ø TEAK OR H. MAHOGANY — MAY BE TURNED TO SUIT — LAND SECURELY ON FLOORS —
20. CARLIN: 1/2" x 1 1/2" D. FIR — NOTCH INTO DECK BEAMS —

0 5' 10'

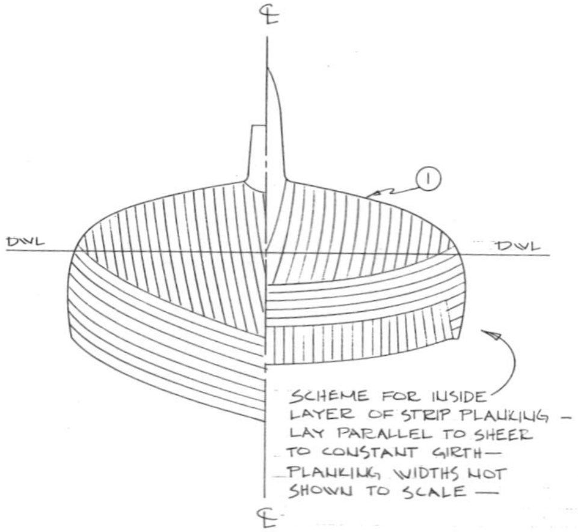

DWL

SCHEME FOR INSIDE LAYER OF STRIP PLANKING — LAY PARALLEL TO SHEER TO CONSTANT GIRTH — PLANKING WIDTHS NOT SHOWN TO SCALE —

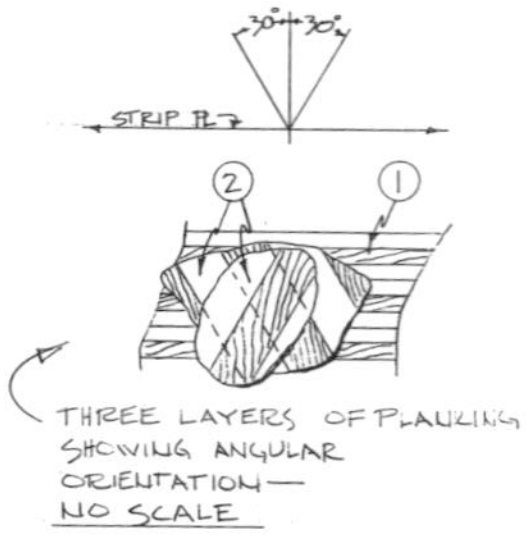

30° 30°
STRIP PL.

THREE LAYERS OF PLANKING SHOWING ANGULAR ORIENTATION — NO SCALE

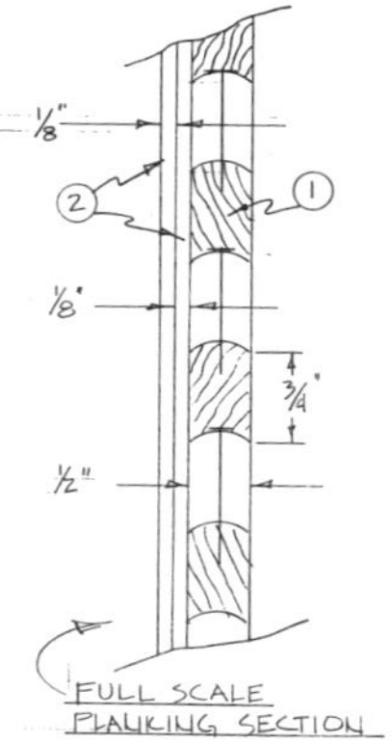

1/8"
1/8"
3/4"
1/2"

FULL SCALE PLANKING SECTION

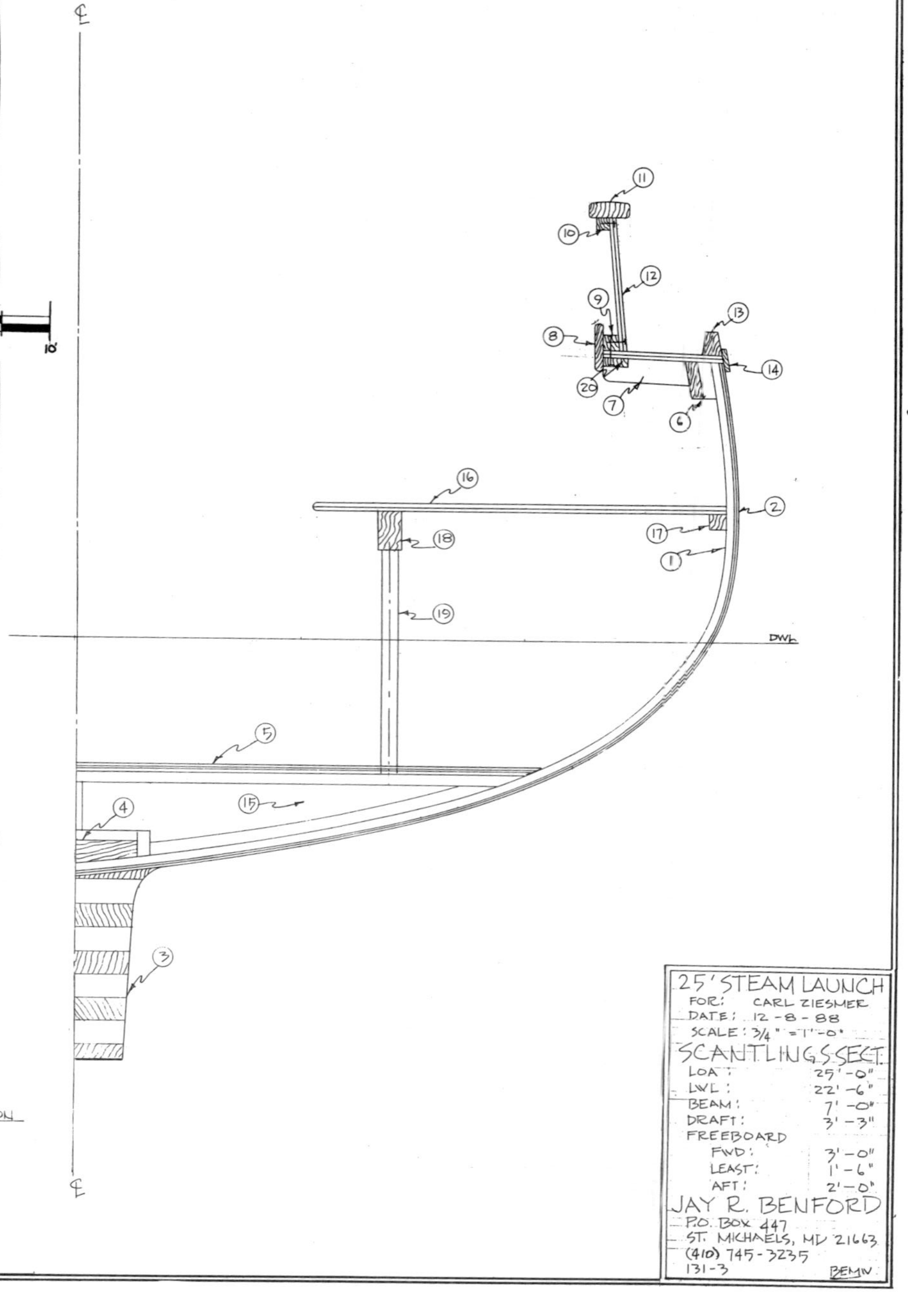

25' STEAM LAUNCH
FOR: CARL ZIESMER
DATE: 12-8-88
SCALE: 3/4" = 1'-0"

SCANTLINGS SECT.

LOA:	25'-0"
LWL:	22'-6"
BEAM:	7'-0"
DRAFT:	3'-3"
FREEBOARD	
FWD:	3'-0"
LEAST:	1'-6"
AFT:	2'-0"

JAY R. BENFORD
P.O. Box 447
ST. MICHAELS, MD 21663
(410) 745-3235
131-3
BEMN

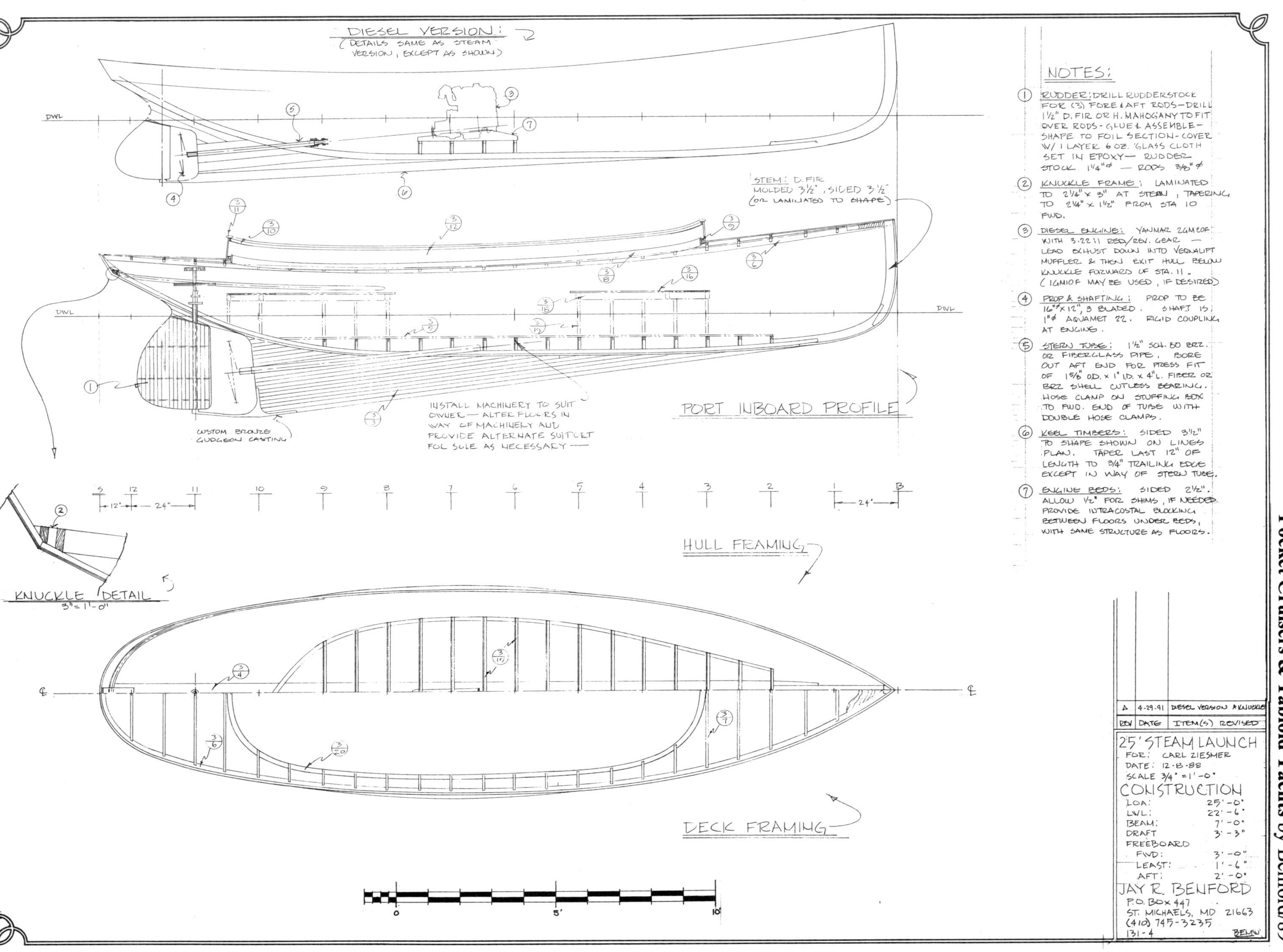

DIESEL VERSION:
(DETAILS SAME AS STEAM VERSION, EXCEPT AS SHOWN)
DWL
STEM: D. FIR
MOLDED 3½", SIDED 3½"
(OR LAMINATED TO SHAPE)
CUSTOM BRONZE GUDGEON CASTING
INSTALL MACHINERY TO SUIT OWNER — ALTER FLOORS IN WAY OF MACHINERY AND PROVIDE ALTERNATE SUPPORT FOR SOLE AS NECESSARY —
PORT INBOARD PROFILE
HULL FRAMING
KNUCKLE DETAIL
3" = 1'-0"
DECK FRAMING
NOTES:
① RUDDER: DRILL RUDDERSTOCK FOR (3) FORE & AFT RODS — DRILL 1½" D. FIR OR H. MAHOGANY TO FIT OVER RODS - GLUE & ASSEMBLE - SHAPE TO FOIL SECTION - COVER W/ 1 LAYER 6 OZ. GLASS CLOTH SET IN EPOXY — RUDDER STOCK 1¼"⌀ — RODS ⅜"⌀
② KNUCKLE FRAME: LAMINATED TO 2¼" x 3" AT STERN, TAPERING TO 2¼" x 1½" FROM STA 10 FWD.
③ DIESEL ENGINE: YANMAR 2GM20F WITH 3.22:1 RED/REV. GEAR — LEAD EXHAUST DOWN INTO VERNALIFT MUFFLER & THEN EXIT HULL BELOW KNUCKLE FORWARD OF STA. 11. (1GM10F MAY BE USED, IF DESIRED)
④ PROP & SHAFTING: PROP TO BE 16"x12", 3 BLADED. SHAFT IS 1"⌀ AQUAMET 22. RIGID COUPLING AT ENGINE.
⑤ STERN TUBE: 1½" SCH. 80 BRZ. OR FIBERGLASS PIPE. BORE OUT AFT END FOR PRESS FIT OF 1⅝" O.D. x 1" I.D. x 4" L. FIBER OR BRZ SHELL CUTLESS BEARING. HOSE CLAMP ON STUFFING BOX TO FWD. END OF TUBE WITH DOUBLE HOSE CLAMPS.
⑥ KEEL TIMBERS: SIDED 3½" TO SHAPE SHOWN ON LINES PLAN. TAPER LAST 12" OF LENGTH TO ¾" TRAILING EDGE EXCEPT IN WAY OF STERN TUBE.
⑦ ENGINE BEDS: SIDED 2½". ALLOW ½" FOR SHIMS, IF NEEDED. PROVIDE INTRACOSTAL BLOCKING BETWEEN FLOORS UNDER BEDS, WITH SAME STRUCTURE AS FLOORS.
A | 4-29-91 | DIESEL VERSION & KNUCKLE
REV | DATE | ITEM(S) REVISED
25' STEAM LAUNCH
FOR: CARL ZIESMER
DATE: 12-8-88
SCALE ¾" = 1'-0"
CONSTRUCTION
LOA: 25'-0"
LWL: 22'-6"
BEAM: 7'-0"
DRAFT 3'-3"
FREEBOARD
FWD: 3'-0"
LEAST: 1'-6"
AFT: 2'-0"
JAY R. BENFORD
P.O. BOX 447
ST. MICHAELS, MD 21663
(410) 745-3235
131-4

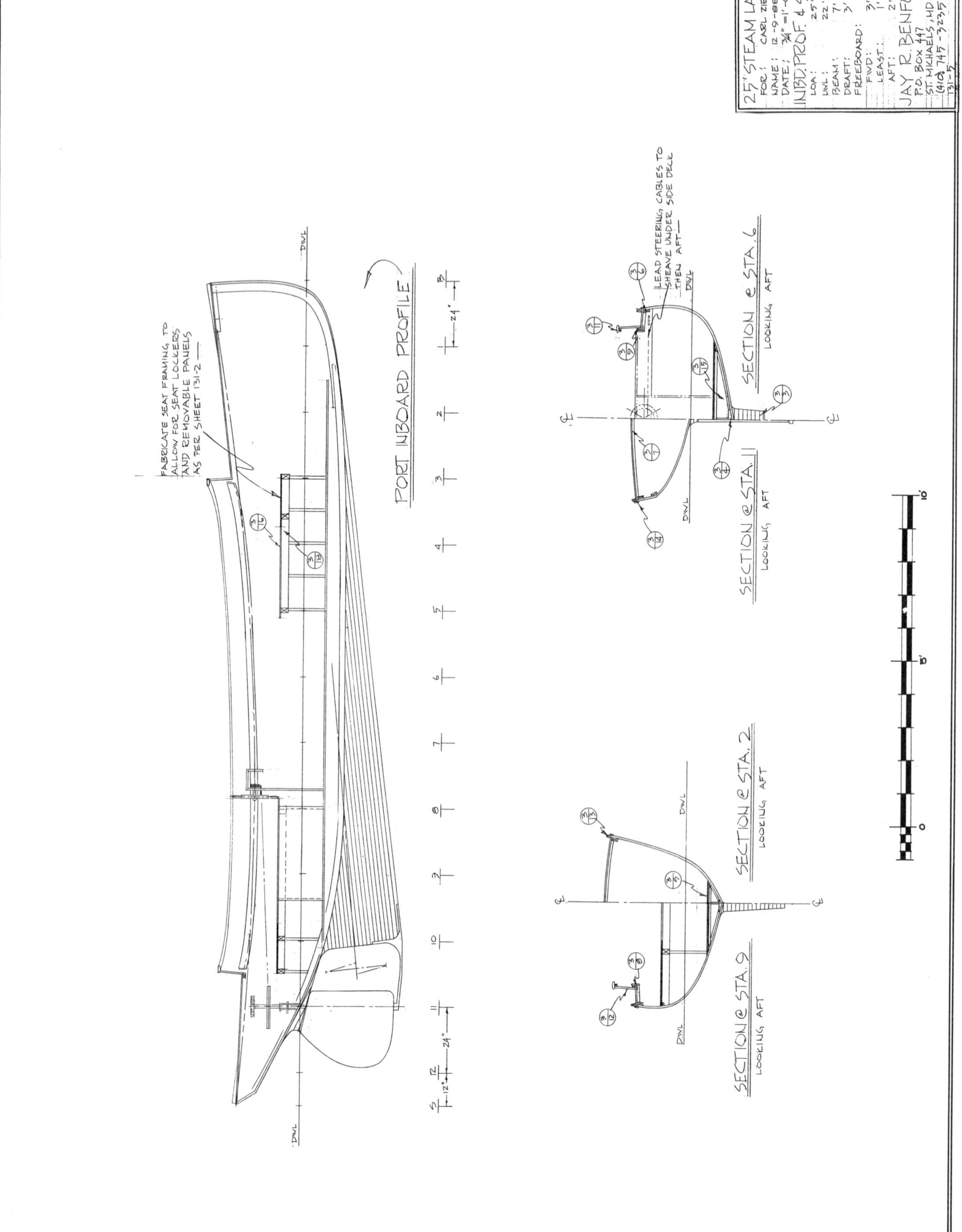
FABRICATE SEAT FRAMING TO ALLOW FOR SEAT LOCKERS AND REMOVABLE PANELS AS PER SHEET 131-2
DWL
PORT INBOARD PROFILE
24"
12"
SECTION @ STA. 9
LOOKING AFT
SECTION @ STA. 2
LOOKING AFT
SECTION @ STA. 11
LOOKING AFT
SECTION @ STA. 6
LOOKING AFT
LEAD STEERING CABLES TO SHEAVE UNDER SIDE DECK THEN AFT
0
5'
10'
25' STEAM LAUNCH
FOR: CARL ZIESMER
NAME: 12-9-88
DATE: 3/4" = 1'-0"
INBD. PROF. & SECTS.
LOA: 25'-0"
LWL: 22'-6"
BEAM: 7'-0"
DRAFT: 3'-3"
FREEBOARD:
FWD: 3'-0"
LEAST: 1'-6"
AFT: 2'-0"
JAY R. BENFORD
P.O. BOX 447
ST. MICHAELS, MD 21663
(410) 745-3235
131-5
BENN

Do You Liveaboard? *Do You* **Want** *To?...*

Ever found yourself out on the water, just wishing you could keep on cruising? What feeling do you have when you leave your boat behind after a pleasant weekend cruise? Have you been thinking that here is ***Something More*** to life?

The Benford Design Group is committed to the advancement of the Liveaboard Yacht. We find this lifestyle to be both challenging and fulfilling, wholly satisfying those wishes for a simpler life.

We can help you in your search. **Small Ships** covers the spectrum of Liveaboard power designs. And these designs are enchanting - having a rare blend of grace and purpose. But we're not done yet! Our current projects continue our thirty-four year history of bringing dreams to life.

Take the 35' Packet (above right) for example. This Small Ship has just what you need for living in comfort, for a long time - like air conditioning, a washer and dryer, and porches. There's room to walk about and room to cook great meals. Room to store your clothes and room to fly a kite. Room for you ***and*** your friends. On this boat the rooms ***are rooms*** - more generous than anything now in production - so it's easy to sprawl out and get comfortable. But even with this unparalleled space and comfort, she's every bit a **boat**, having been conceived as a strong and practical vessel, born to the water.

As is her cousin, our delightful 65' Fantail Motoryacht (below). Equipped for extended cruising and with luxurious accommodations, this ship could be your ***castle***. She has the spirit of an elegant old Trumpy in a new and easily maintainable form. Our modern design and engineering once again give life to these beautiful ships.

So if ***your*** dream combines "man-sized" comfort with solid naval architecture, come and see what we have. Look at the boats we've done. Imagine yourself on board. Think what life on board would be like. We know **you'll feel right at home!**

For more information on these and scores of other liveaboard designs from the Benford Design group, read our **Small Ships** book. Call 1-800-6Tiller with your Visa or Mastercard to order today.

Home is where the chart is....™

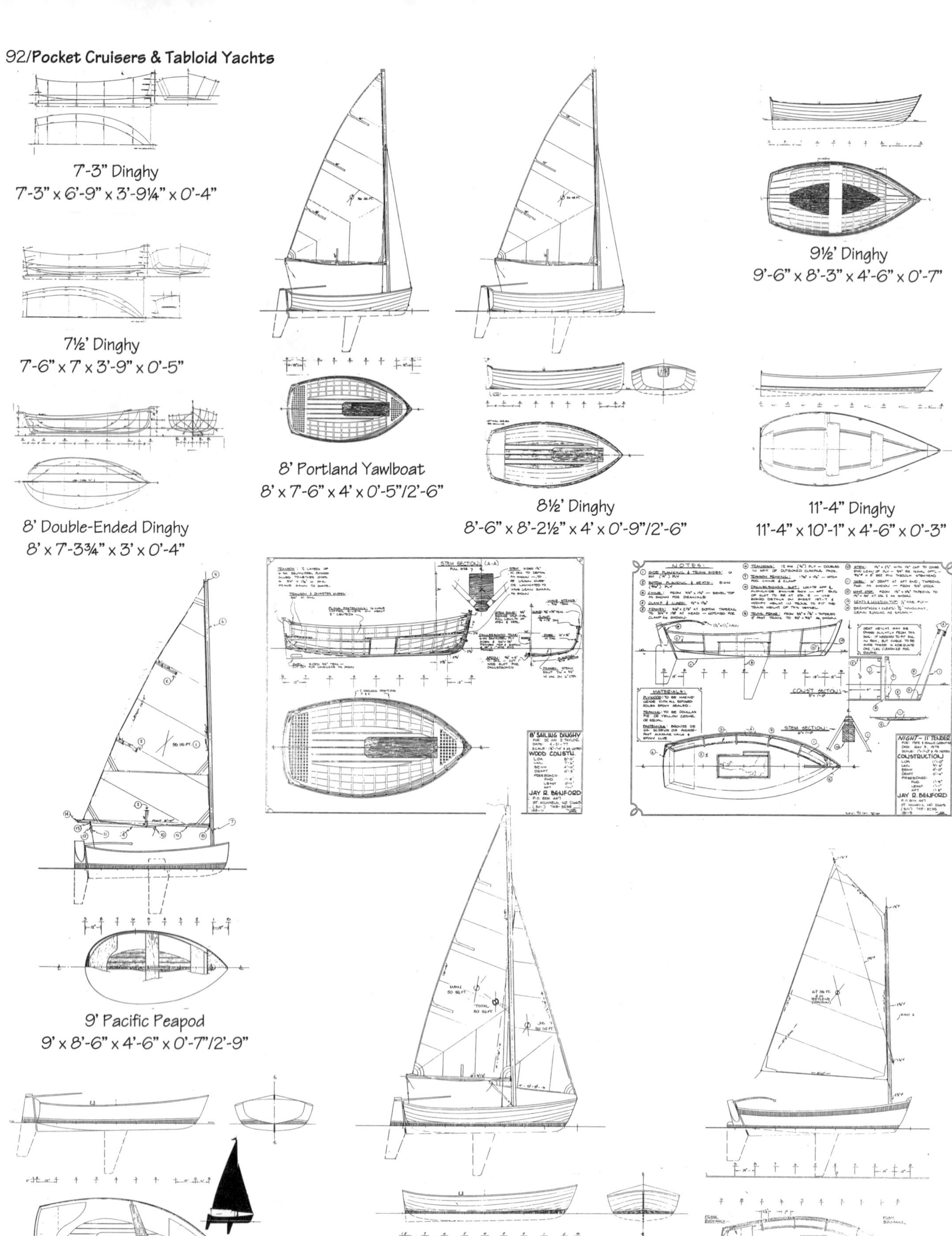

7'-3" Dinghy
7'-3" x 6'-9" x 3'-9¼" x 0'-4"

7½' Dinghy
7'-6" x 7' x 3'-9" x 0'-5"

8' Double-Ended Dinghy
8' x 7'-3¾" x 3' x 0'-4"

8' Portland Yawlboat
8' x 7'-6" x 4' x 0'-5"/2'-6"

8½' Dinghy
8'-6" x 8'-2½" x 4' x 0'-9"/2'-6"

9½' Dinghy
9'-6" x 8'-3" x 4'-6" x 0'-7"

11'-4" Dinghy
11'-4" x 10'-1" x 4'-6" x 0'-3"

9' Pacific Peapod
9' x 8'-6" x 4'-6" x 0'-7"/2'-9"

11' Dinghy
11' x 10' x 5' x0'-6"/3'

11' Oregon Peapod
11' x 10' x 4'-6" x 0'-6"/3'

11' Dinghy **Night**
11' x 9'-6" x 4' 0'-6"/2'-11"

Small Craft Plans

"Let's get it straight up front: This book is more than a catalog of designs. The 96 pages between its covers contain plans for 15 small craft. Designer Jay Benford knows that readers will build directly from the book — bypassing the formality of ordering plans from his office. In fact he encourages the process by including full working drawings and tables of offsets for all of the designs." **WoodenBoat**

The 15 sets of complete plans for skiffs & tenders from the Boards of the Benford Design Group (as shown on these two pages) will help you build your own dinghy, small craft, or tender. Plans for 7'-3" to 18-footers in cold-molded, carvel, lapstrake, plywood, and fiberglass construction are included, along with photos of some completed boats. 96 pages, softcover.

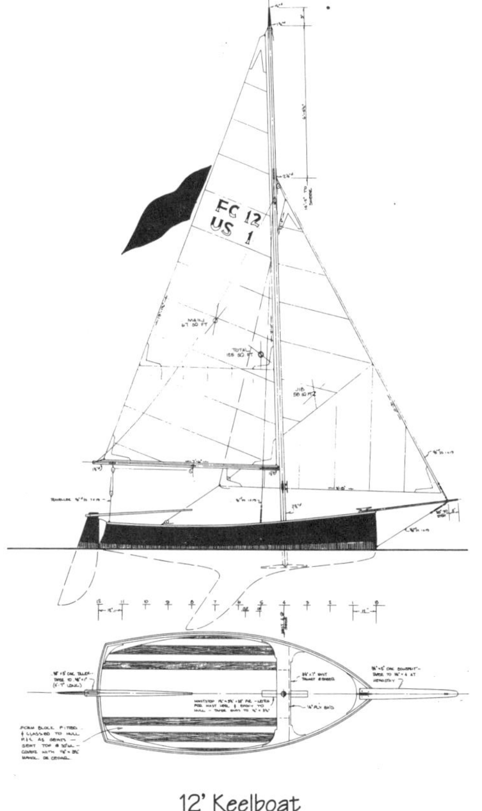

12' Keelboat
12' x 12' x 5' x 3'-4½"

To order this book of plans with your Visa or Mastercard, call our toll-free order line:

1-800-6Tiller.

For a brochure with prices for plans and books, write to us at:

Box 447
St. Michaels, MD 21663

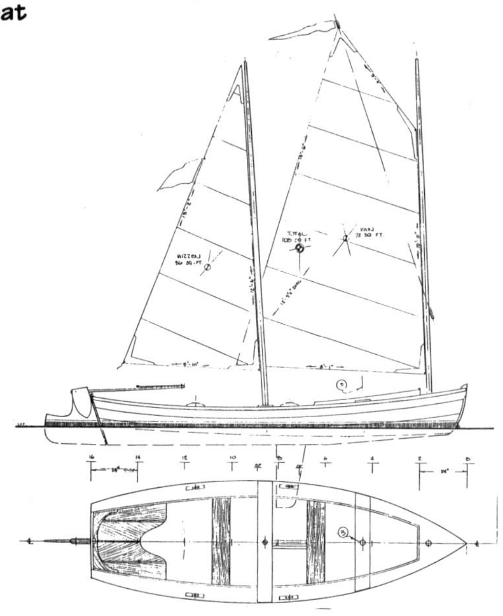

16' *Conch Ad Libitum*
16' x 15' x 5' x 0'-9"/3'-3"

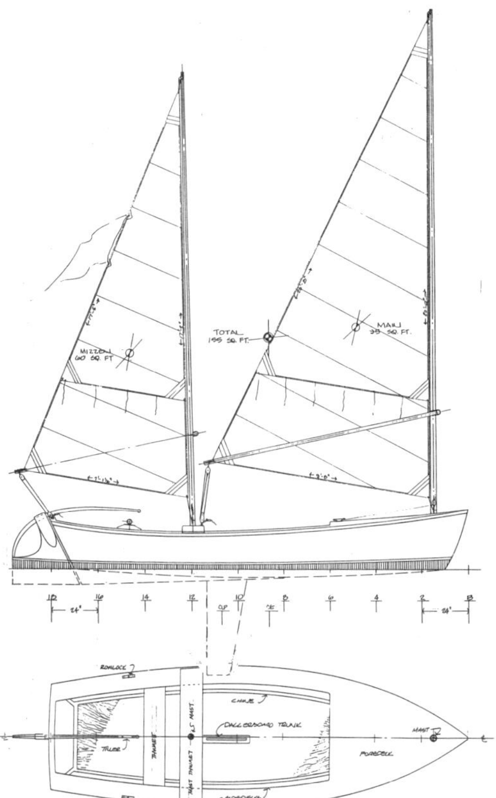

18' Cat Ketch
18' x 16' x 6' x 0'-8"/4'-6"

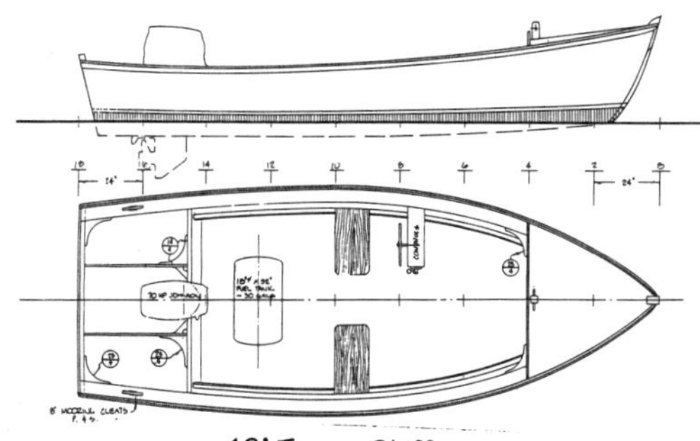

18' Texas Skiff
18' x 16' x 6'-8½" x 0'-5"

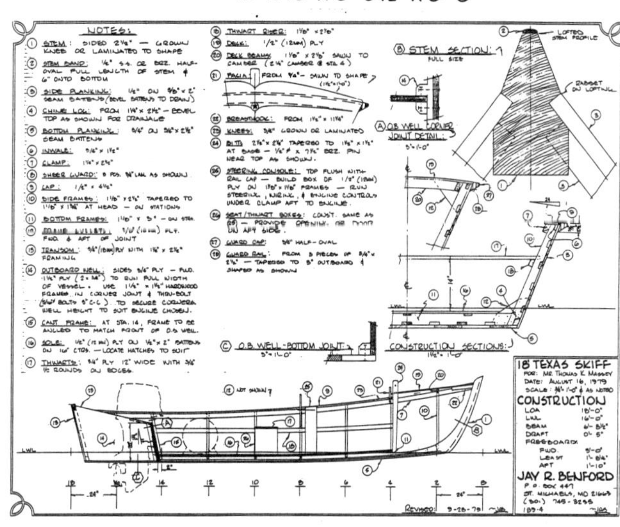

TRUMPY

BY ROBERT TOLF
ILLUSTRATED BY ROBERT PICARDAT

Trumpy celebrates the master craftsmanship and design represented by the renowned Trumpy yachts. In this book, author Robert Tolf traces the Trumpy family from its origins in Switzerland, through Norway and Italy and emigration to the United States. Both as an owner of Mathis Yacht Building Co. and at John Trumpy & Sons, Inc., John Trumpy earned his place in yachting history by creating elegant and well-built yachts of enduring beauty. Trumpy built fine motoryachts, classic houseboats, some boats for the U.S. Government and some sailing vessels. ***Trumpy*** is richly illustrated by marine artist Robert Picardat. His many color illustrations and pen & ink sketches bring the boats to life. Included are some original Trumpy plans, a complete list of all Trumpy yachts built and those known to survive. 11"x8fi", hardcover, 224 pgs, 32 color illus.

"To honor the Trumpy legacy, Tiller Publishing of St. Michaels, MD, has produced its own masterpiece. . . . (Buy two books and cut one up for framing!)"

Chesapeake Bay Magazine

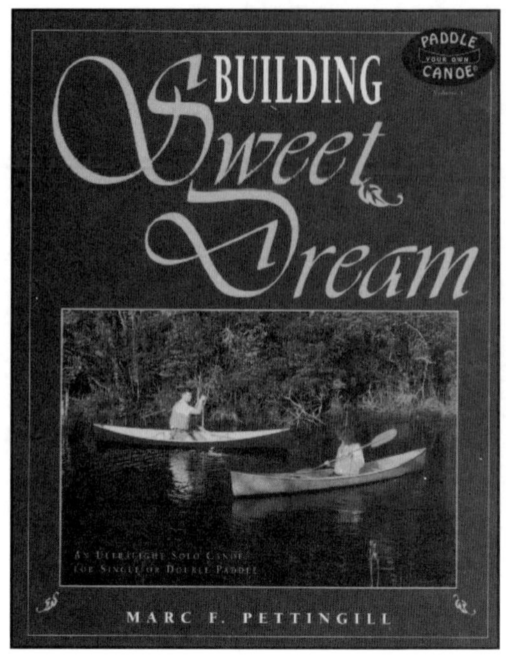

BUILDING SWEET DREAM

AN ULTRALIGHT SOLO CANOE FOR SINGLE AND DOUBLE PADDLE

BY MARC PETTINGILL

Sweet Dream combines an ancient canoe form with contemporary materials and building techniques to create a delightfully light and responsive solo canoe for today's wooden canoe builders and paddlers. ***Building Sweet Dream*** is a complete how-to manual covering all phases of building and finishing. It includes dimensioned hull plans, detailed building sequence heavily illustrated with step-by-step photographs, tips and techniques for painting and varnishing, and hard-to-find background and reference material. ***Sweet Dream*** is easily and quickly built using hand and basic electric tools, by one person in a one-car garage or small workshop. Using "folded plywood" techniques shown in this book, build a 12', 13' or 14' 28-lb. arc-bottom hull canoe. 8fi"x11", softcover, 176 pgs. illus.

SPECIAL OFFER — TRUMPY ART PRINT

This spectacular art print features 25 of the exquisite full-color paintings and drawings from **TRUMPY.** The deep blue background and rich gold type highlight Robert Picardat's stunning renderings of such elegant Trumpy yachts as ***Sequoia II,*** the Presidential Yacht from 1933-1977. Printed on high quality paper, the Trumpy Art Print will grace the walls of any true lover of beautiful boats. Approximate size: 22" x 34". ***Limited Quantity!***

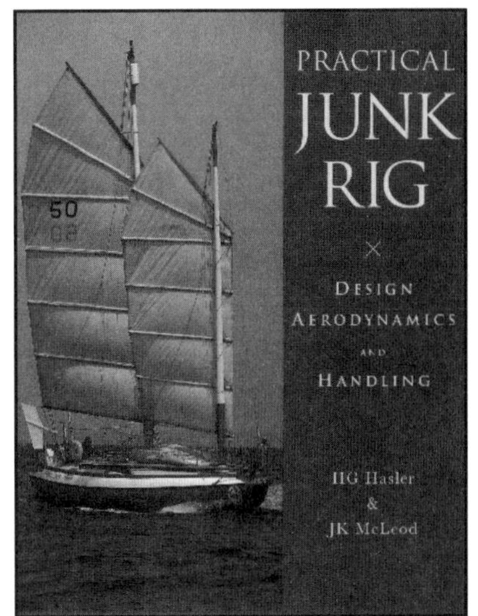

Practical Junk Rig

Design Aerodynamics and Handling

By HG Hasler and JK McLeod

In this encyclopedic volume the late "Blondie" Hasler and his partner Jock McLeod, both pre-eminent in their field, have synthesized 25 years of research and development of the junk rig as adapted to western craft. It is a work which has been welcomed by the growing number of yachtsmen and designers throughout the world who already enjoy the benefits of junk rig or who wish to design one. 9⁄" x11⁄", hardcover, 244 pgs., color & b&w photos, tables & drawings.

"There is no better or more comprehensive work on the subject available . . . it should be considered THE handbook on junk rigs for anyone interested in the subject."

Sailing

*"The depth of knowledge of the two authors, and their fitness to write on such matters, is evident from the moment you start to turn the pages. . . . **Practical Junk Rig** covers all aspects of the design, construction and use of the Chinese lugsail and steers a confident course between the theory and the practices."* **Practical Boat Owner**

Steel Boatbuilding

From Plans To Launching

By Thomas E. Colvin

Colvin's classic as a two-volumes-in-one set; from plans to bare hull & bare hull to launching. 7"x10", softcover, 480 pgs., many illus.

"There is probably no one more uniquely qualified to pen the ultimate book on steel boatbuilding than author, designer, builder and live-aboard cruising man Tom Colvin."

Cruising World

"It's the best I've seen on starting from square one and getting through a completed hull. For people without experience, Colvin's book provides a reasonable substitute, both in terms of understanding the magnitude of the task and how to accomplish it." ***The Houston Post***

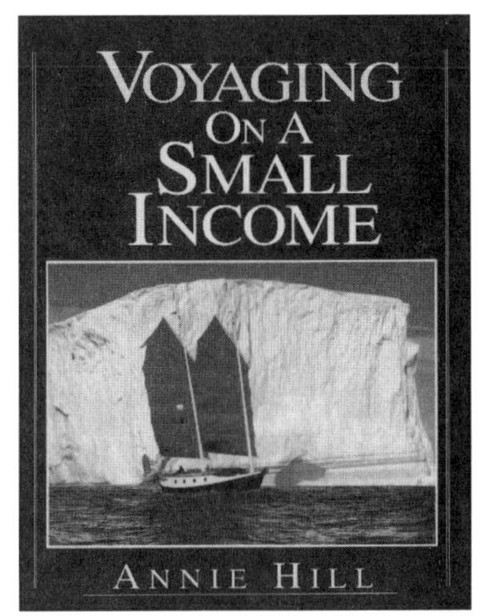

Voyaging on a Small Income

By Annie Hill

Annie and Peter Hill voyage on ***Badger***, a Benford 34' Sailing Dory. An income of £1,300 per year lets them do this without worrying about stopping to work. They built ***Badger*** a decade ago, live aboard her, and have sailed her over 60,000 miles. Annie wrote this book to answer all the questions about what they're doing. If you want to follow their wake or set off on your own adventures, there's a wealth of practical information on how-to-do-it here. 8fi"x11", softcover, 192 pgs, photos, illustrations & drawings. Includes the Benford plywood and epoxy dory designs like the Hill's ***Badger*** and many variations from 26' to 37fi'.

"This book leaps into the 'must read' category for anyone contemplating living aboard and getting about, whether on a small or large income, and the 'should read' category for all cruising people." **Yachting World** • *" An important volume . . . in its ability to communicate how one can cruise to far-off lands simply, inexpensively, safely, and with great joy and comfort."* **Cruising World** • *"The best book we've read to date on liveaboard cruising."* **Messing About in BOATS**

Building the Six-Hour Canoe

By Mike O'Brien and Richard Butz
Illustrations by John Montague
Line Drawings by William Bartoo

Quickly and simply built, the Six-Hour Canoe is suitable for builders and paddlers young and old — a wonderful way to get afloat. This book contains scale plans, specifications, a tool list, step-by-step instructions. All building operations are illustrated with sketches and photographs. 8fi"x11", softcover, 64 pgs. many photos & drawings.

"It's a great how-to, a great read and probably will get as many folks into the wonderful world of modest watercraft as the popular 'Instant Boat' *series. . . . it is easy to build, cheap, a great learning and teaching took and surely something that will help a lot of people get started in the boat hobby."* ***Messing About in BOATS***

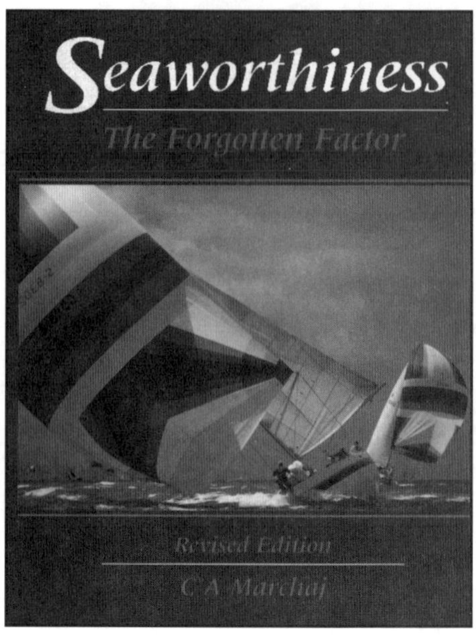

Seaworthiness

The Forgotten Factor

By C.A. Marchaj

Newly updated and revised, this book is a highly readable survey of the seaworthiness of modern yacht designs. Based on the highest degree of practical and academic research, it shows how modern yachts often sacrifice safety for speed and other considerations, and explains how ideas about design still need to be changed to prevent loss of life. 7fl"x10fi"m hardcover, 384 pgs. with 140 line drawings and 50 photos.

"For the first time we are offered logical scientific criteria which help us to assess the likely seaworthiness of one boat or another." ***Practical Boat Owner***

"Probably the most important work on sailing matters that has appeared in the English language since the same author's magisterial **Aero-Hydrodynamics of Sailing** *. . . a first class piece of work, well written, well illustrated, clear and compelling."* ***The Little Ship***